Legalines

Editorial Advisors:
Gloria A. Aluise
  Attorney at Law
Jonathan Neville
  Attorney at Law
Robert A. Wyler
  Attorney at Law

Authors:
Gloria A. Aluise
  Attorney at Law
Daniel O. Bernstine
  Attorney at Law
Roy L. Brooks
  Professor of Law
Scott M. Burbank
  C.P.A.
Charles N. Carnes
  Professor of Law
Paul S. Dempsey
  Professor of Law
Jerome A. Hoffman
  Professor of Law
Mark R. Lee
  Professor of Law
Jonathan Neville
  Attorney at Law
Laurence C. Nolan
  Professor of Law
Arpiar Saunders
  Attorney at Law
Robert A. Wyler
  Attorney at Law

TORTS

Adaptable to Eighth Edition* of Franklin Casebook

By Gloria A. Aluise
Attorney at Law

*If your casebook is a newer edition, go to www.gilbertlaw.com
to see if a supplement is available for this title.

THOMSON

WEST

REGIONAL OFFICES: Chicago, Dallas, Los Angeles, New York, Washington, D.C.

SERIES EDITOR
Linda C. Schneider, J.D.
Attorney at Law

PRODUCTION MANAGER
Elizabeth G. Duke

FIRST PRINTING—2007

Legalines®

**Features Detailed Briefs of Every Major Case,
Plus Summaries of the Black Letter Law**

Titles Available

Administrative Law .... Keyed to Breyer	Criminal Law .... Keyed to Kadish
Administrative Law .... Keyed to Strauss	Criminal Law .... Keyed to LaFave
Administrative Law .... Keyed to Schwartz	Criminal Procedure .... Keyed to Kamisar
Antitrust .... Keyed to Areeda	Decedents' Estates & Trusts ..... Keyed to Dobris
Antitrust .... Keyed to Pitofsky	Domestic Relations .... Keyed to Wadlington
Business Associations .... Keyed to Klein	Evidence .... Keyed to Waltz
Civil Procedure .... Keyed to Cound	Evidence .... Keyed to Weinstein
Civil Procedure .... Keyed to Field	Evidence .... Keyed to Wellborn
Civil Procedure .... Keyed to Hazard	Family Law .... Keyed to Areen
Civil Procecure .... Keyed to Rosenberg	Federal Courts .... Keyed to Wright
Civil Procedure .... Keyed to Yeazell	Income Tax .... Keyed to Freeland
Conflict of Laws .... Keyed to Currie	Income Tax .... Keyed to Klein
Conflict of Laws .... Keyed to Hay	Labor Law .... Keyed to Cox
Constitutional Law .... Keyed to Brest	Labor Law .... Keyed to St. Antoine
Constitutional Law .... Keyed to Choper	Property .... Keyed to Casner
Constitutional Law .... Keyed to Cohen	Property .... Keyed to Cribbet
Constitutional Law .... Keyed to Rotunda	Property .... Keyed to Dukeminier
Constitutional Law .... Keyed to Stone	Property .... Keyed to Nelson
Constitutional Law .... Keyed to Sullivan	Property .... Keyed to Rabin
Contracts .... Keyed to Calamari	Remedies .... Keyed to Re
Contracts .... Keyed to Dawson	Remedies .... Keyed to Rendelman
Contracts .... Keyed to Farnsworth	Sales & Secured Transactions .. Keyed to Speidel
Contracts .... Keyed to Fuller	Securities Regulation .... Keyed to Coffee
Contracts .... Keyed to Kessler	Torts .... Keyed to Dobbs
Contracts .... Keyed to Murphy	Torts .... Keyed to Epstein
Corporations .... Keyed to Choper	Torts .... Keyed to Franklin
Corporations .... Keyed to Eisenberg	Torts .... Keyed to Henderson
Corporations .... Keyed to Hamilton	Torts .... Keyed to Keeton
Corporations .... Keyed to Vagts	Torts .... Keyed to Prosser
Criminal Law .... Keyed to Johnson	Wills, Trusts & Estates .... Keyed to Dukeminier

All Titles Available at Your Law School Bookstore

THOMSON

WEST

SHORT SUMMARY OF CONTENTS

TABLE OF CONTENTS AND SHORT REVIEW OUTLINE

I. INTRODUCTION TO TORT LIABILITY

A. DEFINITIONS AND DISTINCTIONS

The body of law known as "Torts" is concerned with the allocation of losses resulting from the activities of people; it is an attempt to balance the utility of a particular type of conduct against the harm that it may cause, judged by the prevailing social and economic attitudes of the time. The word "tort" was introduced from the French into the English language after the Norman Conquest; it has its roots in the Latin word "tortus," meaning twisted, and in French roughly corresponds to the English word "wrong." In a broad sense, a tort is a wrong, and a tortious act or omission is a wrongful act or omission. While no one definition satisfactorily defines "torts" generally, a tort usually arises through conduct, in the form of an act or omission, affecting a legally protected interest in person or property (or both), usually done with a certain state of mind (*e.g.*, intention, reckless disregard of the consequences, inadvertence, mistake, etc.), which causes damage.

1. **Tort vs. Crime.** A tort is distinguished from a crime in that the latter is a social harm defined and made punishable by the state. While the same act or omission may result in both a crime and a tort, a tort is a wrong to the individual while a crime is a wrong against the public at large for which the state seeks redress. Torts may be committed by individuals, corporations, associations, and other entities. The party who commits a tort is commonly referred to as the "tortfeasor."

2. **Damages.** If the elements of a tort are established by the plaintiff and the defendant fails to raise an adequate defense, a court will award nominal damages if no injury has in fact been sustained, or damages in such amount as it deems reasonable to compensate the plaintiff for the loss suffered. No other special damages (*i.e.*, damages not generally resulting from the tort but suffered by the plaintiff because of his particular circumstances, condition, etc.) need be shown for tort liability to attach to the defendant. However, if liability does attach to the defendant, any special damages caused to the plaintiff as a result of the defendant's act or omission may also be recovered. Furthermore, if it appears that the act or omission of the defendant that forms the basis of the liability was either motivated by an intention to injure or harm the plaintiff or constituted a willful and wanton, or gross, disregard of the consequences, the court may, in addition, award punitive ("exemplary") damages against the defendant. [*See* more detailed discussion, *infra*]

3. **The Policies of Tort Liability.** Judicial opinions resolve controversies between two parties. Thus, the premises underlying tort law are seldom discussed in depth. There are several, sometimes conflicting, values involved:

(i)   Compensating individuals who have been injured;

(ii) Preserving individual choice;

(iii) Determining the social cost-benefit of a given policy;

(iv) The emphasis on value choice; and

(v)   The emphasis on reason to elucidate the premise's underlying choices.

For example, should the legal system force all persons to be vaccinated for polio? Should it do so even if there is some chance that a few will die from the vaccination? Should individual choice be allowed if the benefit to society is greater than the cost of the loss of some individuals?

4. **Objectives of the Tort System.** There are many possible compensation systems: negligence, negligence plus liability insurance, strict liability, strict liability plus insurance, etc. Whatever system is employed, it should fulfill the following objectives:

(i)   Be equitable (among those who receive benefits and those who bear the burden, among beneficiaries, and among the cost bearers);

(ii) Contribute to the wise allocation of human and economic resources;

(iii) Compensate promptly;

(iv) Be reliable;

(v)   Distribute losses rather than leave them on single individuals;

(vi) Be efficient;

(vii) Deter risky conduct; and

(viii)Minimize fraud.

Each compensation system meets these objectives to some extent. For example, negligence law is founded on the notion of compensation-based fault. But fault is objective. Thus, the moral basis of liability is eroded. Objectification may be defended in that it reduces cost and the error in administering the system. Also, fault is supported by commonly shared values of people. Possibly, the system deters risky conduct.

B. UNINTENDED INJURY

1. **Liability Based on Fault.** The most difficult cases are those in which the injury was not intended to occur. The law struggles to deal with two conflict-

ing theories that could be applied in such cases. The courts could apply a theory of strict liability by requiring people to pay for all harms they cause. In the alternative, the courts could require that people only pay for injuries they cause through their own negligence or fault.

2. Strict Liability or Negligence--

Hammontree v. Jenner, 97 Cal. Rptr. 739 (Cal. Ct. App. 1971).

Facts. Jenner (D) had suffered a seizure in 1952 and was subsequently diagnosed as an epileptic. He was given medication and his seizures were brought under control. Beginning in 1955 or 1956, D had to report his condition to the Department of Motor Vehicles on a periodic basis. Since his seizures were under control, he was allowed to keep his driver's license. In 1967, D had a seizure while driving, lost control of his car, hit the Hammontrees' (Ps') shop, and struck Maxine Hammontree. Ps sued for personal injury and property damage. Ps wanted the jury to be instructed on strict liability, but the trial court refused the strict liability instruction and instructed on negligence instead. The jury found for D, and Ps appeal.

Issue. Is strict liability an appropriate theory for recovery when sudden illness renders an automobile driver unconscious?

Held. No. Judgment affirmed.

♦ When products cause injury, strict liability is an appropriate theory. The manufacturers make a profit from sales and should pay for any injuries. Those costs are the costs of doing business.

♦ The theory of negligence, however, is adequate for auto accidents. Drivers share the roads and should allocate damages based on fault. Since D used reasonable care to control his seizures, negligence has not been shown.

C. THE LITIGATION PROCESS

1. **Procedure.** When an injury occurs, the courts are available for the injured party to redress the injury.

    a. **Pretrial.** Prior to the trial, both parties contact attorneys and try to settle the matter. If it cannot be settled, the issues must be litigated.

    b. **Trial.** To initiate the trial, the injured party files a complaint. This complaint lists the bases for the claim. The person who is sued must file an answer. Any factual disputes must be tried to a jury for decision. After the jury's verdict is returned, the trial is over.

c. **Post-trial.** If either party is dissatisfied with the trial's conclusion, an appeal may be taken. The appellate court, however, only reviews issues of law. Appellate decisions explain the proper legal principle and are usually published.

2. **Parties.** The injured party who seeks to recover is called "the plaintiff." The plaintiff will usually be seeking damages for injuries to person or property. The party who is sued for the injury is called "the defendant." A plaintiff's or defendant's death does not stop a lawsuit. A deceased victim has an interest in her bodily security and in continued economic support for her dependents. "Survival" statutes permit the deceased's estate to bring suit for any harm for which the deceased could have sued, such as medical expenses, lost wages, pain and suffering. "Wrongful death" statutes permit suits by and for legally designated beneficiaries to recover financial loss caused by the death.

D. VICARIOUS LIABILITY

Defendants may be held liable for another's torts in many circumstances, *e.g.,* a corporation may be liable for torts of employees.

1. **Scope of Employment--**

Christensen v. Swenson et al., 874 P.2d 125 (Utah 1994).

Facts. Swenson (D), a security guard for Burns (D2), worked eight-hour shifts with no scheduled breaks. Employees were allowed 10-15 minute lunch and bathroom breaks. D left her post to drive across the street to pick up lunch at the only restaurant available to employees, intending to return within the 10-15 minutes allowed. On her return, D collided with Christensen's (P's) motorcycle and several people were hurt. P sued Ds. The trial court granted D2's motion for summary judgment and the appeals court affirmed. P appeals.

Issue. Did the court err in granting summary judgment?

Held. Yes. Judgment reversed and case remanded.

♦ Under respondeat superior, an employer is liable for an employee's torts committed when the employee is acting within the scope of her employment.

♦ Acts falling within the scope of employment are "those acts which are so closely connected with what the servant is employed to do, and so fairly and reasonably incidental to it, that they may be regarded as methods, even though quite improper ones, of carrying out the objectives of employment."

♦ Three factors are helpful in determining scope of employment: (i) the employee's conduct must be the general kind the employee was hired to do, not personal endeavors; (ii) the conduct must occur substantially within the hours and ordinary spatial boundaries of the employment; and (iii) the conduct must be at least partially motivated by the purpose of serving the employer's interest.

♦ Here, the appeals court found D did not meet the second criteria and thus did not address the remaining factors.

♦ However, D maintains she was hired to be seen on and around D2's premises and traveling to the restaurant contributed to the secure atmosphere of the plant. D2 argued that trips to the restaurant are personal. Two of D2's managers testified going to the restaurant was prohibited, but D2 could provide no specific orders to this effect. Thus, reasonable minds could differ on this factor and on whether D2 "tacitly sanctioned" its employees obtaining lunch at the restaurant. A jury might find D was outside the spatial boundaries or within.

♦ D contends she was benefiting D2's business because she phoned in her order, drove to the restaurant and tried to return to her post within the allotted break time. Again, reasonable minds could differ on D's actions. Thus, summary judgment is inappropriate.

---

2. Apparent Authority--

Roessler v. Novak, 858 So. 2d 1158 (Fla. Dist. Ct. App. 2003).

Facts. After being diagnosed as having a perforated viscus, Roessler (P) was referred to the emergency room at Sarasota Memorial Hospital (D), where he was evaluated and admitted. Radiologist Lichtenstein read diagnostic scans of P's abdomen. After surgery, P suffered complications that included renal failure, a heart condition, and several brain abcesses that required surgery and a two and one-half month hospital stay. P alleged that Lichtenstein misinterpreted his scans and failed to include an abdominal abscess in his diagnosis, that he did so while an agent of D and that he did so within the scope of his agency. D contended that Lichtenstein was an independent contractor and filed for summary judgment. The trial court granted D's motion and entered final judgment. P appeals.

Issue. Did D satisfy its burden to establish that no genuine issues of material fact existed regarding its vicarious liability, thereby entitling it to summary judgment as a matter of law?

Held. No. Judgment reversed and case remanded.

♦ While some agencies are based on an express agreement, a principal may be liable for acts within an agent's apparent authority, *i.e.*, the authority the principal tolerates or permits or, by its words or actions, holds the agent out as possessing. Apparent agency is present only if the following elements are met: (i) representation by the purported principal, (ii) reliance on that representation by a third party, and (iii) a change in position by the third party due to the representation. Apparent authority exists only where the principal creates the appearance of an agency relationship.

♦ D and the association of radiologists with which P was affiliated had entered into an independent contractor agreement. However, a hospital may be held vicariously liable for the acts of physicians who are independent contractors if they act with the apparent authority of the hospital. It is often a question of fact for the jury.

♦ Evidence was presented to show that D maintained a radiology department located on its grounds, neither P nor the association of which he was a member had offices outside of the hospital grounds, and the group provided radiology services for D 24 hours a day. D admitted P, provided him with inpatient services, and assigned Lichtenstein to interpret P's scans. P accepted the physicians provided by the hospital and did not attempt to secure the services of a specialist on his own. These facts created a jury question as to whether D represented that Lichtenstein was its apparent agent.

Concurrence. While the apparent agency theory works well to create vicarious liability in negligence cases involving cars or premises liability, it does not work well in the context of a complicated institution like a hospital. Predictable general rules establishing the parameters of vicarious liability are needed in medical situations and institutions. Although I would consider adopting a theory of nondelegable duty, I concur because of the existing precedent.

---

3. **Ostensible Agency.** In *Baptist Memorial Hospital System v. Sampson*, 969 S.W.2d 945 (Tx. 1998), Sampson was treated by Dr. Zakula in Baptist Memorial's emergency room after being bitten by a spider. Sampson alleged that Dr. Zakula's treatment was negligent and led to permanent injuries. Signs were posted in the emergency room indicating that the doctors were independent contractors, and patients were asked to sign forms acknowledging this, but Sampson said she signed without reading the forms and no one explained them to her. After Sampson sued the hospital for Dr. Zakula's negligence on an ostensible agency theory, the trial court granted summary judgment for the hospital. After the appeals court reversed, the trial court judgment was reinstated on appeal. It was found that the hospital's conduct would not lead a reasonable person to believe that emergency room physicians were hospital employees. Citing similar elements as those listed in *Roessler*, above, the court found that even if Sampson's belief that Dr. Zakula was a hospital employee were reasonable, there was no conduct on the

hospital's part to lead to such a conclusion. Sampson had failed to raise an issue of fact on this element of the claim. Furthermore, the court rejected the court of appeal's suggestion that a nondelegable duty be imposed on hospitals for the malpractice of emergency room doctors because patients have a direct cause of action against the negligent physicians.

II. THE NEGLIGENCE PRINCIPLE

A. HISTORICAL DEVELOPMENT OF FAULT LIABILITY

1. **Origins.** Historians have disagreed as to the origins of the law of torts. One theory holds that liability was originally grounded on actual intent or personal fault within a strong moral framework, moving gradually toward the formulation of standards of conduct that were less concerned with subjective fault and more concerned with evaluating the alleged tortfeasor's conduct on the basis of an objective standard. The other and more generally accepted theory is that liability originally was not based upon the immoral conduct of the alleged tortfeasor but upon the causal connection between the conduct and the damage (*i.e.*, a person was deemed to act at her own peril) and gradually evolved to a position where moral standards became the basis of liability. Today, while liability is generally recognized as being based on fault (*e.g.*, where there is intent to injure another, or where there is a breach of a duty owed to another), the "fault" is not necessarily "moral fault" on the part of the tortfeasor, *i.e.*, no personal "immorality" is required; liability may stem from "social fault." "Social fault" will be found where the consequences of the tortfeasor's conduct are deemed by society to be so undesirable that the state of mind of the tortfeasor is immaterial (*e.g.*, liability of the insane for injuries caused to others, strict liability on businesses for placing adulterated foods in the hands of human beings who then suffer food poisonings, etc.).

   a. **Early English law.** In the common law courts of the 13th century, only two writs were available for redressing torts. These were the writ of trespass and the writ of trespass on the case.

      1) **Trespass.** The writ of trespass provided relief for all direct and immediate forcible injuries to person or property. It covered unintentional as well as intentional injuries, required no proof of actual damages, and did not require fault on the part of the defendant (*i.e.*, wrongful intent or negligence was not required).

      2) **Trespass on the case.** The writ of trespass on the case provided relief for injuries that were intended but were either not forcible or not direct. Usually, the plaintiff was required to show actual damages and wrongful intent or negligence on the part of the defendant.

   b. **Present law.** Today, tort liability generally falls into three classes:

      1) Liability based on the intent of the defendant;

      2) Liability based on the negligence of the defendant; and

3) Liability attaching irrespective of the state of mind of the defendant; *i.e.,* strict liability.

c. **American evolution of negligence--**

Brown v. Kendall, 60 Mass. (6 Cush.) 292 (1850).

Facts. Brown's (P's) and Kendall's (D's) dogs were fighting. While attempting to separate the dogs, D accidently struck P (who was standing behind him) in the eye with a stick. The trial court placed the burden on D to show that he had exercised extraordinary care because he was not engaged in a necessary act. D's objection to this requirement was overruled, and judgment was rendered for P. D appeals.

Issue. Was the court correct in requiring D to show that he had exercised extraordinary care?

Held. No. Judgment reversed and new trial ordered.

♦ It was error to overrule D's objection. When a defendant is engaged in a lawful act and injures a plaintiff, the plaintiff may not recover damages if:

(i) The plaintiff and the defendant exercised ordinary care;

(ii) The plaintiff and the defendant failed to exercise ordinary care; or

(iii) The plaintiff alone failed to exercise ordinary care.

♦ If it appears that the defendant was doing a lawful act, and unintentionally hit and hurt the plaintiff, then, unless it also appears to the satisfaction of the jury that the defendant is chargeable with some fault, negligence, carelessness, or want of prudence, the plaintiff fails to sustain the burden of proof, and is not entitled to recover.

Comment. The standard of care referred to by the court was not the subjective standard (*i.e.,* dependent upon the individuals involved), but an objective standard related to the degree of care prudent and cautious persons under similar circumstances would exercise. Furthermore, the court pointed out that the plaintiff, and not the defendant, has the burden of proof—*i.e.,* the plaintiff has the burden of proving negligence or fault on the part of the defendant. The importance of this case is that it indicates the shift to finding liability on the part of a defendant only if he is legally at fault.

---

2. **Elements of Plaintiff's Prima Facie Case.** The elements of a plaintiff's prima facie case based on the negligence of a defendant are the following:

(i)   Act or omission of the defendant;

(ii)   Duty owed by the defendant to exercise due care;

(iii)   Breach of duty by the defendant;

(iv)   Causal relationship between the defendant's conduct and the harm to the plaintiff (both actual and proximate cause); and

(v)   Damages.

Each of the above elements must be alleged by the plaintiff, and the plaintiff has the burden of proving the allegations by a preponderance of the evidence.

B.   THE CENTRAL CONCEPT

1.   **The Standard of Care.** The defendant is bound only to use that care that is commensurate with the hazard involved. The risk, reasonably perceived, defines the duty owed.

2.   **Reasonable Care--**

Adams v. Bullock, 125 N.E. 93 (N.Y. 1919).

Facts. Bullock (D) operated a trolley with overhead wires. At one point the wires crossed near a bridge. Adams (P) was a 12-year-old boy who used the bridge as a shortcut. While P walked along, he swung an eight-foot wire over his head. P's wire contacted D's trolley wire, and P was injured. P successfully sued D. P's verdict was affirmed on appeal, and D appeals.

Issue. Did D breach a duty of reasonable care?

Held. No. Judgment reversed.

◆   D must only exercise ordinary care in light of ordinary risk. In this case, it would take extraordinary foresight to have foreseen this risk. Even if the harm was remote, if the risk was avoidable, liability would attach. Here, however, the trolley line could not have been made safer.

Comment. The opinion seems to suggest a balancing of factors to determine whether a duty was owed. The foreseeability of the harm is balanced against the ability to prevent the injury.

3.   **The Hand Formula--**

United States v. Carroll Towing Co., 159 F.2d 169 (2d Cir. 1947).

Facts. The United States Government's (P's) barge broke from its moorings and sank, allegedly because of Carroll Towing's (D's) negligence. P's employee, who was in charge of the barge, was not on the barge when it broke loose, and had been ashore for 21 hours. The accident occurred in the full tide of war activity when barges were constantly being towed in and out of the harbor. P sued for damages. D contended that P was also negligent in that its employee, the bargee, was not on the barge when it broke loose. P appeals a verdict for D.

Issues.

(i)   Was P's employee negligent in being ashore?

(ii)   If so, did that negligence contribute to the loss of the barge?

Held. (i) Yes. (ii) Yes. Judgment affirmed.

♦   The barge owner's liability depends upon whether his burden of adequate precautions (B) is less than (<) the probability that the barge will break away (P) multiplied by the gravity of resulting injury if it does (L). If B<PL, the barge owner is negligent.

♦   The harbor was crowded; it was not beyond reasonable expectations that work might not be done carefully.

♦   Under such conditions, it is a fair requirement that the barge owner have a bargee aboard during working hours.

Comment. The main question in a negligence case is whether a reasonable person would have realized the risk involved in a course of action but still would not have changed his conduct; in that case, no negligence can be inferred.

---

4.   **Risk-Benefit Analysis.** Because of the balancing of specific factors in *Carroll Towing*, *supra*, analysis of the opinion has frequently centered on economics. The balancing of burdens against risks to be avoided translates easily into a cost-benefit analysis.

5.   **The Reasonable Person.** In general, the standard of care that must be exercised is that conduct that the ***average reasonable person*** of ordinary prudence would follow under the same or similar circumstances. The standard of conduct is an external and objective one, and has nothing to do with indi-

vidual subjective judgment, although higher duties may be imposed by specific statutory provisions or by reason of special knowledge or skill on the part of the actor. Since the standard is an external one, being a fool is no excuse; likewise, being an expert is no excuse if a reasonable person of ordinary prudence would do otherwise. The reasonable person standard takes no account of the personality of the particular person involved.

a. **Best judgment immaterial.** The fact that a defendant used his own best judgment is ordinarily immaterial. The defendant will be held to the standard of a reasonable person.

b. **Physical handicap.** When the defendant suffers a physical handicap, the "reasonable person" will be deemed to have the same handicap.

c. **Mental incapacity.** A person with a mental incapacity is held to the same standard of care as a person of ordinary intelligence because of the difficulties that would occasion determining the degree of disability. Restatement (Second) of Torts section 283B states that insane persons are held in all respects to the reasonableness standard of a sane person, the only exception being where malice or intent is necessary for the cause of action (which is not applicable to negligence).

d. **Children.** The usual objective standard of care has been somewhat modified in the case of children.

   1) **Majority view.** The majority view is that the standard is based on what may be expected of children of like age, intelligence, and experience.

   2) **Common law.** At common law, a child under the age of seven was presumed to be incapable of negligence, between the ages of seven and 14 rebuttably presumed incapable, and over 14 presumed capable.

   3) **Minority rule.** A minority of jurisdictions still have arbitrary age limits.

   4) **When driving a car.** A few jurisdictions still make the age, intelligence, and experience allowance when a child is driving a car or engaging in other "adult" activity, but the majority of cases hold children to an adult standard in such situations. [*Accord* Restatement (Second) of Torts §283A]

6. **Duty of Highest Care Rejected--**

Bethel v. New York City Transit Authority, 703 N.E.2d 1214 (N.Y. 1998).

Facts. Bethel (P) was injured when the wheelchair accessible seat on a New York City Transit Authority's (D's) bus collapsed beneath him. P could not prove D knew of the defect but instead relied on a constructive notice theory based on a computer printout of adjustment and alignment repair made to the seat 11 days earlier. P claimed that, had D properly inspected the repairs, it would have noticed the defect in the seat. The judge instructed the jury on the "highest degree of care that human prudence and fore-sight can suggest" and asked whether, based on this standard of care, a reasonable inspection would have revealed the defect and led to its repair. The jury found for P. The appellate division affirmed. D appeals.

Issue. Should a duty of highest care continue to be applied as a matter of law to common carriers?

Held. No. Judgment reversed and case remanded.

♦   The duty of highest care was adopted in the age of steam engines when primitive safety features led to numerous accident injuries. Today, however, public transportation is at least as safe as private.

♦   The reasonable person standard, which takes into account the circumstances with which the actor was actually confronted when the accident occurred, including the reasonably perceivable risk and gravity of harm to others and any special relationship of dependence between the victim and the actor, provides enough flexibility to address all of the particular circumstances of a case.

C. THE ROLES OF JUDGE AND JURY

1.   **In General.** If an act was negligent as a matter of law (negligent per se), the judge will so instruct the jury. Thus, the "proper" standard of care is given the effect of law by the courts. If an act is not negligent per se, the judge will leave it to the jury to determine whether the act was negligent. This procedure has been adopted in order to prevent juries from being overly swayed by their emotions. The following cases highlight this distinction.

   a.   **Negligence per se--**

Baltimore & Ohio Railroad Co. v. Goodman, 275 U.S. 66 (1927).

Facts. Goodman (the decedent) drove his truck at 10 m.p.h. up to a blind railroad crossing that did not have signals or guard rails. By the time he saw the approaching train operated by the railroad (D), it was too late to stop. Goodman's heir (P) sued in wrongful death. D argued that the decedent's own negligence caused his death. The trial court refused to direct a verdict in favor of D. A jury found for P, and the court of appeals affirmed. D appeals.

Issue. If the evidence shows that a plaintiff failed to take reasonable precautions for his own safety, does the trial court commit error in not directing a verdict for the defendant?

Held. Yes. Judgment reversed and case remanded.

♦ A person approaching a railroad crossing knows that the train cannot stop for him; he must stop for the train.

♦ If a driver cannot be sure of his safety, he has an obligation to get out of his vehicle and look both ways down the track.

♦ Here, the decedent failed to take reasonable precautions for his own safety and is, therefore, negligent; Goodman's own negligence was the proximate cause of his death.

♦ When a plaintiff proximately causes his own injuries, the trial court should direct a verdict for the defendant.

Comment. In *Torgeson v. Missouri-Kansas-Texas Railway Co.*, 124 Kan. 798 (1928), the plaintiff took the Court's advice in *Goodman*. Unfortunately, however, by the time he got back into his vehicle and proceeded, the train had come around the bend and struck him.

---

    b.   **Rule of law--**

Pokora v. Wabash Railway Co., 292 U.S. 98 (1934).

Facts. Pokora (P) approached a railroad crossing in his truck. He stopped, looked, and listened as well as possible, but he did not get out of his truck, which would have been necessary to see sufficiently both ways, as the view was partially blocked by parked boxcars. As P proceeded across the tracks, he was struck by Wabash Railway's (D's) train coming from the direction where his view was partially impaired. The trial court directed a verdict for D, and the court of appeals upheld the directed verdict. P appeals.

Issue. Was P negligent as a matter of law?

Held. No. Judgment reversed. (Dictum from an earlier opinion (*Goodman, supra*) implying that one must always get out and look down the tracks if the view is obstructed is disapproved.)

Comment. The case points out that there are no ironclad rules as to what is negligent conduct; the duty varies with the circumstances. It is usually negligence as a matter of law not to stop, look, and listen, but not always. This holding is the better of the two cases—*Pokora* and *Goodman*. A plaintiff should be given the chance to let the jury decide the extent to which his negligence contributed to his woe.

---

c.   **Common carriers (unfriendly skies)--**

Andrews v. United Airlines, Inc., 24 F.3d 39 (9th Cir. 1994).

Facts. After an airplane's arrival at the gate, Andrews (P) was injured by a briefcase, which fell from an overhead compartment. (Passengers were routinely warned of such a risk before arrival.) P sued United Airlines (D), alleging that her injury was foreseeable and that D did not protect against it. The trial court dismissed the suit on a summary judgment motion, and P appeals.

Issues.

(i)   Does a common carrier owe duties of utmost care and of "the vigilance of a very cautious person" toward its passengers?

(ii)   Is summary judgment precluded under the evidence in this case?

Held. (i) Yes. (ii) Yes. Judgment reversed and case remanded.

♦   D is responsible for even the slightest negligence and is required to do all that with human care and foresight it can reasonably do under the circumstances; however, D is not an insurer of the safety of its passengers.

♦   D must exercise that degree of care and diligence as it can reasonably exercise consistent with the character and method of conveyance adopted and the practical operation of D's business.

♦   There is a genuine issue of material fact as to whether D had a duty to do more than warn its passengers about the possibility of bags falling from overhead bins. P presented witness testimony that D had received reports of items falling from overhead compartments in previous flights, and that D could have refitted the compartments for better safety, as other airlines had. D presented evidence that the number of reports of falling items was trivial considering the number of flights it makes and the fact that many of the reported incidents did not involve injury. Jurors might conclude that D should have done more or that D did enough. In light of the evidence, summary judgment is precluded.

---

2.   **The Role of Custom.** Following custom in the community or trade practice is not conclusive. The custom is merely evidence of the standard of care

owed. The test still is whether the average reasonable person would have so acted under the same or similar circumstances.

a. **Proof of custom--**

Trimarco v. Klein, 436 N.E.2d 502 (N.Y. 1982).

Facts. In 1976, the plaintiff (P), a tenant in the defendant's (D's) apartment building, fell through a glass bathtub enclosure and was injured. Although shatterproof glass had been used in such areas since the 1950s, D had not changed previously installed glass. D claimed that he had no duty to change the glass. P sued D and secured a jury verdict. The Appellate Division reversed, and P appeals.

Issue. Can evidence of business custom be used to indicate D's proper standard of care?

Held. Yes. Judgment reversed; new trial ordered on other grounds.

♦ Evidence of custom or practice is admissible since it tends to show the collective wisdom of a larger group. The custom is, however, merely evidence of reasonable care and is not conclusive.

♦ Evidence of D's conformity to the custom may show due care.

♦ Evidence of D's failure to follow custom may show a failure to use reasonable care.

Comment. There is a definite movement towards imposing a higher standard of care when the defendant knows of inherent dangers in an industry-wide custom. To decide otherwise would allow an entire industry to keep its safety standards artificially low just by refusing to raise the industry-wide standards.

3. **The Role of Statutes.** Statutes that affect a person's conduct may be either civil or criminal. If a plaintiff is provided a civil remedy under the statute, he will not have to be concerned with establishing negligence. When a defendant's conduct violates a criminal statute that does not provide a civil remedy, the plaintiff might still obtain a remedy through a negligence action. When a court adopts a standard of care embodied in a criminal statute, the rationale is that a reasonable person always obeys the criminal law. However, for a plaintiff to support a claim that the violation of the criminal statute by a defendant was negligence, the statute must have clearly defined the conduct or duty required and the class or individual to whom it applies. Failure of a defendant to act as required will constitute a breach of the duty. However, for a plaintiff to establish liability, he must show that he is a mem-

ber of the class protected by the statute and that the statute was enacted to protect members of the class from the type of injury the plaintiff suffered. Depending on the jurisdiction, violation of a statute can have several effects. The *majority view* finds violation of a statute to give rise to a conclusive presumption of negligence. In other jurisdictions, violation is deemed *merely evidence of negligence*. However, when a plaintiff's claim is based on violation of the statute as negligence, a defendant generally has available to him the defenses of contributory negligence and assumption of risk (*see infra*).

a.   Violation of safety legislation--

Martin v. Herzog, 126 N.E. 814 (N.Y. 1920).

Facts. Mr. Martin was thrown from the wagon he was driving and was killed when Herzog (D) failed to drive his car to the right of the center of the highway and struck the wagon. The accident occurred at night. The wagon had no lights, which was a statutory violation. Mrs. Martin (P) sued D for damages resulting from his negligence in driving on the wrong side of the street. D was denied a jury instruction that the absence of a light on the wagon was prima facie evidence of contributory negligence. The trial court found for P, and the Appellate Division reversed and ordered a new trial. P appeals the reversal.

Issue. Is the unexcused violation of a statute contributory negligence in itself (per se)?

Held. Yes. Judgment affirmed.

♦   Unexcused omission of the statutorily required lighting is negligence per se.

♦   To omit safeguards prescribed by statute for the benefit of others is to fall short of the duty of diligence owed toward the rest of society.

♦   The trial court erred in giving the jury the power to relax the duty that P's intestate owed to other travelers.

Comment. Note that the majority rule—that violation of a safety statute is negligence per se—may have an exception: it may not be negligence where, under all of the circumstances, actions that violate a statute are the most reasonable thing to do.

b.   Exceptions to the general rule--

Tedla v. Ellman, 19 N.E.2d 987 (N.Y. 1939).

Facts. Tedla (P) and her brother were wheeling carriages loaded with junk along the right edge of a highway when they were struck by a vehicle driven by Ellman (D). P was injured, and her brother was killed. There were no footpaths along the highway, but P and her brother were probably carrying a light. Nevertheless, D moved to dismiss P's complaint for damages on the ground that P and her brother were contributorily negligent as a matter of law because they violated a statute requiring that they walk on the left side of the highway. P introduced evidence that the traffic was very heavy on the other side of the road, whereas the traffic was light on the side on which she walked. D appeals the verdict for P, which was affirmed by the Appellate Division.

Issue. If a statute sets forth a general rule of conduct without fixing a standard of care that would, under all circumstances, tend to protect life, will a justifiable deviation from the general rule be regarded as negligence per se?

Held. No. Judgment affirmed.

♦   The legislature intended to set forth a general rule that would provide for the safety of pedestrians.

♦   Nevertheless, in this situation, obedience to the rule would have subjected the pedestrians to great danger.

♦   We cannot reasonably assume that the legislature intended that a statute enacted for the safety of pedestrians must be observed when observance would subject them to more imminent danger.

♦   Negligence is the failure to exercise the care required by law.

♦   Statutes such as the one in question may be properly construed as intended to apply only to ordinary situations. Thus, the statute may be subject to an exception if disobedience is likely to prevent rather than cause the accidents that the statute seeks to prevent.

---

   c.   **Licensing statutes.** Licensing statutes are not ordinarily used to set standards of care. Accordingly, failure to obtain a license is not negligence per se.

D. PROOF OF NEGLIGENCE

1.   **Plaintiff's Burden.** If persons of reasonable intelligence may differ as to the conclusion to be drawn, the issue must be left to the jury; if not, the court will decide. Generally, the burden of proof, *i.e.,* the risk of nonpersuasion, is on the plaintiff, and if the evidence he introduces is not greater or more persuasive than that of his adversary, he must lose. The burden of going forward with presenting proof, on the other hand, is established by presumptions, and the failure to rebut a presumption may result in a directed verdict.

a.   **Circumstantial evidence.** Circumstantial evidence is the proof of one fact, or group of facts, that gives rise to an inference by reasoning that another fact must be true.

2.   **Res Ipsa Loquitur ("RIL").** RIL, directly translated, means "the thing speaks for itself." In situations where (i) it is highly probable that the injury would not have occurred in the absence of someone's negligence, (ii) the indicated source of the negligence is within the scope of a duty owed by the defendant to the plaintiff, and (iii) neither the plaintiff nor any third party appears to have contributed to the plaintiff's injuries, an inference is permitted that the defendant was negligent, without any ***direct proof***. The defendant then has the burden of going forward and introducing evidence to overthrow the inference.

   a.   **Rationale.** The courts recognize RIL because of the existence of an injured plaintiff and a defendant who has better access to the evidence concerning the cause of injury.

   b.   **Burden on defendant.** RIL puts the burden on the defendant to explain away the negligence. However, the doctrine does not apply if negligence by the defendant is no more likely than another explanation; *e.g.,* where an auto unexplainably runs off the road, but is subsequently found to have a flat tire.

      1)   There must be some evidence of negligence, but control of the instrumentality by the defendant gives rise to an inference that it happened from lack of care if it would not ordinarily happen without a lack of care.

      2)   The doctrine does not apply unless reasonable persons could not disagree that 51% of the probabilities point to the defendant's liability.

   c.   **Three views of the effect of RIL.** The effect of RIL varies depending on the jurisdiction.

      1)   It may create a ***permissible inference***, the strength of which varies with the circumstances of the case. The jury may accept or reject the inference. This is the majority view.

      2)   A ***presumption of negligence*** may be raised by RIL and, unless the defendant shows evidence to rebut, the court must find negligence as a matter of law.

      3)   The ***burden of proof shifts*** to the defendant, requiring the defendant to introduce evidence to support his defense. If the defendant's evidence is sufficient to support a finding of fact in his favor, the burden of proof shifts back to the plaintiff, who then must prove the defendant's negligence.

d.   Illustrative cases.

1)   Constructive notice--

Negri v. Stop & Shop, Inc., 480 N.E.2d 740 (N.Y. 1985).

Facts. Negri (P) was shopping in a store owned by Stop and Shop (D). P slipped and fell, striking her head on broken baby food jars on the floor. The evidence indicated that the baby food jars were broken, the food was dirty and messy, no one had heard jars breaking for 15 to 20 minutes prior to the accident, and the aisle had not been cleaned or inspected for 50 minutes to two hours prior to the accident. P received a jury verdict, and judgment was entered for P by the trial court. The Appellate Division reversed and dismissed the complaint. P appeals.

Issue. Is the evidence sufficient to submit the case to the jury?

Held. Yes. Judgment reversed and case remanded.

- ♦   There was sufficient evidence that the jury could find that the broken baby food jars had been on the floor for an extended period of time. During this time, D's employees could have discovered and remedied the situation.

- ♦   If the Appellate Division finds that the jury verdict was against the weight of the evidence, the appropriate action would be to order a new trial.

---

2)   No evidence of constructive notice--

Gordon v. American Museum of Natural History, 492 N.E.2d 774 (N.Y. 1986).

Facts. Gordon (P) fell while on the front steps of the American Museum of Natural History (D). P claimed to have seen a piece of paper on the steps that came from D's concession stand. P claimed that D's employees should have discovered and removed the paper. The jury found for P, and the Appellate Division affirmed. D appeals.

Issue. Is there sufficient evidence to submit the case to the jury?

Held. No. Judgment reversed and complaint dismissed.

- ♦   There is no evidence in the case indicating how long the piece of paper could have been on the steps. This absence of evidence offers no way to determine whether D's employees should have had constructive notice of its presence.

♦   In the absence of evidence on a material issue, a court should not submit the case to the jury.

Comment. *Negri*, *supra*, and *Gordon* may be distinguished by the amount of evidence that was offered by each plaintiff. In *Negri*, there was sufficient evidence offered to give rise to an inference that the employees should have discovered the danger. In *Gordon*, there was no evidence offered that would give rise to such an inference. Although res ipsa loquitur may be used to infer issues that are not subject to direct proof, there must be sufficient circumstantial evidence offered to give rise to those inferences.

3)   Early case--

Byrne v. Boadle, 2 H. & C. 722, 159 Eng. Rep. 299 (Ct. Ex. 1863).

Facts. The plaintiff (P) was walking on the street when a barrel rolled out of the defendant's (D's) window, striking and injuring P. There was no other evidence. P was nonsuited by the trial court.

Issue. Can P get the case to the jury by showing only that there was an accident and that it was caused by the barrel?

Held. Yes. Verdict for P.

♦   All that is necessary is that reasonable persons would say that more likely than not there was negligence. The fact of the barrel falling is prima facie evidence of negligence. If there are any facts inconsistent with negligence, it is up to the defendant to prove them.

4)   Recent case--

McDougald v. Perry, 716 So. 2d 783 (Fla. 1998).

Facts. McDougald (P) sued Perry (D) and D's employer for personal injuries sustained in an accident. P was driving behind a tractor-trailer, which was driven by D. As D drove over some railroad tracks, the 130-pound spare tire came out of its cradle underneath the trailer and fell to the ground. The trailer's rear tires then ran over the spare, causing the spare to bounce into the air and strike the windshield of P's vehicle. The spare tire was stored in an angled holding case underneath the trailer and was held in place by its own weight. It was secured by a four-to six-foot long chain with one-inch links, which was wrapped around the tire. D testified that he believed the chain to be the original chain that came with the trailer in 1969. D also stated that originally the chain was secured to the body of the trailer by a latch device but that, at the time of the accident, the chain was attached to the body of the trailer with a nut and bolt. D had inspected the chain prior to the trip, but did not inspect each link. Although the chain could not be found at time of trial, D's opinion was that a link had stretched and slipped from the nut and bolt. The judge instructed the jury regarding res ipsa loquitur and the jury found for P. The district court reversed. P petitioned for review.

Issue. Did the trial court properly instruct the jury on the issue of res ispa loquitur?

Held. Yes. Judgment reversed.

♦ The doctrine of res ispa loquitur provides an injured plaintiff with a common-sense inference of negligence where direct proof of negligence is wanting, provided certain elements consistent with negligent behavior are present. Essentially the injured plaintiff must establish that the instrumentality causing his injury was under the exclusive control of the defendant, and that the accident is one that would not, in the ordinary course of events, have occurred without negligence on the part of the one in control.

♦ We have held that an injury standing alone ordinarily does not indicate negligence. The doctrine of res ipsa loquitur simply recognizes that in rare instances an injury may permit an inference of negligence if coupled with a sufficient showing of its immediate, precipitating cause.

♦ A proper analysis of this issue is provided in section 328D of Restatement (Second) of Torts (1965):

> Type of event. The first requirement for the application of the rule stated in this Section is a basis of past experience which reasonably permits the conclusion that such events do not ordinarily occur unless someone has been negligent. There are many types of accidents which commonly occur without the fault of anyone. The fact that a tire blows out, or that a man falls down stairs is not, in the absence of anything more, enough to permit the conclusion that there was negligence in inspecting the tire, or in the construction of the stairs, because it is common human experience that such events all too frequently occur without such negligence. On the other hand there are many events, such as those of objects falling from the defendant's premises, the fall of an elevator, the escape of gas or water from mains or of electricity from wires or appliances, the derailment of trains or the explosion of boilers, where the conclusion is at least permissible that such things do not usually happen unless someone has been negligent. To such events res ipsa loquitur may apply.

Basis of conclusion. In the usual case the basis of past experience from which this conclusion may be drawn is common to the community, and is a matter of general knowledge, which the court recognizes on much the same basis as when it takes judicial notice of facts which everyone knows. It may, however, be supplied by the evidence of the parties; and expert testimony that such an event usually does not occur without negligence may afford a sufficient basis for the inference. Such testimony may be essential to the plaintiff's case where, as for example in some actions for medical malpractice, there is no fund of common knowledge which may permit laymen reasonably to draw the conclusion. On the other hand there are other kinds of medical malpractice, as where a sponge is left in the plaintiff's abdomen after an operation, where no expert is needed to tell the jury that such events do not usually occur in the absence of negligence.

♦ The accident that occurred here is the type that would not occur but for the failure to exercise reasonable care on the part of the person in control. The district court found there were other possible explanations, but even this speculation does not defeat the doctrine in this case. P does not have to eliminate all possible causes. P has only to provide evidence based upon which reasonable persons can say it is more likely than not there was negligence associated with the event.

---

e. **Defenses against RIL.**

1) Inspection is no defense.

2) How can a defendant defend against RIL?

   a) Offer alternate explanations for the injury to the plaintiff other than the defendant's negligence.

   b) Show that such injuries happen frequently without the negligence of anyone.

   c) Show that the defendant did not have control of the situation or that another person had control.

f. **Departure from the rule of exclusive control--**

Ybarra v. Spangard, 154 P.2d 687 (Cal. 1944).

Facts. Ybarra (P) consulted Dr. Tilley (D), who diagnosed P as having appendicitis and arranged for an appendectomy, which was performed by Dr. Spangard (D) at a hospital owned by Dr. Swift (D). Prior to the operation, P was wheeled into the operating room by Gisler (D), a nurse, and his body was adjusted on the operating table by Dr. Reser (D), an anesthetist, who pulled P to the head of the operating table and laid him back against two hard objects at the top of his shoulders. P awoke the next morning attended by Thompson (D) and another nurse. P immediately felt sharp pain between his neck and right shoulder, which spread to his lower right arm, although he had never suffered pain or injury there before. P's condition worsened (after his release from the hospital) to paralysis and atrophy. P sued to recover damages for personal injuries due to negligent malpractice. Dr. Reser (D) and the nurses were employees of Dr. Swift; the other doctors were independent contractors. They contended that P must show by what instrumentality he was injured and which D controlled it. The lower court entered a judgment of nonsuit as to all Ds, and P appeals.

Issue. When a person is rendered unconscious in order to undergo surgical treatment and in the course of the treatment receives an unexplained injury to a part of his body not the subject of treatment, is it the burden of each of those who were charged with the patient's well-being to demonstrate that they exercised due care toward the patient?

Held. Yes. Judgment reversed.

♦   When a person is rendered unconscious to receive medical treatment and an untreated part of his body is injured, those entrusted with his care have the burden of initial explanation.

♦   Every D in whose custody P was placed for any period had a duty of ordinary care to see that he was not unnecessarily injured.

♦   Any D who negligently injured P or neglected P so that he could be injured would be liable.

♦   An employer would be liable for the negligence of his employees; a doctor in charge of the operation would be liable for negligence of anyone who assisted in the operation.

♦   Each D had had within his control one or more instrumentalities by which P might have been injured.

♦   It is unreasonable to insist that P, who had been rendered unconscious, identify the negligent defendant.

Comment. Since the court believes that all of the defendants would protect each other, the court departs from the normal res ipsa doctrine (*i.e.,* the plaintiff must show that the cause of the harm is under the exclusive control of the defendant) in order to smoke out the evidence.

E. MEDICAL MALPRACTICE

1. **The Professional Standard.** A doctor or other professional is required to have the same skill and learning as average members of the profession and to apply that skill and learning with the same care as is generally exercised by other members of his profession.

    a. **Example of the standard.** In *Robbins v. Footer*, 553 F.2d 123 (D.C. Cir. 1977), the locality rule was rejected. Robbins's baby died a few hours after birth. Robbins alleged that Dr. Footer had given the mother a drug that affected the baby's oxygen supply and caused the death. Robbins offered two experts who testified to a national standard of care. One of those experts admitted that local practice recognized a lesser standard, and his testimony was stricken from the record. The trial court instructed the jury to apply a standard "similar" to a local standard. The trial court found for the defendant, but the appeals court vacated and remanded. The court reasoned that the medical profession is held to the customary practice of a physician in good standing. Early cases allowed the customary practice standard to be limited to that practice of the local community, but these cases are no longer followed. At least with respect to certified specialists, the court rejected the locality rule and held that the defendant must exercise that degree of care and skill that a reasonably competent practitioner in his field exercises under similar circumstances.

    b. **Exceptions to the standard.** Although the medical profession may ordinarily set its own standard by customary practice, exceptions do occur. Where the practice appears to be unreasonable even to lay people, a higher standard will be set.

2. **National Standard Adopted--**

Sheeley v. Memorial Hospital, 710 A.2d 161 (R.I. 1998).

Facts. Sheeley (P) delivered a healthy child at Memorial Hospital. At the time of the birth, P was under the care of Dr. Ryder, a second-year family practice resident. Dr. Ryder performed an episiotomy on P. This procedure involves a cut into the perineum of the mother to prevent tearing during the delivery. After the baby had been delivered, Dr. Ryder performed a repair of the episiotomy, stitching the incision previously made. After her discharge from the hospital, P developed complications in the area in which the episiotomy had been performed and required corrective surgery. P filed suit against the hospital and Dr. Ryder (Ds), alleging negligence. The trial judge excluded the testimony of P's expert witness and granted Ds' motion for a directed verdict against P. P appeals.

Issue. Did the trial justice err in excluding the testimony of P's expert witness, which exclusion resulted in the entry of the directed verdict?

Held. Yes. Judgment reversed.

- P was not permitted to introduce the expert testimony of a New York board certified OB/GYN regarding Dr. Ryder's alleged malpractice and the applicable standard of care for an episiotomy. Dr. Ryder is a family practice resident, not in the same medical field as P's expert.

- We have held that only where a physician-expert lacks knowledge, skill, or experience in the same field as the alleged malpractice is it required that the testifying expert be in the same medical field as the defendant.

- Ds' argument that P's expert lacks any knowledge about Rhode Island's standard of care in this matter prompts us to reexamine the proper standard of care to be applied in medical malpractice cases and to abandon the "similar locality" rule, which previously governed the admissibility of expert testimony in such actions.

- The "similar locality" rule legitimized a low standard of care in certain smaller communities and failed to address or to compensate for the potential so-called conspiracy of silence in a plaintiff's locality that would preclude any possibility of obtaining expert testimony.

- Geographical impediments that may previously have justified the need for a "similar locality" analysis are no longer applicable in view of the present-day realities of the medical profession.

- In enacting the relevant statute, the legislature did not provide any reference to the "similar locality" rule. We conclude that this omission was deliberate and constitutes a recognition of the national approach to the delivery of medical services, especially in the urban centers of this country, of which Rhode Island is certainly one.

- Accordingly we join the growing number of jurisdictions that have repudiated the "same or similar" communities test in favor of a national standard and hold that a physician is under a duty to use the degree of care and skill that is expected of a reasonably competent practitioner in the same class to which he belongs, acting in the same or similar circumstances.

---

3. **Res Ipsa Loquitur Supported by Expert Witness--**

States v. Lourdes Hospital, 792 N.E.2d 151 (N.Y. 2003).

Facts. States (P) successfully underwent surgery at Lourdes Hospital for removal of an ovarian cyst. However, P alleges that the anesthesiologist and his practice group (Ds) injured her right arm. When Ds inserted a needle into P's right arm to administer anesthesia, P complained of pain and burning, but the surgery continued. After surgery, P complained of increasing pain. Finally, she was diagnosed with right thoracic outlet syndrome and reflex sympathetic dystrophy. While the cause of P's injury is disputed, P alleges that her arm was negligently positioned during surgery. Ds moved for summary judgment at the close of discovery, based on the absence of evidence. P conceded the absence of direct evidence, but submitted expert medical opinion that her injuries would not have happened in the absence of negligence and argued that this testimony could be used to support a res ipsa loquitur theory. The trial court denied D's motion. A divided appeals court reversed. P appeals.

Issue. May expert testimony be used to educate a jury as to the likelihood that the occurrence would take place without negligence where a basis of common knowledge is lacking?

Held. Yes. Judgment reversed.

♦   A plaintiff may invoke the doctrine of res ipsa loquitur if she establishes that: (i) the occurrence would not have taken place in the absence of negligence; (ii) the injury was caused by an agent or instrumentality within the exclusive control of the defendant; and (iii) no act or negligence on the plaintiff's part contributed to the happening of the event.

♦   We are concerned here with the first of the three required elements of res ipsa loquitur. In order to satisfy this element in this case, P must rely on expert testimony, not merely everyday experience.

♦   D argues that res ipsa loquitur only applies to matters of general knowledge. However, expert testimony may be used by the jury to bridge the gap between the expert's specialized knowledge and its own common knowledge. A majority of courts that have considered this question agree. Our society has become more sophisticated and specialized, and there are many people with proper training and experience in all professions who can aid and educate a jury. This does not negate the jury's ultimate responsibility to draw the necessary conclusion.

---

4.   **Informed Consent in Invasive and Noninvasive Treatment--**

Matthies v. Mastromonaco, 733 A.2d 456 (N.J. 1999).

Facts. Matthies (P), 81, living alone and maintaining an independent lifestyle, fell in her apartment and fractured her right hip. Dr. Mastromonaco (D), an osteopath and board-certified orthopedic surgeon, was called in to consult on P's care and treatment. D reviewed P's medical history and condition and, based on three factors, decided against pinning her hip: (i) P was elderly and in a weakened condition, making surgery risky; (ii) P had osteoporosis, and D determined P's bones were too porous to hold the steel screws; and (iii) 40 years earlier, P had suffered a stroke that left her partially paralyzed on her right side, resulting in its limited use. D concluded that bed rest would allow P's hip to heal enough to restore her leg to its limited function. Soon after P began her bed rest treatment, the head of her right femur displaced, resulting in a shortening of her right leg and her continued inability to walk. At trial, P's expert testified that bed rest was an inappropriate treatment unless the patient does not expect to walk again and because of the risk of dislocation of the hip. D's expert agreed that pinning P's hip would have decreased the risk of displacement, but he also agreed that P's bones were too porous to withstand insertion of the pins. P now lives in a nursing home confined to a bed or chair, and is completely dependent on others. P sued D. The trial court accepted D's argument that informed consent is irrelevant in noninvasive treatment cases. The court refused to charge the jury on the issue of lack of informed consent and did not allow P's attorney to question on the issue of disclosure of alternative procedures. The jury returned a verdict of no cause of action. The Appellate Division reversed and remanded the matter to the trial court for a new trial on both issues. The state supreme court granted D's petition for certification.

Issues.

(i)   Does the doctrine of informed consent require a doctor to obtain the patient's consent before implementing a nonsurgical procedure?

(ii)   Should a doctor, in discussing with the patient treatment alternatives that he recommends, discuss medically reasonable alternative courses of treatment that the doctor does not recommend?

Held. (i) Yes. (ii) Yes. Judgment affirmed.

♦   Even when the chosen treatment is noninvasive, to obtain a patient's informed consent to one of several alternative courses of treatment, the physician should explain the medically reasonable invasive and noninvasive alternatives, including the risks and the likely outcomes of those alternatives.

♦   A patient has a duty to provide her doctor with all information necessary for the doctor to make a diagnosis and determine a course of treatment. In turn, the doctor has the duty to evaluate the relevant information and disclose all courses of treatment that are medically reasonable under the circumstances. The patient must make the ultimate decision regarding treatment based on the doctor's recommendation. Informed consent applies to both invasive and noninvasive procedures.

♦   Under the negligence theory of informed consent, the analysis centers on whether the physician adequately presents the material facts so that the patient can make an informed decision. The reasonable patient standard provides the physician is obligated to disclose only that information material to a reasonable patient's informed decision.

♦ To insure informed consent, the physician must inform patients of medically reasonable treatment alternatives and their risks and outcomes. The test for measuring the materiality of the risk of a treatment is whether a reasonable patient in the patient's position would have considered the risk material. A physician should discuss the medically reasonable courses of treatment, including nontreatment. Physicians do not adequately discharge that duty by disclosing only treatment alternatives that they recommend.

♦ The duty to inform is especially critical when the choice of one alternative precludes the choice of another, as in this case, or when it increases the risks attendant on the other alternatives. That need further intensifies when the choice turns not so much on purely medical considerations as on the choice of one lifestyle or set of values over another.

♦ A cause of action based on the doctor's breach of the standard of care does not adequately protect the patient's right to be informed of treatment alternatives. Like the deviation from the standard of care, the doctor's failure to obtain informed consent is a form of medical negligence. Recognition of a separate duty emphasizes the doctor's obligation to inform, as well as treat, the patient.

♦ Here, the jury did not have the opportunity to consider whether D had obtained P's informed consent to the treatment he recommended. Because the issues of informed consent and deviation from the standard of care are interrelated, the jury should consider both issues on retrial.

III. THE DUTY REQUIREMENT: PHYSICAL INJURIES

A. INTRODUCTION

1. **Limited Duty.** A duty is a legal obligation imposed on one person for the benefit of another. In negligence cases, the duty owed by the defendant is to conform to the legal standard of reasonable conduct in light of the apparent risk; *i.e.,* conduct that a reasonable person of ordinary prudence would follow under the same or similar circumstances. In some situations, however, the defendant will not be under the full obligation of reasonable conduct toward the plaintiff even in light of a foreseeable and quite reasonable risk. In these situations, the defendant has only a limited duty.

2. **Privity Requirement.** The privity of contract theory developed in the English courts in the early 1800s as a shield for manufacturers and suppliers against injured users and parties other than the buyer. In *Winterbottom v. Wright* (Eng. 1842), *infra*, Lord Abinger rejected the claim against a coach repairman by a passenger injured when the coach collapsed (the repairman had agreed with the owner to keep the coach in repair), stating that the most absurd and outrageous consequences would result if those not in privity of contract were allowed to sue in contract. Unless the injured plaintiff was the buyer, no recovery could be had either in tort or contract, no matter how negligent the seller's conduct. Modern developments distinguish between nonfeasance and misfeasance—where breach of contract constitutes misfeasance, such breach may also constitute a tort. The privity limitation was abolished as to sellers of negligently made goods in *MacPherson v. Buick Motor Co.*, *infra*.

B. OBLIGATIONS TO OTHERS

1. **No Duty to Act.**

    a. **Misfeasance vs. nonfeasance.** One must distinguish between nonfeasance and misfeasance—between failing to act and acting negligently. Although a person may be under no duty to take affirmative action in the first instance, if she undertakes assistance and is thereafter negligent in what she does or does not do, she is liable.

    b. **Act or omission of defendant.** The act of the defendant must be the external manifestation of her will, *i.e.,* volitional movement, in order to support a cause of action based on negligence. However, liability in negligence can also be based on the failure or omission of the defendant to act if she is under an affirmative duty to act.

2. Defendant's Relationship to Plaintiff.

a. **Undertaking a duty.** Nonfeasance creates no duty for the defendant. Under certain circumstances, however, a duty may arise. If a defendant undertakes a duty, that act must be performed with reasonable care.

b. **Superior knowledge--**

Harper v. Herman, 499 N.W.2d 472 (Minn. 1993).

Facts. Harper (P), a 20-year-old, was a guest on Herman's (D's) boat on Lake Minnetonka. P was seriously injured while diving into shallow water. D, 64, was an experienced boat owner and had spent hundreds of hours operating boats on Lake Minnetonka. P had some experience swimming in lakes, but no formal diving training. When D stopped the boat for swimming and was lowering the boat's ladder, P dove into the water, without warning, and severed his spinal cord. P sued D. The trial court granted D's motion for summary judgment, finding that D had no duty to warn P, and the court of appeals reversed. D appeals.

Issues.

(i) Does a boat owner who is a social host owe a duty of care to warn his guests on the boat that water is too shallow for diving?

(ii) Does a boat owner's superior knowledge that water is shallow give rise to a duty to warn?

Held. (i) No. (ii) No. Judgment reversed and original judgment reinstated.

◆ An affirmative duty to act arises only when there is a special relationship between parties. This relationship is generally found only on the part of common carriers, innkeepers, possessors of land who hold land open to the public, and persons who have custody of another person under circumstances in which that other person is deprived of normal opportunities to protect himself.

◆ Here, P was not vulnerable and he had the ability to protect himself. D did not hold power over his guests' welfare, and the guests did not expect D's protection.

◆ In the absence of a duty to provide protection, superior knowledge of a dangerous condition by itself does not establish liability in negligence.

c. Social venture--

Farwell v. Keaton, 240 N.W.2d 217 (Mich. 1976).

Facts. Siegrist (D) and Farwell (the decedent) were drinking beer near a drive-in restaurant. When they saw several girls, they began to follow them. The girls complained to some friends and six boys chased D and Farwell. D escaped unharmed, but Farwell was severely beaten. D drove Farwell around for several hours and then drove him home. Farwell was left in the back seat of the car, and he was not discovered until the next day. Farwell died three days later. Farwell's father (P) sued D for Farwell's wrongful death, claiming that D had a duty to render aid to Farwell. The jury found for P, and the court of appeals reversed. P appeals.

Issue. Did D owe P's son a duty of reasonable care?

Held. Yes. Judgment reversed and jury verdict reinstated.

♦ D and Farwell were companions on a social venture. Because of this common venture, a special relationship arose between them. When D knew or should have known of Farwell's peril, he had a duty to render aid. In addition, D undertook a duty of care and must fulfill it reasonably.

Dissent. There was no special relationship in this case that would give rise to a duty of care. In addition, D undertook no duty and, therefore, owed no duty. Finally, the issue of duty is a question of law to be decided by the court and not the jury.

---

d. Negligent misrepresentation--

Randi W. v. Muroc Joint Unified School District, 929 P.2d 582 (Cal. 1997).

Facts. Randi W. (P) alleged that vice principal Robert Gadams molested her in his office at a middle school in the Muroc school district. P also alleged that four school districts and their employees (Ds) had supplied unreservedly positive letters of recommendation to the placement office at the college where Gadams received his teaching credentials even though those defendants allegedly knew of prior charges or complaints of sexual misconduct and knew that the college would provide their letters to prospective employers. P alleged the school district relied on the letters of recommendation. Among P's theories of liability were negligent misrepresentation, fraud, and negligence per se. The trial court granted demurrers on all three claims. The appeals court reversed on these claims and affirmed on P's remaining claims. P appeals.

Issues.

(i)   Although Ds made no representations to P, was P entitled to protection, since she suffered physical injury resulting from the reliance of the district that ultimately hired Gadams?

(ii)   Did P state causes of action for fraud and negligent misrepresentation?

(iii)   Did P adequately plead causation between Ds' misconduct and her injuries?

(iv)   Did P state a cause of action for negligence per se based on violation of a child abuse reporting statute?

Held. (i) Yes. (ii) Yes. (iii) Yes. (iv) No. Judgment affirmed as to negligent misrepresentation and fraud and reversed as to negligence per se.

♦   The Restatement (Second) of Torts section 311 provides for liability in the absence of reliance, where the plaintiff suffers physical harm as a result of a misstatement that threatened physical danger to others.

♦   The assault on P was reasonably foreseeable. Ds could see that a school district would rely on their letters when deciding to hire Gadams. Ds could foresee Gadams might not be hired if he were not unqualifiedly recommended. Ds could foresee that Gadams might molest or injure a student such as P.

♦   Ds' letters constituted "misleading half-truths" rather than mere nondisclosures. Ds made positive assertions, including implied representations that Gadams would interact appropriately with female students. Thus, Ds were obliged to disclose all facts that materially qualified the limited facts disclosed.

♦   P was not a member of the class for whose protection the Child Abuse and Neglect Reporting Act was enacted. The act was intended to protect only those children in the custodial care of the person charged with reporting the abuse and not all children who may at some future time be abused by the same offender. Ds were never the "custodians" of P and accordingly owed her no obligations under the act.

Comment. This holding could have wide implications. If an employee had been terminated for sexual harassment of a physical nature, it would clearly apply. Because of the "foreseeable risk of physical injury," an employer in such a situation would be wise to provide only job title and dates of employment when giving a job reference.

---

e.   Duty to warn--

Tarasoff v. Regents of the University of California, 551 P.2d 334 (Cal. 1976).

Facts. The Tarasoffs (Ps) are the parents of a girl who was murdered by a patient of a psychologist employed by the University of California (D). Ps alleged that the murderer confided his intent to kill their daughter to the psychologist two months before the killing and that although the killer was briefly detained, no further action was taken to restrain him or to warn Ps or their daughter. D demurred to the complaint. The trial court and lower appellate court upheld the demurrer, and Ps appeal.

Issue. Does a therapist who determines that a patient poses a serious danger of violence to others have a duty to exercise reasonable care to protect the foreseeable victim of that danger?

Held. Yes. Judgment reversed.

♦ When prevention of a foreseeable harm requires a defendant to control the conduct of another person or to warn of such conduct, the common law imposes liability only if the defendant bears some special relationship to the dangerous person or to the potential victim. D's therapist had such a relationship with the murderer.

♦ D claims that therapists cannot accurately predict violent behavior and in fact are more often wrong than right. We do not require perfection, but once the existence of a serious danger of violence is determined or should have been determined, the therapist has a duty to exercise reasonable care to protect the foreseeable victims. If such care includes warning the victim, the therapist is liable for his failure to do so.

♦ D claims that such a warning could damage the professional relationship with the patient. Weighing this uncertain damage against the peril to the victim's life compels the conclusion that inaccuracy in predicting violence cannot negate the therapist's duty to protect the threatened victim. The containment of such risks lies in the public interest.

Concurrence and dissent. Since the therapist did in fact predict the danger, he had a duty to warn. There is no liability, however, if a therapist fails to predict the harm.

Dissent. Both legislation and general tort theory favor nondisclosure.

---

f.   **Private right of action denied--**

Uhr v. East Greenbush Central School District, 720 N.E.2d 886 (N.Y. 1999).

Facts. Parents and their child (Ps) sued East Greenbush Central School District (D), alleging that D was negligent in failing to test the child annually for scoliosis in violation of a state statute, and that this failure in the 1993-1994 school year caused her to undergo surgery that could have been avoided. The trial court granted D's motion for summary judgment. The Appellate Division affirmed. Ps appeal.

Issues.

(i)   Does the statute create a private right of action?

(ii)   Did Ps state a claim for common law negligence?

Held. (i) No. (ii) No. Judgment affirmed.

♦   Education Law section 905(1) states that "[m]edical inspectors or principals and teachers in charge of schools in this state shall . . . examine all . . . pupils between eight and sixteen years of age for scoliosis, at least once in each school year." Section (2) provides that "[n]otwithstanding any other provisions of any general, special or local law, the school authorities charged with the duty of making such tests or examinations of pupils for the presence of scoliosis pursuant to this section shall not suffer any liability to any person as a result of making such test or examination, which liability would not have existed by any provision of law, statutory or otherwise, in the absence of this section."

♦   D's obligation to examine for scoliosis is clear, but a statutory command does not necessarily carry with it a right of private enforcement. When a statute is silent, as here, courts have had to determine whether a private right of action may be fairly implied. We must apply the test of *Sheehy v. Big Flats Community Day*, 73 N.Y.2d 629 (1989). In making the determination, we ask:

(i)   Whether the plaintiff is one of the class for whose particular benefit the statute was enacted;

(ii)   Whether recognition of a private right of action would promote the legislative purpose; and

(iii)   Whether creation of such a right would be consistent with the legislative scheme.

♦   P is a member of the class.

♦   The second prong requires that we first discern the legislature's objective when it enacted the statute, and then determine whether a private right of action would promote that objective. Scoliosis, if detected early, can be treated successfully, often without the need for surgery. It is obvious that the legislature was seeking to benefit public health and reducing the cost of medical care. Ps argue a private right of action would aid the legislative purpose; the risk of liability for failure to screen will encourage compliance with the statute. D argues that the risk of liability will prompt school districts to seek waivers of the requirement to screen and thus defeat the statute's purpose. We conclude that a private right of action would promote the legislative purpose; the second prong is satisfied.

♦ We conclude that a private right of action would not be consistent with the statutory scheme. The statute expressly charges the Commissioner of Education with the duty to implement the law and gives the commissioner authority to adopt rules and regulations for that purpose. Also, the commissioner has power to withhold public funding from noncompliant school districts. We can conclude that the legislature contemplated administrative enforcement of this statute. An implied private right of action would be inconsistent with the legislative scheme. The statute provides that the school district "shall not suffer any liability to any person as a result of *making* such test or examination" (emphasis added). Ps interpret the statute as conferring immunity for misfeasance but not nonfeasance. We agree with D's position, however, that it would be incongruous for the legislature to provide immunity for one circumstance but not the other.

♦ Ps have failed as a matter of law to state a claim for common law negligence.

C. POLICY BASES FOR INVOKING NO DUTY

There are some cases in which the defendant's negligence played a part in creating the risk that injured the plaintiff, but for specific policy reasons, such as to keep liability within manageable bounds, courts determine that no duty exists.

1. Contractual Relationship--

Strauss v. Belle Realty Co., 482 N.E.2d 34 (N.Y. 1985).

Facts. Strauss (P) was a resident of an apartment building that had its electrical power supplied by Consolidated Edison (D). Both P's own apartment and the common areas of the apartment were supplied power by D. During the power blackout of New York City in 1977, P's apartment building lost its power. P fell in a dark stairway and sued D and Belle Realty Company. D moved to dismiss the complaint, and the trial court denied the motion. The Appellate Division reversed and dismissed the complaint, and P appeals.

Issue. Did D owe P a duty of reasonable care in providing power to light the stairway in a common area of the apartment?

Held. No. Judgment affirmed.

♦ The contractual relationship to light the common area was with the apartment owner. D had no contractual relationship with P to light that area. Under these circumstances, D owes no additional duties outside of those defined in the contract.

- Substantial public policy lends aid to D's claim of no duty. The blackout was system-wide and had an impact on millions of people. Although P may be a foreseeable plaintiff, he was not a member of a narrow class. There were millions in the same group. To allow recovery here would extend liability to millions of people.

Dissent. The public policy claims ignore the other public policy problems. The extensive liability could well be paid by a reduction of the return on shareholder's equity or by raising rates. In addition, granting immunity in this case places the total cost of the injury on the injured party.

---

2. Social Host Liability Not Extended to Injured Third Persons--

Reynolds v. Hicks, 951 P.2d 761 (Wash. 1998).

Facts. After Jamie and Anna Hicks (Ds) were married, several hundred people, including Anna's under-age nephew, Steven, attended a dinner reception where wine and champagne were served. After dinner, drinks were available at a hosted bar. At approximately midnight, Steven left the reception in his sister's car and was involved in an automobile accident with Reynolds (P). P was seriously injured. P and his family sued Steven, his sister, and Ds, alleging that they were "negligent in serving alcoholic beverages to Defendant [Steven] with knowledge and/or reason to believe that [he] was below the age of 21 years and/or became intoxicated." Steven and his sister settled with Ps. Ds' motion for summary judgment was granted on the issue that Ds, as social hosts, did not owe a duty to third parties injured by the intoxicated minor. Ps appealed to the court of appeals. The court of appeals certified the case to this court and direct review was granted.

Issue. Does Washington law extend social host liability for furnishing alcohol to a minor to third persons injured by the intoxicated minor?

Held. No. Trial court's dismissal affirmed.

- Social hosts are ill-equipped to handle the responsibilities of guests' alcohol consumption; unlike commercial vendors, social hosts have no profit motive. Commercial vendors are better organized to control customers and have the financial resources to do so.

- The results would be sweeping and unpredictable if liability were imposed. Commercial vendors are responsible for a narrow group of people. Liability for social hosts, on the other hand, would touch most adults frequently and because they are not accustomed to handling intoxicated guests, we cannot predict how they would respond to ill-defined duties.

- Minors are protected from their own injuries as a result of their intoxication.

Concurrence. I agree that Ds are not liable, but my reasons are those expressed by the dissent in *Hansen v. Friend*, 824 P.2d 483 (Wash. 1992). ("I have consistently held to the belief that without legislative mandate no tort action should lie against a host, either commercial or social . . . , and continue to do so.")

Dissent. The legislature has established the public policy of criminalizing the furnishing of alcohol to a minor. The majority ignores this established policy and replaces it with its own version of policy, based on the fact that an expanded duty to protect third persons raises problematic questions for social hosts in all contexts.

---

3.   Negligent Entrustment--

Vince v. Wilson, 561 A.2d 103 (Vt. 1989).

Facts. Vince (P) was injured in an auto accident. P sued Wilson (D), who had provided funds for her grandnephew, the driver of the car at the time of the accident, to purchase the vehicle. Later, Ace Auto Sales, Inc. and its president, Gardner, were added as defendants. D had communicated to Ace and Gardner prior to the sale of the vehicle that her grandnephew had no license and had failed his driver's test; D also knew that he had abused alcohol and other drugs. The trial court directed a verdict for Ace and Gardner, and P appeals. The jury returned a verdict against D, and D appeals.

Issues.

(i)   Should recovery under a claim of negligent entrustment be limited to those situations in which the defendant is the owner or has the right to control the instrumentality entrusted?

(ii)   Did the trial court err in directing verdicts for Ace and Gardner?

Held. (i) No. (ii) Yes. Case remanded.

- The Restatement (Second) of Torts section 390 provides that "[o]ne who supplies directly or through a third person a chattel for the use of another whom the supplier knows or has reason to know to be likely because of his youth, inexperience, or otherwise, to use it in a manner involving unreasonable risk of physical harm to himself and others whom the supplier should expect to share in or be endangered by its use, is subject to liability for physical harm resulting to them."

- The issue is clearly one of negligence to be determined by the jury under proper instruction; the relationship of D to the particular instrumentality is but one factor to be considered. The key factor is that the theory requires a showing that the "entrustor knew or should have known some reason why entrusting the item to another was foolish or negligent."

♦ Insofar as D is concerned, the evidence was significant to make out a prima facie case of negligent entrustment and the trial court properly submitted the question to the jury.

♦ Regarding Ace and Gardner, there was evidence that, if believed by the jury, would establish that Ace and Gardner knew that the operator had no license and had failed his driver's test. The question should have been determined by a jury.

D. LANDOWNERS AND OCCUPIERS

1. **Duty of Owners and Occupants of Land.** In this area, duties are divided into fairly rigid arbitrary categories, depending on the type of landowner or occupier and the plaintiff involved. These duties are generally the result of historical precedent and often would be considered inconsistent with what reasonable persons under the same or similar circumstances would do.

   a. **Trespassing adult.** Trespassing adults enter the land of another with no right or privilege; they must take the premises as found and are presumed to assume the risk of looking out for themselves. Thus, the general rule is that a landowner/occupier is not liable for injuries to adult trespassers caused by her failure to exercise due care, put her land in a safe condition for them, or carry on her activities in such a manner as not to endanger them. In most jurisdictions, the foreseeability of a trespass is deemed to create no duty on the part of the landowner/occupier. However, where the trespassers are known generally (even though the identity or presence of a particular trespasser is unknown), the trespass occurs on a particular part of the property (*e.g.,* walking path, etc.), and the trespassers are tolerated, there is a tendency on the part of many courts to treat the trespasser (called a "discovered" trespasser) as a licensee, requiring the landowner/occupier to warn the trespasser of, or make safe, known natural or artificial conditions or activities involving any risk of harm that the trespasser is unlikely to discover. Other courts limit the obligation of the landowner/occupier to a duty to discover and warn the discovered trespasser of, or make safe, known artificial conditions and activities that could seriously injure the trespasser. Under this position, there is no duty with respect to natural conditions or artificial conditions presenting a risk less than death or serious bodily injury.

   b. **Licensees.** A licensee is one who goes on the land of another with the consent of the owner/occupier, through authority of law or by necessity, and is deemed to take the land as the occupier uses it. However, the landowner/occupier must warn the licensee of, or make safe, known natural or artificial conditions or activities involving any risk of harm that the licensee is unlikely to discover, whether existing at the time of entry or arising thereafter. The licensee has the occupier's consent and nothing more.

1) **Social guest.** "Invitee" (defined *infra*) is a word of art; it does not include all persons invited onto the premises. A social guest, though invited, is only a licensee. The fact that a guest renders some incidental service or was invited out of economic motives does not remove the guest from the status of licensee.

2) **Known danger.** The owner of premises is under a duty either to warn a known licensee of known dangerous conditions that the owner cannot reasonably assume that the licensee knows or should reasonably detect, or to make such conditions safe.

3) **Duty to inspect.** The duty of a landowner/occupier extends only to known dangerous conditions; there is no duty to inspect in order to discover dangerous conditions.

4) **Licensee-invitee distinction--**

Carter v. Kinney, 896 S.W.2d 926 (Mo. 1995).

Facts. The Kinneys (Ds) hosted a Bible study at their home. Mr. Kinney had shoveled snow on the driveway the previous evening, but was unaware that ice had formed overnight. Carter (P) slipped and fell, breaking his leg. Ds had offered their home as other church members did; interested members signed up on a sheet at the church to attend. P had no social relationship with Ds, and Ds received no financial benefit from P. P filed suit, and Ds were granted summary judgment. P appeals.

Issue. Was P a licensee and, therefore, owed no duty of protection from Ds as to unknown dangerous conditions?

Held. Yes. Judgment affirmed.

♦ All visitors who enter another's premises with permission are licensees unless the possessor has an interest in any visits such that a visitor has reason to believe that the premises have been made safe for his sake, in which case a visitor is an invitee.

♦ A possessor of land owes a licensee a duty to make him safe only from those dangers of which the possessor is aware.

♦ A possessor of land owes invitees a duty to exercise reasonable care to protect invitees against dangers of which he is aware and those that an inspection would reveal.

♦ A social guest is a subclass of licensee rather than invitee, under Missouri law. In this case, P was clearly only a licensee.

Comment. *Rowland v. Christian*, 443 P.2d 561 (Cal. 1968), rejected the categories and the respective duties owed to each. *Rowland* has met with complete acceptance in some states, partial acceptance in others, and rejection in most states. Under *Rowland*, one's status as a trespasser or an invitee is just one factor to consider in determining negligence.

---

5) Rejection of common law categories--

Heins v. Webster County, 552 N.W.2d 51 (Neb. 1966).

Facts. After a heavy snowfall, Heins (P) and his family visited the Webster County Hospital (D). D claims that P was merely paying a social visit to his daughter Julie, the director of nursing for the hospital. P claims he was visiting, but he was also checking on plans for him to play Santa at the hospital Christmas party. While P and his family were leaving the hospital through the main door, P fell. At trial, P testified that he held the front entrance door open for others and then slipped as he stepped onto the landing. P blames his fall on a patch of ice on the landing. P sued D, claiming D failed to properly inspect the entrance, failed to warn P of the dangerous condition, allowed the ice to accumulate, and failed to remove the ice and snow. After a bench trial, the court found P was a licensee and entered judgment for D. P appeals.

Issue. Should this court abolish the common law classifications of licensee and invitee and require a duty of reasonable care to all nontrespassers?

Held. Yes. Judgment reversed and case remanded.

♦ Our present law limits the duty that a landowner owes to a licensee to refrain from injuring a licensee by willful or wanton negligence or designed injury, or to warn him, as a licensee, of a hidden danger or peril known to the owner or occupant but unknown to or unobservable by the licensee, who is required to exercise ordinary care. A business visitor, or invitee, receives a higher degree of care, reasonable care. Therefore, under present law, the trial court correctly found for D based on its finding that P was a licensee.

♦ Many states have abandoned the classifications with regard to licensees and invitees but retained them with regard to trespassers. Unlike a trespasser, who has no basis to claim protection from a landowner, invitees and licensees enter another's land "under color of right."

♦ Many of the states that have retained the distinctions have done so because of the predictability of the common law. They have noted the concern that the absence of a stable and established system of loss allocation would result in the establishment of a system devoid of standards for liability. Further, they cite statutory refinements that ameliorate the harshness of the common law. The most often cited reason for abandoning the categories is that an entrant's status should not determine the duty that the landowner owes to him.

♦ To focus upon the categories is contrary to our modern social mores and humanitarian values.

♦ While the common law classifications as determinants of liability have been abandoned by many states, they have found that the classifications remain relevant in determining the foreseeability of the harm under ordinary negligence principles.

♦ Here, P was denied the opportunity to recover because of his status at the moment of his fall; had he been a patient, he would have been able to recover. D would undergo no additional burden in exercising reasonable care for a social visitor such as P because it had the duty to exercise reasonable care for its invitees.

♦ The common law status classifications should not be able to shield those who would otherwise be held to a standard of reasonable care but for the arbitrary classification of the visitor as a licensee. We conclude that we should eliminate the distinction between licensees and invitees by requiring a standard of reasonable care for all lawful visitors. We retain a separate classification for trespassers because we conclude that one should not owe a duty to exercise reasonable care to those not lawfully on one's property. Adopting this rule places the focus where it should be, on the foreseeability of the injury, rather than on allowing the duty in a particular case to be determined by the status of the person who enters upon the property.

♦ We impose upon owners and occupiers only the duty to exercise reasonable care in the maintenance of their premises for the protection of lawful visitors. Among the factors to be considered in evaluating whether a landowner or occupier has exercised reasonable care for the protection of lawful visitors will be (1) the foreseeability or possibility of harm; (2) the purpose for which the entrant entered the premises; (3) the time, manner, and circumstances under which the entrant entered the premises; (4) the use to which the premises are put or are expected to be put; (5) the reasonableness of the inspection, repair, or warning; (6) the opportunity and ease of repair or correction or giving of the warning; and (7) the burden on the land occupier and/or community in terms of inconvenience or cost in providing adequate protection.

Dissent. It is not the function of the court to create a liability where the law creates none. Under the majority's opinion, a homeowner would have potential liability for any number of not only uninvited but unwanted solicitors or visitors coming to the homeowner's door.

---

c. **Invitees.** An invitee is one who goes upon the land of another with the consent of the owner/occupier for some purpose connected with the use of the premises, *e.g.,* a business or a public invitee. The duty owed is co-extensive with the invitation. The basis of liability is an implied promise that the premises are, or will be, safe or reasonably so. This means that the invitor is under a duty to make a reasonable inspection of the premises and discover any dangers that may exist. Thereafter, the duty owed to the invitee is one of ordinary care. The limitations of responsibility of the invitor in the case of the business invitee are generally determined by specific time or length of stay, part of premises visited, etc. Generally, those entering under public authority during non-business hours (*e.g.,* firefighters) are deemed licensees; others entering for a business purpose, such as postal workers, are seen as invitees under the modern view.

1) **Business invitees.** One of the older theories was that to be a business invitee, one must be invited on the premises for potential pecuniary benefit to the owner. Potential gain was not difficult to find; one who loitered in a store was held to be an invitee because she might buy something.

2) **Limitation on invitation.** A person remains an invitee only while in those areas or parts of the premises held open to her for the purposes for which she came. If an invitee goes outside the area of invitation, but under consent of the owner, she becomes a licensee, and if no permission is involved, she may be a trespasser.

3) **Reasonable care required.** The legal obligation of the defendant in all of these situations is only to exercise reasonable care. The duty arises only when danger is to be anticipated (*i.e.,* is reasonably foreseeable), and the owner/occupier is not required to do anything unreasonable or risk personal harm.

4) **Protection against third persons.** The owner/occupier must exercise whatever power of control the landowner has over the conduct of third persons to protect an invitee who may be injured by such conduct.

Posecai v. Wal-Mart Stores, Inc., 752 So. 2d 762 (La. 1999).

Facts. After Posecai (P) exited Sam's Club (D) and returned to her parked car, she was robbed at gunpoint by a man who had been hiding under her car. P was wearing jewelry valued close to $19,000. After P was released, she ran back to the store for help. A security guard posted inside the store could not see outside. No security guards patrolled the parking lot. There was conflicting testimony as to whether the parking area was a high crime area. To one testifying officer's knowledge, no other stores in the area employed security guards. P's expert testified that the robbery could have been prevented by an outside security guard. During the six years prior to the incident, there were three robberies or "predatory offenses" on D's premises, one related to a domestic dispute. P contends that D was negligent in failing to provide adequate security in the parking lot. P filed suit to recover for mental anguish as well as for her property loss. Following a bench trial, judgment was rendered in P's favor. P was awarded $18,968 for her lost jewelry and $10,000 in general damages for her mental anguish. The appeals court affirmed the judgment but modified the allocation of damages. The state supreme court granted certiorari.

Issue. Did D owe a duty to protect P from the criminal acts of third parties under the facts and circumstances of this case?

Held. No. Judgment reversed.

◆   Under the duty-risk analysis used to determine whether liability exists under the facts presented, P must prove that the conduct in question was the cause-in-fact of the resulting harm, D owed a duty of care to P, the requisite duty was breached by D, and the risk of harm was within the scope of protection afforded by the duty breached.

◆   We now adopt the rule that although business owners are not the insurers of customers' safety, under limited circumstances they do have a duty to implement reasonable measures to protect customers from foreseeable criminal acts.

◆   To determine foreseeability, jurisdictions have used four basic approaches: (i) the specific harm rule (considered too restrictive by many courts), under which a landowner owes a duty to protect patrons from the violent acts of third parties only if he is aware of specific, imminent harm about to befall them; (ii) the prior similar incidents test (considered arbitrary by some), which looks to prior incidents of crime near the premises, their frequency, and their similarity to the crime in question in establishing foreseeability; (iii) the totality of the circumstances test (most commonly used, but considered too broad by some), which takes into account additional factors such as the nature, condition, and location of the land, as well as any other relevant factual circumstances including property crimes or minor crimes that may be precursors to more violent crimes; and

(iv) the balancing test, which addresses the interests of both business owners and customers by balancing the foreseeability of harm against the burden of imposing a duty to protect against the criminal acts of third persons.

♦ We adopt the balancing test to be used in deciding whether a business owes a duty of care to protect its customers from the criminal acts of third parties. The foreseeability of the crime risk on the defendant's property and the gravity of the risk determine the existence and the extent of the defendant's duty. The greater the foreseeability and gravity of the harm, the greater the duty of care that will be imposed on the business. A very high degree of foreseeability is required to give rise to a duty to post security guards, but a lower degree of foreseeability may support a duty to implement lesser security measures such as using surveillance cameras, installing improved lighting or fencing, or trimming shrubbery. The plaintiff has the burden of establishing the duty the defendant owed under the circumstances. The foreseeability and gravity of the harm are to be determined by the facts and circumstances of the case. The most important factor to be considered is the existence, frequency, and similarity of prior incidents of crime on the premises, but the location, nature, and condition of the property should also be taken into account.

♦ In the instant case, of the three predatory offenses that occurred, only one was similar to the crime involving P. The foreseeability and gravity of harm in D's parking lot remained slight. D did not possess the requisite degree of foreseeability for the imposition of a duty to provide security patrols in its parking lot.

Concurrence. I agree that D did not have a duty to provide security patrols in its parking lot under the facts of this case, but I would adopt the totality of circumstances test to determine the defendant's duty.

---

d. **Trespassing children.** Except with respect to extrahazardous activities or conditions, such as maintaining a railroad turntable, children were treated like adults until about the 1920s, when trespassing children began to be recognized as a special class. The rationale for the special classification lies in the fact that (i) children are often incapable of protecting themselves because of their inability to perceive a risk, (ii) parents cannot be expected to follow the child around all day, (iii) maintaining an "attractive nuisance" is deemed undesirable, and (iv) the costs to alleviate the risk of harm is usually slight in comparison with the damages that might be suffered.

1) **Restatement rule.** Restatement (Second) of Torts section 339 sets forth the duty of a property owner with respect to artificial conditions when infant trespassers are involved. A property owner will be liable for injuries to infant trespassers from dangerous artificial

conditions on his land under the following circumstances:

a) If he knows or should know that infants are likely to trespass upon the places where the dangerous condition is maintained;

b) If he knows or should know that the condition involves an unreasonable risk of injury to them;

c) If the infants, because of their immaturity, do not realize the danger involved;

d) If the utility of maintaining the condition is slight in relation to the risk of injury to the infants; and

e) If he fails to exercise reasonable care to eliminate the dangers or otherwise protect the infants.

e. **Persons outside of the premises.** The person in possession of land is required to exercise reasonable care with regard to his activities on the land for the protection of those outside the premises.

1) **Natural conditions.** A landowner/occupier is not liable for damages resulting from conditions on the premises arising in a state of nature.

2) **Public highways or walkways.** The public right of passage on a highway carries with it an obligation on the part of the adjacent landowners to use reasonable care for the protection of those on the highway.

3) **Artificial conditions.** If the landowner/occupier creates artificial conditions on the land, he is obligated to inspect them and protect against danger to others.

2. **Landlord and Tenant.**

a. **Duty owed by landlord to persons outside the land.**

1) The landlord has a duty to repair or warn the tenant of known dangerous artificial conditions or of conditions that may become dangerous.

2) This duty continues only until the tenant has reasonable opportunity to discover the condition and remedy it. If the landlord actively conceals the danger, the duty continues until the tenant actually discovers and has time to remedy it.

3) The landlord has no duty with respect to dangers arising after the property is leased unless the landlord covenants to repair or voluntarily undertakes to do so.

b. **Duty owed by landlord to the lessee.**

1) **Latent dangerous conditions.** The landlord has a duty to repair or warn of known latent dangerous conditions. If the condition is reasonably apparent, no duty is owed.

2) **Failure to make repairs promised.** The landlord has no duty with respect to conditions arising after the property is leased, except that the landlord is liable for her negligent repairs and, under modern cases, the landlord is liable in tort for failure to make repairs covenanted in the lease.

3. **Intrafamily Duties.** At common law, spouses were generally barred from suing one another for personal injury. When 19th century legislatures gave married women the right to own property and to sue over property and contract disputes, state courts began eliminating spousal immunity from tort liability. Intentional torts were the first claims allowed because they indicated the absence of the underlying spousal harmony sought to be preserved. Today, all remnants of spousal immunity have disappeared. Claims by children against parents for intentional harm are also almost universally permitted today. The major area of dispute in parent-child injuries has been over negligently inflicted harms.

a. **Parental immunity abolished--**

Broadbent v. Broadbent, 907 P.2d 43 (Ariz. 1995).

Facts. Laura Broadbent (D) left her two-and-a-half-year-old son Christopher alone by the pool to answer the phone. When D could not see Christopher, she dropped the phone, ran toward the pool, and found him in the bottom of the pool. Christopher was revived, but he suffered severe brain damage from lack of oxygen and lost his motor skills and voluntary movement. Christopher's father (P), as conservator, sued D on Christopher's behalf, alleging negligence. The trial court granted D's motion for summary judgment based on the parental immunity doctrine. P appealed. The parties stipulated that: (i) the real party in interest was Northbrook Indemnity Company, which provided personal umbrella liability insurance coverage for D on the date of the accident; (ii) D may be entitled to indemnity from Northbrook if she is liable for the injuries to Christopher; (iii) D did not want to defend the action but agreed that Northbrook should be permitted to defend; and (iv) the only issue in the case was whether the doctrine of parental immunity applied. The court of appeals ordered that Northbrook be permitted to appear and defend the case. The court of appeals affirmed the parental immunity finding and noted that any change in the parental immunity doctrine was for the supreme court to determine. The case is before the state supreme court.

Issue. Does the doctrine of parental immunity bar an action against Christopher's mother for negligence?

Held. No. Judgment vacated and case remanded.

♦ The primary justifications for this immunity are: (i) parental suits would disturb domestic tranquility; (ii) there is a danger of fraud and collusion; (iii) damages awarded to the child would deplete family resources; (iv) if the child predeceases the parent and the parent inherits the child's damages, the parent would benefit; and (v) suits against parents would interfere with parental care, discipline, and control.

♦ These justifications are weak. A tortiously injured child who receives no compensation upsets the family more than a lawsuit. The possibility of fraud is present in all lawsuits; that can be addressed as in other situations. Because it is unlikely suits will be brought if there is no insurance, there is little chance that family resources will be depleted. The parent inheriting from a child is a remote possibility; however, the solution to this problem is to prohibit inheritance by the parent.

♦ The rationale with the greatest appeal is that allowing children to sue their parents would undercut parental authority and discretion. However, if a child were beaten by a parent, that would be willful conduct, and parents are not immune from suit for willful, wanton, or malicious conduct. While we agree that parents should have the right to determine how much independence, supervision, and control a child should have, they do not possess "unfettered discretion" in raising their children. We need to fashion an objective standard that does not result in second-guessing parents in the management of their family affairs. We reject other tests and approve of the "reasonable parent test," in which a parent's conduct is judged by whether that parent's conduct comported with that of a reasonable and prudent parent in a similar situation.

♦ Here, the jury must determine whether the mother acted as a reasonable and prudent parent in this situation.

♦ A parent may avoid liability because there is no negligence, but not merely because of the status as parent.

Concurrence. Because alleged tortious conduct does not grow out of the family relationship, the question of negligence may be determined as if the parties were not related. However, there are areas of broad discretion in which only parents have authority to make decisions. In these areas, I agree with the Restatement's view that "the standard of a reasonable prudent parent . . . recognizes the existence of that discretion and thus . . . requires that the [parent's] conduct be palpably unreasonable in order to impose liability." If, however, the charged breach of duty falls outside the area of a parent's discretionary authority and is, instead, within the obligation of due care owed by anyone who has supervisory or other responsibility for another's safety, then the test should be much more flexible.

E. GOVERNMENTAL ENTITIES

1. **Historical.** At common law, the doctrine evolved that "the King can do no wrong." Thus, when a plaintiff attempted to sue the state for a wrong done to him, the state was held to be immune from tort liability.

2. **Statement of Doctrine.** Whereas the government is liable or may consent to liability in suits of some other nature, its tort immunity is said to rest upon public policy; *i.e.,* the idea that the people as a whole cannot be guilty of a tort.

    a. **State and federal immunity.** Following this doctrine, it was held that not only are state and federal governments immune from tort liability, but so are various state and federal agencies (*e.g.,* hospitals and schools).

    b. **Status of doctrine today.** The doctrine of sovereign immunity has been abrogated to a great extent by the federal government (under the Federal Tort Claims Act, discussed *infra*) and by a majority of states. However, immunity in these jurisdictions still exists for "discretionary" acts and basic policy decisions.

    c. **Municipalities.** A great deal of law has developed regarding the tort liability of municipal corporations, resulting from the dual character of such entities. On the one hand, they are subdivisions of the state and therefore its agents in the exercise of certain functions and responsibilities; on the other hand, they are also corporate bodies capable of the same acts as private corporations and having certain local interests not shared by the state. For those jurisdictions retaining municipal immunity (about half the states), the law has attempted to distinguish between the two aspects of municipalities and limits tort immunity to the "*governmental*" or "public" functions. A municipality's "*proprietary*" or "private" functions are not immune and may therefore result in tort liability. (The difficulty arises, of course, in attempting to determine which city functions are "governmental" and which are "proprietary.")

    d. **Not applicable when state sues.** Most modern jurisdictions take the position that sovereign immunity applies only when an individual is suing the state. It does not apply when the state has sued the individual defendant, who then seeks to assert a counterclaim or offset against the state. In such a case, it would be unfair to allow the state to assert its immunity to bar the individual defendant's counterclaim.

3.   State and Municipal Liability.

   a.   Doctrine retained--

Riss v. City of New York, 240 N.E.2d 860 (N.Y. 1968).

Facts. Riss (P) repeatedly asked the police department for the city of New York (D) to provide her with protection. She had been threatened by a rejected suitor and feared for her safety. D refused to provide personal protection, and the rejected suitor had someone throw lye in P's face, scarring and blinding her. P sued D for her injuries, claiming that D had a duty to protect her once D was put on notice of the danger. The trial court dismissed the action, and the Appellate Division affirmed. P appeals.

Issue. Did D owe P a duty of care?

Held. No. Judgment affirmed.

♦   The decision to provide police protection is discretionary with the official who must decide how to allocate resources. Individual citizens may not bring actions claiming that they wanted some different allocation. If the immunity the city enjoys is to be abolished, that action is for the legislature to take.

Dissent. The majority opinion is based on nothing more than old tradition. There is no indication that allowing recovery in such actions would cause substantial problems. Such recovery would also encourage cities to provide better services. Finally, the claim that such decisions cannot be made where they have an impact on the allocation of resources is inconsistent. Every decision that concerns dangerous sidewalks, for example, requires a city to allocate more resources to sidewalk repair.

   b.   No liability--

Lauer v. City of New York, 733 N.E.2d 184 (N.Y. 2000).

Facts. After three-year-old Andrew Lauer died, an autopsy revealed that his death was a homicide caused by "blunt injuries" to the neck and brain. The report further indicated that the brain was being preserved for further examination. The police began investigating, focusing primarily on Andrew's father (P). Weeks later, after a more detailed study of Andrew's brain, the medical examiner and a neuropathologist concluded that a ruptured brain aneurysm caused Andrew's death. The medical examiner did not correct the autopsy report or death certificate, and did not notify law enforcement authorities. After a 17-month police investigation, the autopsy findings were finally revealed and a new death certificate issued. P sought $10 million in damages against the city (D), alleging defamation, violation of his civil rights, and negligent and intentional infliction of emotional distress. The trial court dismissed P's claims. The Appellate Division affirmed, except for the negligent infliction of emotional distress claim. D appeals.

Issue. May a member of the public recover damages against a municipality for its employee's negligence?

Held. No. Judgment reversed.

♦ In the area of governmental immunity, a distinction is made between discretionary acts and ministerial acts. A public employee's discretionary acts—meaning conduct involving the exercise of reasoned judgment—may not result in the municipality's liability even when the conduct is negligent. By contrast, ministerial acts—meaning conduct requiring adherence to a governing rule, with a compulsory result—may subject the municipal employer to liability for negligence. It is undisputed that the medical examiner's failure to correct the record and notify the authorities was ministerial.

♦ While a ministerial act is not immunized, it is not necessarily tortious.

♦ Without a duty running directly to the injured person there can be no liability in damages, however careless the conduct or foreseeable the harm. When a plaintiff seeks to sustain liability against a municipality, the duty breached must be more than that owed the public generally.

♦ Based on a statute that charges the chief medical examiner with examining "bodies of persons dying from criminal violence" or other suspicious circumstances, keeping "full and complete records in such form as may be provided by law," and promptly delivering "to the appropriate district attorney copies of all records relating to every death as to which there is, in the judgment of the medical examiner in charge, any indication of criminality," P argues he is owed a duty.

♦ Absent clear and specific language imposing an obligation on D, we cannot impute that obligation. The city charter establishes the office of the chief medical examiner and requires performance of autopsies and preparation of reports for the benefit of the "public at large." The medical examiner must report only to the district attorney.

♦ Further, there is no "special relationship" with P. A special relationship requires: (i) an assumption by the municipality, through promises or actions, of an affirmative duty to act on behalf of the party who was injured; (ii) knowledge on the part of the municipality's agents that inaction could lead to harm; (iii) some form of direct contact between the municipality's agents and the injured party; and (iv) that party's justifiable reliance on the municipality's affirmative undertaking.

♦ We refuse to impose a new duty on the office of the chief medical examiner, which for the future would run to members of the public who may become subjects of a criminal investigation into a death.

Dissent. P has adequately pleaded a prima facie case.

Dissent. The public servant here was the catalyst for the police investigation of P as a murder suspect. He possessed exclusive power to correct the wrong. To immunize this type of alleged misconduct rewards government employees who hide the truth with impunity.

———————————

c.   **Liability allowed--**

Friedman v. State of New York, 493 N.E.2d 893 (N.Y. 1986).

Facts. This opinion discusses three separate cases. Friedman (P1) was injured when her car was forced across a median and was struck head-on. The state of New York (D) had determined five years earlier that a median barrier was needed in this particular location, but none had been built. The trial court found for P, and the Appellate Division affirmed. D appeals. Muller (P2) suffered injury in a similar median cross-over accident at a different location. The state (D) had determined three years earlier that a median barrier was necessary in this location, but none had been built. P2 sued D, but the claim was dismissed. The dismissal was affirmed by the Appellate Division, and P2 appeals. Cataldo (P3) was injured in a similar accident. The state (D) had studied the location of P3's injury and decided that no median barrier was needed. P3's action was dismissed, and this dismissal was affirmed by the Appellate Division. P3 appeals.

Issues.

(i)   May the state be held liable for the decision that a median barrier was not needed in a particular location?

(ii)   May the state be held liable for the failure to install a barrier once a determination has been made that a barrier is necessary?

Held. (i) No. (ii) Yes. Judgment in *Cataldo v. New York State Thruway Authority* affirmed. Judgment affirmed in *Friedman* and reversed in *Muller v. State of New York.*

♦ The state has the authority to make decisions concerning public safety. There is a qualified immunity for such discretionary decisionmaking as long as the study being done was not wholly inadequate. The study in *Cataldo* was consistent with expert opinion.

♦   Once D is made aware of a dangerous highway condition, however, repairs must be made within a reasonable time. In *Friedman* and *Muller*, three and five years are unreasonable delays.

---

4. **Liability of Government Officers.**

   a. **High-ranking officers.** Judges, legislators, and high-ranking members of the executive branch (*e.g.,* cabinet members and department heads) are totally immune from tort liability for acts carried out within the scope of their duties, even if the acts involve "malice" or "abuse of discretion."

   b. **Lower-level administrative officers.** Lower-level officers or employees are immune from claims of negligence under *federal law*, and some states also follow this position.

   c. **Common law rule.** Other states retain the common law rule, which granted immunity to lower-level government officers or employees only when performing "discretionary," as opposed to "ministerial," functions.

      1) **Discretionary functions.** "Discretionary" functions are those in which the officer has some element of personal judgment or decisionmaking, such as evaluating property for assessment purposes or designing or routing a highway. In carrying out these functions, the officer is granted immunity as long as he was acting *honestly and in good faith*.

      2) **Ministerial functions.** "Ministerial" functions are those in which the officer is left no choice of his own; he is merely carrying out orders of others or established duties of his office; *e.g.,* repairing roads or driving vehicles. Here, there is no tort immunity. If the officer fails to perform his required duties properly, he can be held personally liable for any damages resulting therefrom, regardless of whether he was acting in good faith.

5. **The Federal Tort Claims Act.**

   a. **Introduction.** Under the Federal Tort Claims Act ("FTCA") [28 U.S.C. §§1346, 2671 *et seq.*], the federal government, by its consent, is stripped of all immunities with regard to negligent or wrongful acts or omissions by government employees. Still, one cannot maintain an action for intentional torts, strict liability, or discretionary acts by government agents. ("Discretionary" acts have been defined by case law to mean administrative decisions at the "planning" level as opposed to those at the "operational" level.)

b.   **Discretionary function exception of the Federal Tort Claims Act--**

Cope v. Scott, 45 F.3d 445 (D.C. 1995).

Facts. Beach Drive, a two-way, two-lane road, is maintained by the National Park Service. The road was originally designed for pleasure driving because of its many sharp curves, but it has become an important and heavily trafficked commuter route. It carries two to three times its recommended load of 8,000 vehicles a day. On a rainy spring night, Cope (P) was driving north along Beach Drive and suffered neck and back injuries when Scott's southbound vehicle rounded a curve, slid into P's lane and hit his car. The officer at the scene said the road had a "worn polished surface" that was "slick when wet." P sued Scott and the National Park Service (D), alleging that D was negligent "in failing to appropriately and adequately maintain the roadway of Beach Drive . . . and failing to place and maintain appropriate and adequate warning signs along the roadway." During discovery, P found an engineering study that identified this stretch of Beach Drive as one of nine "high accident areas" in the park, and noted that sections of the Drive, including the location of the accident, fell below "acceptable skid-resistance levels" in a test conducted five months after the accident. The study recommended specific material for future repaving on the most dangerous curves, and noted that "the curves should be adequately signed and the skid resistance maintained with an opened graded friction course." The road was 33 on a list of 80 maintenance projects; 15 of the projects that preceded the Beach Drive project were of equal or less cost. There were "Slippery When Wet" signs posted, but the record is unclear as to the exact placement. D argued its action (or inaction) with respect to the road was discretionary and therefore exempt from suit. D's motion for summary judgment was granted. P settled with Scott and appeals.

Issues.

(i)   Did the district court err in dismissing P's claim regarding negligent maintenance of the road surface?

(ii)   Did the district court have jurisdiction over the allegations that D failed to warn adequately of dangers on Beach Drive?

Held. (i) No. (ii) Yes. Judgment affirmed in part and reversed in part.

♦   The "discretionary function" exception to governmental liability is at the heart of this case. The policy underlying this exception is to prevent the courts from "second guessing," through decisions in tort actions, the way that government officials choose to balance economic, social, and political factors as they carry out their official duties.

- In determining whether an action is exempt from suit under the discretionary function exemption, we ask whether any federal statute, regulation, or policy specifically prescribes a course of action for an employee to follow. If it does, then the employee had no "choice." If the employee followed the directive, he is exempt; if he did not follow the directive, he may open the government to suit. The discretionary function exception *may* apply where there is no specific prescription and the government employee has a "choice." If the choice led to the events being litigated, the exception may apply. But not all actions that require choice—actions that are, in one sense, "discretionary"—are protected as "discretionary functions" under the FTCA.

- Following this inquiry, we must determine whether the challenged discretionary acts of a government employee "are of the nature and quality that Congress intended to shield from tort liability." If decisions involving choice are "susceptible to policy judgment" and involve an exercise of "political, social, [or] economic judgment," they are exempt. If the discretion is *grounded* in the policy of the regulatory regime," the exception applies.

- No matter the level at which the decision was made, the nature of the decision, or the impact it had on others, we have consistently held that the discretionary function exception applies only where the question is not negligence but social wisdom, not due care but political practicability, not reasonableness but economic expediency.

- Regarding the state of the road surface, we do not agree with P's assessment of the manual entitled "Park Road Standards," which P interprets as setting forth "specific prescriptions" regarding skid resistance and surface type. The manual standards apply to "new construction and reconstruction" of park roads. Beach Drive was neither. The manual also notes that the standards apply only "to the extent practicable." To us, this caveat means that the standards are applicable only when no competing priorities exist. Such flexibility is the essence of discretion.

- Rather than debating the question of whether the failure to maintain was a matter of "design" or "maintenance" as the district court did, we must look at whether the "failure to maintain adequate skid resistance" is the kind of discretion that implicates "social, economic, or political" judgment. The situation here does not involve routine decisions like filling potholes. To correct the "inadequate skid resistance," the traffic load would have had to be reduced, the road would have had to have been paved initially with a different surface, or the curve resurfaced entirely, or at least milled to create grooves in the surface. The proper course of action would emerge as a result of balancing factors such as the road's purpose, cost and allocation of funds, safety, and inconvenience. Such decisions require the establishment of priorities, and we decline to "second guess" the agency's judgment here.

♦ In contrast, however, the discretion regarding where and what type of signs to post is not the kind of discretion protected by the discretionary function exception. Placing of signs may involve judgment, but this type of judgment is not "fraught with public policy considerations."

IV. THE DUTY REQUIREMENT: NONPHYSICAL HARM

A. EMOTIONAL HARM

1. **Mental Disturbance.** Mental disturbance is the negligent infliction of severe mental suffering on the plaintiff. Under the older view, some physical impact or contact was required before the courts would allow recovery by the plaintiff. The rationale was that this gives the defendant reasonable grounds for declaring a defense and acts as a deterrent to fraudulent claims. Today, as with the tort of intentional infliction of mental distress, there seems to be a move away from the requirement that there must be physical impact before the tort will be recognized. However, physical injury manifestations from the emotional disturbance caused by the defendant's negligent act are still required for the plaintiff to be entitled to any damages.

    a. **Bodily injury resulting from fear--**

Falzone v. Busch, 214 A.2d 12 (N.J. 1965).

Facts. Falzone, when standing in a field next to the road, was struck and injured by Busch's (D's) car. Falzone's wife (P) was sitting in a parked car at the time, and D's car came so close to her car as it veered across the road that it caused her to fear for her safety. As a result, she became ill and required medical care. The trial court granted summary judgment for D on P's claim. P appeals.

Issue. May a plaintiff recover for bodily injury or sickness resulting from fear for her safety caused by a negligent defendant, where the plaintiff was placed in danger by such negligence, although there was no physical impact?

Held. Yes. Judgment reversed.

◆ Since 1900, *Ward v. West Jersey & Seashore Railroad Co.*, 65 N.J.L. 383, has set forth the law in this state that a physical impact upon the plaintiff is necessary to sustain a negligence action. The court denied recovery in *Ward* for three reasons: (i) there was no physical injury as the proximate result of the negligent act; (ii) the court concluded that because *Ward* was the first case on this issue, general agreement among the bar must have been that no liability exists without impact; and (iii) "public policy" concerns about the flood of litigation and feigned cases.

◆ Recovery has been allowed in this state where there was only slight impact (a small injury to the plaintiff's neck and dust in her eyes), where a person was injured while trying to avoid a hazard, and for physical suffering resulting from a willfully caused emotional disturbance. The medical community has broadened its knowledge of the relationship between emotional disturbance and physical injury, and the relationship seems no longer open to serious challenge.

♦   The opinion of lawyers is not a sufficient bar to suit.

♦   Difficulty of proof should not be a bar to suit. Furthermore, in other states where impact is not required as a basis of recovery, there is no indication of a flood of litigation.

b.   Recovery denied for fear of disease alone--

Metro-North Commuter Railroad Company v. Buckley, 521 U.S. 424 (1997).

Facts. Buckley (P), a pipefitter, was exposed to dust that contained asbestos but had no physical symptoms of exposure. Because he feared he would develop cancer, P sued Metro-North (D) under the Federal Employers' Liability Act ("FELA"), seeking damages for negligently inflicted emotional distress, and to cover the costs of future medical checkups for cancer and asbestosis. D conceded negligence, but argued that P had not suffered emotional distress, and because P had suffered no physical harm, he was not entitled to recover. The district court dismissed. The court of appeals reversed. The Supreme Court granted certiorari.

Issue. May a worker recover damages under FELA for negligently inflicted emotional distress if the employee manifested no symptoms of an asbestos-related disease?

Held. No. Judgment reversed and remanded.

♦   In *Consolidated Rail Corporation v. Gottshall,* 512 U.S. 532 (1994), we held that FELA permits recovery for such emotional distress where a plaintiff meets the "zone of danger" test, which permits plaintiffs to recover for emotional injury if they "sustain a physical impact from, or are placed in immediate risk of physical harm by, a defendant's negligence."

♦   The "physical impact" to which *Gottshall* referred involves a threatened physical contact that caused, or might have caused, immediate traumatic harm. We decline to adopt the Second Circuit's interpretation of those words as "including a simple physical contact with a substance that might cause a disease at a future time, so long as the contact was of a kind that would 'cause fear in a reasonable person.'"

♦   Physical impact does not include exposure to a substance that may pose some risk of disease in the future, and which causes a worker some distress because he may become ill after a substantial period of time.

- With only a few exceptions, common law courts have denied recovery for emotional distress to plaintiffs who are disease- and symptom-free.

- Policy reasons referred to in *Gottshall* to support restricting recovery are present here. Those reasons include: (i) special "difficulty for judges and juries" in separating valid, important claims from those that are invalid or "trivial," (ii) a threat of unlimited and unpredictable liability, and (iii) the potential for a flood of comparatively unimportant, or trivial claims.

Concurrence and dissent (Ginsburg, Stevens, JJ). Contact with asbestos particles constitutes "physical impact," but P's emotional distress claim should be denied because P did not present objective evidence of severe emotional distress.

---

c.   **Severe emotional distress--**

Gammon v. Osteopathic Hospital of Maine, Inc., 534 A.2d 1282 (Me. 1987).

Facts. Gammon's (P's) father died in the Osteopathic Hospital of Maine (D), and P asked a funeral home (D) to make funeral arrangements. P alleged that Ds negligently conducted their operations because when P received what he thought were his father's personal effects, he opened the bag to find a bloodied leg, severed below the knee. P yelled to an aunt that the hospital had taken his father's leg off and the aunt testified that P was "as white as a ghost." The leg was actually a pathology specimen removed from another person. P began having nightmares, his personality was affected, and his relationship with his family deteriorated. P's condition began to improve after several months, although there were occasional nightmares. P sought no medical or psychiatric attention and offered no medical evidence at trial. The trial court granted a directed verdict on P's negligence claim for severe emotional distress. On other counts, the trial judge charged the jury that "'severe emotional distress' was distress 'such that no reasonable man should be expected to endure it.'" P appeals.

Issue. Did the trial court err in directing a verdict on P's claim for negligent infliction of severe emotional distress?

Held. Yes. Judgment vacated and case remanded.

- A person is entitled to the protection of his psychic well-being as much as his physical well-being. We have previously required a showing of physical impact, objective manifestation, underlying or accompanying tort, or special circumstances to ensure that a claim for emotional distress without physical injury is not spurious. These more or less arbitrary requirements should not bar P's claim.

- In abandoning these artificial devices, we rely on the trial process for protection against fraudulent claims and upon the principle of foreseeability to provide adequate protection against unduly burdensome liability claims.

- Courts have concluded that the exceptional vulnerability of the family of recent decedents makes it highly probable that emotional distress will result from any mishandling of the body. That high probability provides sufficient trustworthiness to allay the court's fear of fraudulent claims. This rationale is but another way of determining that the defendant reasonably should have foreseen that mental distress would result from his negligence. In this case, the evidence would support a jury finding that either or both Ds failed to exercise reasonable care to prevent such an occurrence.

---

d. Test for bystander recovery--

Portee v. Jaffee, 417 A.2d 521 (N.J. 1980).

Facts. Portee's (P's) seven-year-old son was trapped in Jaffee's (D's) building between the outer door of the elevator and the shaft. When the elevator was activated, the boy was dragged to the third floor. P watched throughout a four-and-one-half-hour rescue attempt while the boy moaned, cried out, and flailed his arms. The boy suffered multiple bone fractures and internal injuries and died during the rescue attempt. After the boy's death, P became severely depressed and self-destructive, attempted suicide, and required extensive counseling and psychotherapy. P sued D and the companies involved in designing and maintaining the elevator. The trial court granted summary judgment for Ds on P's claim for mental and emotional distress. The dismissal was directly reviewed by the supreme court.

Issue. May a court impose liability for negligently causing mental or emotional distress where the defendant's conduct creates neither the risk nor the occurrence of physical harm but where emotional injury is foreseeable?

Held. Yes. Judgment reversed.

- Courts in other jurisdictions that have found liability in the circumstances before us have followed the test set forth in *Dillon v. Legg*, 441 P.2d 912 (Cal. 1968), where the California Supreme Court identified three factors that would determine whether an emotional injury would be compensable because it was foreseeable. We agree that those factors together create a strong case for negligence liability and we add a fourth factor to the cause of action we approve for negligent infliction of emotional distress: "[i] the death or serious physical injury of another caused by [the] defendant's negligence; [ii] a marital or intimate familial relationship between [the] plaintiff and the injured person; [iii]

observation of the death or injury at the scene of the accident; and [iv] resulting severe emotional distress. We find that a defendant's duty of reasonable care to avoid physical harm to others extends to the avoidance of this type of mental and emotional harm."

---

e. Direct and indirect injuries--

Johnson v. Jamaica Hospital, 467 N.E.2d 502 (N.Y. 1984).

Facts. The Johnsons' (Ps') newborn daughter was abducted from Jamaica Hospital (D) a short time after her birth. The baby was recovered by police and returned to Ps after four-and-one-half months. During the time that the child was missing, Ps brought suit for the emotional distress brought about by D's negligence. The trial court denied D's motion to dismiss Ps' action for failure to state a cause of action. The appellate division affirmed by a divided vote and certified to the court of appeals the question of whether it had acted properly.

Issue. May Ps recover damages from D for mental distress or emotional disturbances they may have suffered as a result of the direct injury inflicted upon their daughter by D's breach of its duty of care to her?

Held. No. Order reversed and complaint dismissed.

♦　Ps contend that their complaint states a cause of action because D owed a duty directly to them, as parents, to care properly for their child, and that it was or should have been foreseeable to D that any injury to Ps' child, such as abduction, would cause Ps mental distress. The court has refused to recognize such a duty on the part of a hospital, and there is no reason to depart from that rule here.

♦　The direct injury allegedly caused by D's negligence (abduction) was sustained by the infant, and the foreseeability that psychic injuries such as Ps' would result from injury to the infant does not establish a duty running from D to Ps. In the absence of such a duty, there can be no liability.

♦　To permit Ps to recover would be to invite "open-ended liability for indirect emotional injury suffered by families in every instance in which the very young, very elderly, or incapacitated experience negligent care or treatment."

Dissent. I had thought that the fear of "open-ended liability for indirect emotional injury" had long ago been laid to rest, and that *Bovsun v. Sanperi*, 461 N.E.2d 843 (N.Y. 1984), with its recognition that severe emotional distress suffered by an immediate family member was a compensable injury, marked the start of a new rationale for determining when freedom from mental disturbance is a protected interest in this state.

B. ECONOMIC HARM

1. **Creation of Risk.** When a negligent defendant causes an injury to a plaintiff that includes only pure economic losses, substantial problems arise. Recovery for those losses may be obtained, but courts usually require a strict showing of foreseeable plaintiffs and foreseeable harm.

2. **Foreseeable Plaintiff.** In order for a plaintiff to recover for a negligently caused economic harm, there must be proof that a duty was owed specifically to that plaintiff.

    a. **Privity requirement--**

Nycal Corporation v. KPMG Peat Marwick LLP., 688 N.E.2d 1368 (Mass. 1998).

Facts. Nycal (P), relying on KPMG's (D's) report of the financial statements of Gulf Resources & Chemical Corporation ("Gulf"), entered into an agreement with Gulf's controlling shareholders to purchase controlling stock. D did not learn of the transaction until a few days before the closing. The sale was completed in 1991. In 1993, Gulf filed for bankruptcy. P's investment was worthless. P sued D, alleging that P had relied on D's report and claiming that D had materially misrepresented Gulf's financial condition. Summary judgment was granted for D in the trial court. P and D appeal.

Issue. Is an accountant liable to persons with whom the accountant is not in privity?

Held. No. Judgment affirmed.

♦   Three common law or statutory tests that have been applied in other jurisdictions to determine the duty of care owed by accountants to nonclients include the foreseeability test, the near-privity test, and the test contained in section 552 of the Restatement.

♦   Traditional tort law principles in negligence cases, *i.e.*, holding an accountant liable to anyone who the accountant could reasonably foresee would obtain and rely on his opinion, are not suitable for accountants because no efforts of the auditor can remove primary control of the financial reporting process from the client. Such liability is too expansive. Massachusetts law does not protect every reasonably foreseeable user of an inaccurate audit report.

- The near-privity test requires reliance by the third party, knowledge that the party intended to rely, and conduct by the accountant providing a direct linkage to the third party. We have previously applied the reliance and knowledge components of this test, but not the conduct. The leading Massachusetts case on the duty owed by a professional to persons with whom the professional is not in privity, *Craig v. Everett M. Brooks Co.*, 222 N.E.2d 752 (Mass. 1967), limits recovery for negligent misrepresentation situations where the defendant knew that a particular plaintiff would rely on the defendant's services.

- We have applied a liability standard most like that taken from section 552 of the Restatement (Second) of Torts (1977). Section 552 describes the tort of negligent misrepresentation committed in the process of supplying information for the guidance of others as follows:

  > One who, in the course of his business, profession or employment, or in any other transaction in which he has a pecuniary interest, supplies false information for the guidance of others in their business transactions, is subject to liability for pecuniary loss caused to them by their justifiable reliance upon the information, if he fails to exercise reasonable care or competence in obtaining or communicating the information.

- Liability is limited to:

  > Loss suffered (a) by the person or one of a limited group of persons for whose benefit and guidance he intends to supply the information or knows that the recipient intends to supply it; and (b) through reliance upon it in a transaction that he intends the information to influence or knows that the recipient so intends or in a substantially similar transaction.

That test avoids both unlimited and uncertain liability for economic losses in cases of professional mistake and exoneration of the auditor in situations where he clearly intended to undertake the responsibility of influencing particular business transactions involving third persons. Better reasoned opinions limit liability to noncontractual third parties who can demonstrate actual knowledge on the part of accountants of the limited, though unnamed, group of potential third parties who will rely upon the report, as well as actual knowledge of the particular financial transaction that such information is designed to influence. The accountant's knowledge is to be measured at the moment the audit report is published, not by the foreseeable path of harm envisioned by litigants years following an unfortunate business decision.

- D did not know of the transaction between P and Gulf until after the purchase agreement had been signed, and D never intended to influence the transaction, nor did D know Gulf intended to use the report to influence P.

b. Personal injury or property damage required--

532 Madison Avenue Gourmet Foods, Inc. v. Finlandia Center, Inc., 750 N.E.2d 1097 (N.Y. 2001).

Facts. Three cases are involved in this appeal, two of which involve the same events. When a section of a wall of a 39-story office tower broke loose, bricks, mortar, and other material fell onto a busy commercial location crammed with stores and skyscrapers. Fifteen blocks on Madison Avenue and adjacent streets were closed for two weeks; some businesses closest to the incident stayed closed longer. In one case, *532 Madison Ave. Gourmet Foods v. Finlandia Center, Inc.,* the plaintiff's 24-hour delicatessen was closed for five weeks. In *5th Ave. Chocolatiere v. 540 Acquisition Co.,* two retailers sued on behalf of themselves and a putative class of all other business entities in a specified geographical area. They alleged that shoppers and others had no access to their stores during the time Madison Avenue was closed to traffic. The defendants in both of these cases are Finlandia Center (the building owner), 540 Acquisition Company (the ground lessee), and Manhattan Pacific Management (the managing agent) (Ds). In both cases, Ds' motions to dismiss the plaintiffs' negligence claims were granted on the ground that the plaintiffs could not establish that Ds owed a duty of care for purely economic loss absent personal injury or property damage, and the public nuisance claims were dismissed on the ground that the "injuries were the same in kind as those suffered by all of the businesses in the community." Additional claims in *5th Ave. Chocolatiere,* for gross negligence and negligence per se, were dismissed on the ground that the plaintiffs could not establish a duty owed by Ds, and their private nuisance cause of action was dismissed on the ground that they could not establish either intentional or negligent wrongdoing. The third case, *Goldberg Weprin & Ustin v. Tishman Construction* involves the collapse of a 48-story construction elevator tower in the heart of Times Square. Following the accident, all traffic was prohibited in the area and nearby buildings were evacuated for varying time periods. Three actions were consolidated—the first by a law firm, the second by a public relations firm, and the third by a clothing manufacturer, all located within the affected area. The law firm sought damages for economic loss on behalf of itself and a proposed class of persons whose businesses were closed and a subclass of area residents who were evacuated from their homes. The law firm alleged gross negligence, strict liability, and public and private nuisance. The trial court found that failure to allege personal injury or property damage barred recovery in negligence and rejected the remaining claims for strict liability and public and private nuisance. The appeals court affirmed dismissal of the *Goldberg Weprin* complaint, but reinstated the negligence and public nuisance claims of *532 Madison* and *5th Ave. Chocolatiere,* holding that Ds' duty to keep their premises in reasonably safe condition extended to "those businesses in such close proximity that their negligent acts could be reasonably foreseen to cause injury" and that, as such, they established a special injury distinct from the general inconvenience to the community at large. Ds in *532 Madison* and *5th Ave. Chocolatiere* appeal. Ps in *Goldberg Weprin* appeal.

Issue. Did the defendants' liability extend to the plaintiffs whose negligence claims were based solely on economic loss, without any personal injury or property damage claims?

Held. No. Judgment in *532 Madison* and *5th Ave. Chocolatiere* reversed. Judgment in *Goldberg Weprin & Ustin* affirmed.

♦ Determining the scope of a tortfeasor's duty involves balancing such factors as the reasonable expectations of parties and society in general, the proliferation of claims, the likelihood of unlimited or insurer-like liability, disproportionate risk and reparation allocation, and public policies affecting the expansion or limitation of new channels of liability. In apportioning risks and allocating the burden of loss, courts must always be aware of the precedential effects of their decisions.

♦ Foreseeability of harm alone does not create a duty. Absent a duty owed directly to the party harmed, there can be no liability in damages. For example, a landowner has a duty to protect tenants, patrons, and invitees from the foreseeable harm resulting from the criminal conduct of another while on the landowner's premises because he is in the best position to protect against this risk, but his duty does not extend to members of the public. His liability is limited because the special relationship defines the class of plaintiffs to whom he owes the duty. In *Strauss v. Belle Realty Co.*, *supra*, we found that no duty was owed by a utility to a plaintiff hurt in a fall on a staircase in a building during a citywide blackout. The injuries were foreseeable, but we restricted negligence liability for damages to direct customers, those who had a contractual relationship with the defendant, in order to avoid crushing exposure to the lawsuits of millions of electricity consumers. Likewise, while a landowner owes persons on adjoining premises a duty to take reasonable precautions to avoid injuring them, he does not have a duty to protect an entire urban neighborhood against purely economic losses. Policy-driven line-drawing is arbitrary because the line invariably cuts off liability to persons who foreseeably might be plaintiffs. On the other hand, in cases such as this, if all of those who suffered economic losses were allowed to sue, Ds' liability would extend to an indeterminate group in the affected areas. Limiting the scope of Ds' duty to those who have suffered personal injury or property damage reasonably apportions liability. And if a plaintiff falls within the scope of a defendant's duty of care, he may seek damages for economic loss as well as recovery for personal injury or property damage.

---

    c.   **Landmark decisions.** In *Glanzer v. Shepard*, 135 N.E. 275 (N.Y. 1922), a public weigher had been contacted to weigh beans and supply the weight ticket to the buyer. Since the weigher was conducting a public calling and knew the specific use of the ticket, the weigher was liable to the buyer for an economic loss. In *Ultramares Corp. v. Touche*, 174 N.E. 441 (N.Y. 1931), an accounting firm supplied financial statements. When an audited company defaulted on loans, the creditor, who had relied on the statements, sued the accounting firm. Since the accounting firm did not know the specific identity of the party who was to use the statement and had merely supplied it for the audited company's use, there was no liability for negligence. The court found that the accounting firm's actions were so reckless as to amount to fraud. Under fraud principles, the plaintiff could recover by merely showing that he was one of a class of people that the accounting firm should have foreseen would receive the statements.

    d.   **Legal malpractice.** When a lawyer negligently fails to perform, the usual injury is an economic loss. When that economic loss falls on the lawyer's client, the courts have no difficulty in finding that a duty was owed to the client, and liability results. When that loss falls on some third party, the courts are less inclined to find the duty. In the absence of some special relationship with the third party, the lawyer will not be liable for economic losses suffered by the third party.

C. WRONGFUL BIRTH AND WRONGFUL LIFE

    1.   **Introduction.** Advances in science, law and technology have brought to the fore discussions of the types and extent of legal obligations medical personnel incur when they become involved in procreation decisions such as genetic counseling, or diagnoses during pregnancy and end-of-life decisions. "Wrongful pregnancy" or "wrongful birth" suits have been brought by parents, and "wrongful life" suits have been brought by children. These cases have prompted discussion regarding categorization. Will the traditional negligence or medical malpractice theories apply, or will it be necessary to recognize new causes of action, "wrongful living" for example, to compensate parties whose end-of-life choices have been ignored?

    2.   **Prenatal Injuries.** Today, seemingly all jurisdictions allow recovery for prenatal injuries. Medical science has advanced to the point where causation of injury to a fetus in the early stage of development can be ascertained.

        a.   **Stillborn children.** Most courts do not require that the child be born alive in order for an action to be brought.

        b.   **Wrongful death actions.** Actions for wrongful death are purely statutory—there is great variance among the statutes and the interpretations of the statutes.

3.   **Birth Defects.** Parents have begun suing when their children are born with birth defects. The claim is usually that the child would have been better off not to have been born. The alternative to the birth is, of course, abortion. Courts have generally denied recovery by the child (wrongful life), but permitted recovery by the parents (wrongful birth). Courts disagree on the proper measure of damages.

4.   **Negligent Performance of Sterilization Procedure--**

Emerson v. Magendantz, 689 A.2d 409 (R.I. 1997).

Facts. For financial reasons, after the birth of their first child, the Emersons (Ps) decided to limit their family, and Diane Emerson consulted Magendantz (D), a gynecological specialist. D performed a tubal ligation upon Diane. Diane later became pregnant and gave birth to Kirsten, alleged to have congenital problems. Diane underwent a second tubal ligation. Ps sued D, alleging Kirsten's birth was proximately caused by D's negligence and that D had failed properly to inform Diane and to obtain her consent before surgery. Ps alleged that Diane suffered severe physical pain and required additional invasive medical treatment as a result of D's negligence, that they have suffered mental anguish and distress, and that they have suffered financial loss and lost earning capacity as a result of Diane's unanticipated pregnancy. Ps also sued for compensation for Kirsten's medical care and maintenance. The trial judge certified two questions to the state supreme court.

Issues.

(i)   Is there a cause of action under Rhode Island law when a physician negligently performs a sterilization procedure and the patient subsequently becomes pregnant and delivers a child from that pregnancy?

(ii)   If so, should the damages be limited?

Held. (i) Yes. (ii) Yes.

♦   The overwhelming majority of opinions of other states recognize negligent performance of a sterilization procedure as a tort for which recovery may be allowed. Because we are persuaded by these opinions, we answer the first question in the affirmative.

♦   Courts that have recognized the cause of action have adopted three types of remedies: (i) limited recovery, which includes physician and hospital costs, loss of wages, and sometimes recovery for emotional distress, loss of consortium, and medical expenses for prenatal care, delivery, and postnatal care; (ii) recovery of medical costs plus the costs of child rearing balanced against the economic or emotional benefits derived by the parents by having the child; and (iii) full recovery without benefit offsets.

- We adopt the limited-recovery rule, except for the element of emotional distress arising out of an unwanted pregnancy that results in the birth of a healthy child.

- Our public policy would preclude allowing costs for raising a healthy child after the parents have decided to keep the child and not opt for adoption. All the joys and benefits that come from parenthood along with the decision not to release the child for adoption provide the most persuasive evidence that the parents consider the benefit of retaining the child to outweigh the economic costs of child rearing.

- We acknowledge that in the case of a physically or a mentally handicapped child, special medical and educational expenses beyond normal rearing costs should be allowed. There is an overwhelming financial and emotional drain connected with raising such a child.

- Furthermore, when a physician, in performing a sterilization procedure, has notice that the parents have a reasonable expectation of giving birth to a physically or a mentally handicapped child, or by reason of statistical information he is or should be aware of such a risk, then the entire cost of raising such a child would be within the ambit of recoverable damages.

- Neither the extraordinary costs of maintaining a handicapped child nor the physician's liability would end when the child reached majority. Economic benefits from governmental or other agencies would be offset.

- In the event of the birth of a physically, or a mentally, handicapped child, the parents should be entitled to compensation for emotional distress.

Concurrence and dissent. The true nature of this action is medical malpractice, and the patient should be allowed to recover for all of the injuries and damages that can be proven to have been reasonably foreseeable and proximately caused by the tortfeasor's negligence.

V. CAUSATION

A causal relationship must exist between the defendant's conduct and the harm to the plaintiff (both actual and proximate cause). If the defendant did not cause the injury *in fact*, he is not liable, but even if the defendant did cause the injury in fact, he is not liable if he was not the *proximate cause* of injury or damage. This may be thought of in terms of the following diagram, with liability accruing to the defendant only if the circumstances are within both circles.

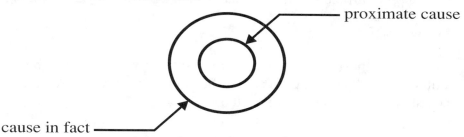

Actual causation is always a question of fact for the jury. The court enters into the decision only in deciding if reasonable persons could find such a fact. Proximate cause is a question of law, not concerning facts; it involves conflicting considerations of policy—it comes into consideration only after causation in fact is established. In order to recover, a plaintiff must sustain the burden of proof as to both.

A. CAUSE IN FACT

1. **Sine Qua Non (But For) Rule.** If the injury to the plaintiff would not have happened "but for" the act or omission of the defendant, such conduct is the cause in fact of the injury.

   a. The failure of one driver to give a turn signal is not a cause of an automobile collision when the driver of the other automobile was not looking and would not have seen it even if it had been given. In such a case, the defendant was negligent, but his negligence in not signaling his intention to turn was not the actual cause of the damage.

   b. Likewise, the failure to supply firefighting equipment that could not have been used because no water was available is not the actual cause of the plaintiff's loss when his building burns down.

2. **Proof of Causation.** The plaintiff ordinarily has the burden to prove that, more likely than not, the defendant was a substantial factor in bringing about the result.

   a. **Plaintiff's burden--**

Stubbs v. City of Rochester, 124 N.E. 137 (N.Y. 1919).

Facts. The city of Rochester (D) supplied Hemlock system water for drinking and Holly system water for firefighting. The Hemlock water was pure but the Holly water was contaminated and unfit. D negligently intermingled the systems. Stubbs (P) contracted typhoid and alleged that the disease was caused by contaminated water. P presented experts who agreed that typhoid could be caused by the water, and statistics showed that a greater number of cases of typhoid were reported after the water was intermingled. The trial court dismissed the claim, and the Appellate Division affirmed. P appeals.

Issue. Did P supply sufficient evidence that D's negligence caused his injury?

Held. Yes. Judgment reversed.

♦ The plaintiff must show sufficient proof so that a reasonable inference of causation can be drawn. In this case, sufficient evidence was introduced, and the case should have been submitted to a jury.

---

b.   **Increased risk of harm--**

Zuchowicz v. United States, 140 F.3d 381 (2d Cir. 1998).

Facts. At the local naval hospital, Mrs. Zuchowicz was prescribed, and for a month took, twice the maximum dosage of Danocrine. For two months thereafter she took half the amount prescribed. She experienced bloating, weight gain, edema, hot flashes, a racing heart, chest pains, dizziness, headaches, acne, and fatigue. After being advised by a private physician to stop taking the drug, Mrs. Zuchowicz experienced symptoms and was diagnosed with primary pulmonary hypertension ("PPH"). The average life expectancy for sufferers of PPH was two-and-a-half years at the time of the diagnosis. Mrs. Zuchowicz became ineligible for a lung transplant because she became pregnant while on the waiting list. One month after giving birth, she died. Mr. Zuchowicz (P) continued his wife's case under the Federal Tort Claims Act ("FTCA"), claiming the U.S. Naval Hospital (D) was at fault. Following a bench trial, the district court awarded P damages. D appeals.

Issues.

(i)   Was the factfinder clearly erroneous in determining that, more probably than not, Mrs. Zuchowicz's illness was caused by Danocrine?

(ii)   Was the factfinder able to conclude more probably than not that it was a negligently prescribed overdose that was the cause of Mrs. Zuchowicz's illness and subsequent death?

Held. (i) No. (ii) Yes. Judgment affirmed.

- P's expert testified that, based on the time factor between the prescription of the overdose and the start of PPH, and the exclusion of other causes, he believed to a reasonable medical certainty that Mrs. Zuchowicz had suffered from drug-induced PPH.

- Under Connecticut law, on the basis of this testimony alone, the trier of fact could have concluded that it was more likely than not that the drug caused the PPH.

- This case is a classic example of the tort principle that: if (i) a negligent act was deemed wrongful because that act increased the chances that a particular type of accident would occur, and (ii) a mishap of that very sort did happen, this was enough to support a finding by the trier of fact that the negligent behavior caused the harm. Where such a strong causal link exists, it is up to the negligent party to bring in evidence denying *but for* cause and suggesting that in the actual case the wrongful conduct had not been a substantial factor.

- When a drug has been prescribed in greater than approved dosages, and negative side effects have been shown to be the result, a strong enough causal link has been shown to permit the finder of fact to conclude the overdosage was a substantial factor in producing the harm.

c.   **Lost chance--**

Alberts v. Schultz, 975 P.2d 1279 (N.M. 1999).

Facts. Alberts (P) suffered from a narrowing of the blood vessels restricting blood flow to a particular area of the body. P sought treatment from Schultz (D1) for severe [pain] in his right foot. P had pain when he had no activity or exercise, a sign of impending [gan]grene that could lead to the amputation of the affected limb. D1 did not order an [exam] or conduct a motor sensory examination. Thirteen days later P saw another [doctor (D]2), who immediately sent P to the hospital and tried several procedures to [save P'] s leg, including bypass surgery, but ultimately, P's right leg was amputated [bel]ow the knee. P sued Ds for medical malpractice. The trial court granted partial [s]ummary judgment for Ds because P could not establish to a reasonable degree of medical probability that Ds' conduct proximately caused the amputation of P's leg. The trial court certified two questions for appeal and the court of appeals certified those questions to the state supreme court.

Issues.

(i)   Should New Mexico recognize a patient's claim that, in the treatment of a medical condition, a healthcare provider's negligence has resulted in the loss of a chance for a better result?

(ii)   If New Mexico does recognize loss of chance, may P recover under such a claim?

Held. (i) Yes. (ii) No.

♦   The appeals court has adopted the lost-chance concept and we affirm.

♦   This claim involves a patient seeking medical help for a specific problem. The claim is based on the negligent denial by a healthcare provider of the most effective therapy for a patient's presenting medical problem. A substantial opportunity for improvement is obliterated by a medical person's failure to give timely treatment. The core of the claim is that prior to the negligence, there is a chance the patient would have been better off with adequate care. The item for which the patient seeks compensation is the chance to avoid the presenting problem and achieve a better result, not for the entire injury. Also, compensation should be provided for malpractice that increases the probability that the patient will suffer from the effects of the presenting problem.

♦   The plaintiff in a loss of chance case bears the burden of proving the same elements as those required in other medical malpractice actions, or in negligence suits in general: duty, breach, loss or damage, and causation.

♦   The injury is the lost opportunity of a better result, and the causal connection between the negligence and the resultant injury must be medically probable. The injury is in no way speculative. This is not a matter where one is exposed to a harmful substance and may experience injury in the future. The patient must show that the harm for which treatment was sought was in fact made worse by the lost chance.

♦   Lost-chance claims are not limited to those cases in which the chance of a better result has been utterly lost. Diminution may lead to unreasonable hair-splitting. Evidence of the physical progression of the patient's disease during a negligent delay in diagnosis or treatment may be sufficient to establish that the plaintiff was "injured" by the delay.

♦   In order to prove proximate cause, the plaintiff must show by a preponderance of the evidence that the defendant's negligence resulted in the lost chance for a better result. Causation must be proved to a probability, but not to a certainty. The standard of proof is to a "reasonable degree of medical probability."

♦   Damages should be awarded on a proportional basis as determined by the percentage value of the patient's chance for a better outcome prior to the negligent act.

♦   Here, P cannot show there was a window of time during which measures could have been taken to prevent the amputation of P's leg. P cannot show, to a reasonable degree of medical probability, that timely and proper medical intervention would have saved his leg, that an earlier bypass would have precluded the amputation, and that P was a suitable candidate for a bypass at an earlier time but became unsuitable by the day when the bypass was actually performed.

Dissent. P's expert presented enough evidence to present to the jury on the issue of causation.

---

d. **Alternative liability.** Where there is undoubtedly fault and alternative liability, the rule of causation is relaxed.

1) **The landmark case--**

Summers v. Tice, 199 P.2d 1 (Cal. 1948).

Facts. Tice and Simonson (Ds), hunting quail, shot in Summers's (P's) direction with their shotguns at the same time and a shot hit P in the eye. Obviously, only one of the Ds shot P, but P could not tell which one. Ds argued that therefore P could not show which D was negligent (*i.e.,* that the "but for" test could not be satisfied). From judgment for P against both Ds, Ds appeal.

Issue. Has P shown causation?

Held. Yes. Judgment affirmed.

♦ Ds' acts of shooting in P's direction were negligent and P's injury would not have resulted but for Ds' acts. Ds are joint tortfeasors and each is liable (joint and several liability), even though only one inflicted the injury. Ds brought about the harm, so they can untangle the facts.

---

2) **Applying the rule.**

a) The effect of this rule (alternative liability rule) is to shift the burden of causation to defendants; each must absolve himself. This is similar to *Ybarra v. Spangard, supra,* where each defendant was required to absolve himself from the breach of the duty. This shift of the burden is based on policy and justice, not logic.

b) The rule applies when there is no evidence as to which of the possible defendants is responsible for the injury.

(1) Two defendants negligently sell bullets to boys and one bullet kills a boy. There is joint and several liability.

(2) Two negligently driven cars, A and B, collide. Then a negligent third driver, C, runs into the wreck and a passenger in car A is hurt. The result is that all three drivers are liable (absent guest statute protection for driver A, etc.), but only because all three were negligent and there is no evidence as to which driver caused the injury.

c) Distinguish the case where a plaintiff does not prove a case against one or more defendants from the alternative liability case where a plaintiff proves he was injured by *one* of several negligent defendants, but does not know which one. The difference is that under the alternative liability rule, both defendants are negligent and only one caused the injury, whereas under the other rule, only one defendant was negligent. Both defendants must be negligent to apply *Summers v. Tice, supra.*

e. **Market-share analysis--**

Hymowitz v. Eli Lilly & Co., 539 N.E.2d 1069 (N.Y. 1989), *cert. denied,* 493 U.S. 944 (1989).

Facts. From 1941 to 1971, the drug diethylstilbestrol ("DES") was marketed for treatment of various maladies, including preventing human miscarriages. In 1971, the FDA banned the use of DES as a miscarriage preventative when studies established that DES caused vaginal cancer and a precancerous vaginal or cervical growth in offspring of mothers who took the drug. Some of these offspring (Ps) brought suit against the DES manufacturers (Ds). Ps faced two barriers to recovery: identification of the particular manufacturer of the drug, and claims barred by the statute of limitations before the injury was discovered. The appeals in this case are representative of nearly 500 similar actions pending in state courts and the rules articulated by the court here must be administratively feasible in the context of this mass litigation. In the present appeals, Ds moved for summary judgment because Ps could not identify the manufacturer of the drug, and the complaints were time barred. The trial court denied these motions; on the statute of limitations issue, the court granted Ps' cross-motions, dismissing Ds' affirmative defenses because of the legislature's provision that the statute began to run upon the discovery of "the latent effects of exposure to any substance" and its one-year revival of causes of action for exposure to DES. The Appellate Division affirmed and certified to this court the questions of whether the orders of the trial court were properly made.

Issue. May a DES plaintiff recover against a DES manufacturer when identification of the producer of the specific drug that caused the injury is impossible?

Held. Yes. Certified questions answered in the affirmative.

♦ The doctrines of alternative liability and concerted action in their unaltered common law forms do not permit recovery in DES cases. Alternative liability generally requires that defendants have better access to information than does the plaintiff, and that all tortfeasors are before the court; it also rests on the premise that where there is a small number of possible wrongdoers, all of whom breached a duty to the plaintiff, the likelihood that any one of them injured the plaintiff is relatively high. In DES cases, however, there is a great number of wrongdoers, many years elapse between taking the drug and injury, there is no real possibility of having all possible producers before the court, and DES defendants are in no better position than are plaintiffs to identify the manufacturer of the DES ingested in any given case.

♦ Insofar as concerted action is concerned, there is nothing in the record to show any agreement, tacit or otherwise, to market DES for pregnancy use without taking proper steps to ensure the drug's safety.

♦ We conclude that the best solution rests on a market share theory, based upon a national market. We choose to apportion liability so as to correspond to the overall culpability of each defendant, measured by the amount of risk of injury of each defendant created to the public at large.

♦ A defendant cannot be held liable if it satisfies its burden of proof showing that it did not market DES for pregnancy use. However, there should be no exculpation of a defendant who, although a member of the market producing DES for pregnancy use, appears not to have caused a particular plaintiff's injury.

♦ The liability of DES producers is several only and should not be inflated when all participants in the market are not before the court in a particular case.

Concurrence and dissent. I agree with the market share theory, but, in my view, the liability for Ps' damages of those Ds who are unable to exculpate themselves should be joint and several, thereby insuring that Ps will receive full recovery of their damages.

─────────────

B. PROXIMATE CAUSE

1. **Introduction.** Proximate cause is used to determine the extent of the defendant's liability after actual causation (*i.e.,* causation in fact) is established. It is an attempt to deal with the problem of liability for unforeseeable or unusual consequences following the defendant's acts. "Proximate cause" is an unfortunate term since closeness in time and space have nothing to do with the consideration here, which really deals with how far public policy will extend liability to the defendant for the consequences of his act. The Restatement uses the term "legal cause," but this term is not much better.

a. **Direct results of the defendant's act.** When there is no intervening force between the defendant's negligent act and the harm to the plaintiff, such harm is said to be the direct result of the defendant's act. For example, if the defendant negligently reaches for his cigarette lighter while driving his car and the car hits a telephone pole that falls onto the plaintiff's house, the damage to the plaintiff's house is the direct result of the defendant's negligence. Indirect results (discussed *infra*) occur when there is an intervening force (or forces) between the defendant's act and harm to the plaintiff.

1) **Foreseeability of harm.** The harm caused the plaintiff as a direct result of the defendant's acts may be either foreseeable (*e.g.,* it is foreseeable that pedestrians and other drivers may be injured if the defendant negligently runs a red traffic light) or unforeseeable (*e.g.,* it is unforeseeable in the preceding example that buildings in the neighborhood will have all their windows blown out by an explosion caused by the defendant running into another vehicle, which turns out to be a gasoline truck).

2) **The opposing views.** There are two opposing views on foreseeability of consequences of a defendant's act. One view is that the defendant's acts will be considered to be the proximate cause of the plaintiff's injury only if such consequences, judged by time, place, and the circumstances under which the defendant acted, were reasonably foreseeable. Essentially, this view uses the same criteria for foreseeability to determine the extent of liability as is used to determine whether the defendant's act is negligent—is the injury reasonably foreseeable as something likely to happen? The other view, where the injury to the plaintiff is the direct result of the defendant's act, is that foreseeability is important only in determining whether there is negligence; if the injury follows in an unbroken sequence of events, the defendant will be liable for the consequences, regardless of the remoteness of the injury.

2. **Unexpected Harm.** The defendant's act may be negligent. In addition, some harm may result. The harm, however, may be different than foreseen due to some preexisting condition or subsequent circumstances. As noted *supra*, courts have taken different positions on this issue.

a. **Preexisting condition--**

Benn v. Thomas, 512 N.W.2d 537 (Iowa 1994).

Facts. Benn's executor (P) sued Thomas (D) after D's semi rear-ended a van in which Benn was a passenger. Benn suffered a bruised chest and a fractured ankle; he died six days later of a heart attack. At trial, P's medical expert testified that Benn had a history of coronary disease and insulin-dependent diabetes. He had had a previous heart attack and was at risk of having a second. The expert viewed the accident and Benn's injuries as "the straw that broke the camel's back" and the cause of his death. Other medical evidence indicated the accident did not cause his death. The trial court denied P's request that the jury be instructed that the defendant must take his plaintiff as he finds him, even if that means that the defendant must compensate the plaintiff for harm an ordinary person would not have suffered (the "eggshell plaintiff" rule). The jury awarded P $17,000 for Benn's injuries but nothing for his death. In the special verdict, the jury determined D's negligence did not proximately cause Benn's death. P's motion for a new trial was denied. P appealed. The court of appeals reversed the trial court. D appeals.

Issue. Did the trial court err in refusing to instruct the jury on the "eggshell plaintiff" rule in view of the fact that the plaintiff's decedent, who had a history of coronary disease, died of a heart attack six days after suffering a bruised chest and fractured ankle in a motor vehicle accident caused by the defendant's negligence?

Held. Yes. Appeals court affirmed.

♦ The proposed instruction stated: "If Loras Benn had a prior heart condition making him more susceptible to injury than a person in normal health, then the Defendant is responsible for all injuries and damages which are experienced by Loras Benn, proximately caused by the Defendant's actions, even though the injuries claimed produced a greater injury than those which might have been experienced by a normal person under the same circumstances."

♦ The proximate cause instruction in this case provided: "The conduct of a party is a proximate cause of damage when it is a substantial factor in producing damage and when the damage would not have happened except for the conduct. 'Substantial' means the party's conduct has such an effect in producing damage as to lead a reasonable person to regard it as a cause."

♦ The "eggshell plaintiff" rule provides that a tortious act, superimposed upon a prior latent condition, that results in an injury, may impose liability for the full disability.

♦ While the jury might have found D liable for Benn's death as well as his injuries under the instructions given, the instructions do not reflect existing law. Under the eggshell plaintiff rule, a defendant is liable for unusual results of personal injuries that may be unforeseeable. Once it is established that the defendant injured the plaintiff, liability is imposed for the full extent of those injuries.

♦ Although there was conflicting evidence, it was sufficient to present to a jury to determine whether Benn's heart attack and death were the direct result of the injury caused by D.

♦   To deprive P of the requested instruction under this record would fail to convey to the jury a central principle of tort liability.

---

b.   Different injury foreseeable--

In re **Polemis,** 3 K.B. 560 (1921).

Facts. Owners of a vessel (Ps) chartered it to the defendants (Ds). While unloading cargo, Ds' servants dropped a plank into the hold of the vessel. Apparently, it caused a spark that ignited petrol vapors. The resulting fire destroyed the vessel. Arbitrators also found that the longshoreman who dropped the plank had been negligent. Although the spark could not have been anticipated, some damage could have been. The court affirmed the arbitrators' award of damages to Ps and Ds appeal, arguing that the particular damage could not have been anticipated.

Issue. Is a defendant liable for unforeseeable consequences of his acts if *some* damage is foreseeable, but not the damage that actually occurred?

Held. Yes. Judgment affirmed.

♦   The foreseeability of damages may be important in determining the existence of negligence. But once negligence is established, the negligent party is liable for all damages, regardless of foreseeability.

♦   Here, the arbitrators found that the plank fell due to the negligence of Ds' servants. They also found that, although the creation of a spark could not be reasonably anticipated, some damage could be foreseen.

♦   Ds are liable for the damage actually caused, even though it was not the type foreseen.

Concurrence. If a negligent act is likely to cause damage, the fact that the damage actually caused is different from that anticipated is immaterial, as long as the actual damage is a direct result of the negligent act.

---

c.   Actual results must be foreseeable--

Overseas Tankship (U.K.) Ltd. v. Morts Dock & Engineering Co. (Wagon Mound I), [1961] A.C. 338.

Facts. The defendant's (D's) freighter, Wagon Mound, was moored approximately 600 feet away from the plaintiff's (P's) wharf. D's ship negligently discharged oil, which spread across the harbor and under P's wharf. P's workers were welding on the wharf. Molten metal dripped from the welding job and set fire to cotton that was floating on the surface of the water, and this in turn ignited the oil. The ensuing fire damaged the wharf and two ships docked alongside. From a judgment for P, D appeals.

Issue. Must the actual damage or results be foreseeable?

Held. Yes. Judgment reversed.

♦ The actual type of damage or results must be foreseeable. It is not enough that just any damage or results are foreseeable or follow in an unbroken sequence. Some limitation must be imposed upon the consequence for which a negligent actor is to be held responsible; therefore, we choose to adopt the better view of reasonable foreseeability, *i.e.,* liability limited to what the reasonable person ought to foresee.

Comment. This case represented a repudiation of the direct causation rule of *Polemis, supra*.

---

       d.   **Balancing test.** *Overseas Tankship (U.K.), Ltd. v. Miller Steamship Co. (Wagon Mound II)*, [1967] 1 A.C. 617, involved the same facts as in *Wagon Mound I, supra*. Here, the suit was brought by the owners of the ships damaged in the fire, and the court held for the plaintiffs on reasoning similar to that in *Carroll Towing, supra; i.e.,* the burden of eliminating a risk must be balanced against the probability of its materializing times the potential gravity of the harm. The court stated that the defendant should have known that there was a serious risk of the oil on the water catching fire in some way and that if it did, serious damage to ships or other property was not only foreseeable, but very likely, thus making it unreasonable to dismiss such a risk.

            1)   **Comment.** This case can be viewed as consistent with its sister case involving the wharf by finding that the court in that case erred in determining what a reasonable person would foresee. Here, the result in *Polemis, supra,* is approached by charging the reasonable person with the recognition of slight or extremely remote risks.

    3.   **Superseding Causes.**

       a.   **Indirect results of defendant's act.** As discussed *supra*, indirect results occur when there is an intervening force (or forces) between the defendant's act and the harm caused to the plaintiff. Such forces or causes are of external origin, and do not come into operation until after the defendant's negligent act has occurred. Intervening causes generally do not relieve the defendant of liability unless they are both unforeseeable and bring about unforeseeable results. In such cases, the intervening causes are said to be "superseding." However, the test in every case where there is an intervening force or cause is whether the average, reasonable person faced with like or similar circumstances would have foreseen the likelihood that the force or cause would intervene.

1) Intervening criminal act--

Doe v. Manheimer, 563 A.2d 699 (Conn. 1989).

Facts. While a meter reader (P) was working in a high crime area, she was confronted and raped by a man with a gun and other items that indicated he had planned a rape. P was forced from the sidewalk to an area of property owned by Manheimer (D), which had overgrown sumac bushes and tall grass that shielded the area from view from the street. P suffered serious emotional and psychiatric problems, was hospitalized, and attempted suicide several times. P sued D for personal injuries sustained in the attack. P claimed that D should have removed the overgrowth because the neighborhood was a high crime area and the overgrowth caused and contributed to her assault. At trial, an environmental psychologist testified that it was his opinion that the physical configuration of the site increased the risk of violent crimes by creating a protective zone that reduced or eliminated visibility and served as an inducement for crime. The jury found for P, but the trial court set aside the verdict. P appeals.

Issue. May a landowner be liable in tort for damages arising from a rape committed on the landowner's property behind brush and trees that hid the area from view from the public sidewalk and street?

Held. No. Judgment affirmed.

♦   Except in circumstances where there is no room for reasonable disagreement, the trier of fact determines questions of proximate cause.

♦   Proximate cause is an actual cause that is a substantial factor in the resulting harm. The substantial factor test is whether the harm that occurred was of the same general nature as the foreseeable risk created by the defendant's negligence. To make this determination, we look from the injury to the negligent act for the necessary causal connection.

♦   Where the risk of harm created by the defendant's negligence allegedly extends to an intervening criminal act by a third party, as here, we also apply the "scope of the risk" analysis. A negligent defendant who has increased the risk of harm and is a substantial factor in causing the harm is not relieved from liability where there is intervention, except when the intervenor intentionally causes the harm and that harm is not within the scope of the risk created by the defendant's actions. In a situation like this, the third party intervenor has deliberately assumed control of the situation; all responsibility shifts to him. The tortious or criminal acts may be foreseeable, however, and thus within the scope of the created risk.

◆   In this case, D has not argued that his conduct was not a "cause in fact" of P's injuries, and the trial court found that the rape probably would not have occurred where it did if it were not for the overgrowth. The jury could have found that the attacker had planned for the attack to occur in that exact location. They could have concluded that the attack may not have lasted as long as it did were it not for the overgrowth. We do not question these findings.

◆   However, we do not agree with P's contention that there was room for reasonable disagreement over the question of proximate cause. The harm that P suffered cannot reasonably be understood to be within the scope of risk created by D's conduct. The scope of risk analysis contemplates reasonably foreseeable intervening misconduct, not all conduct that actually arises from a situation created by the defendant. Furthermore, to be within the scope of risk, the harm actually suffered must be of the same general type as that which makes the defendant negligent in the first place. Here, it was not reasonably foreseeable to D that the overgrowth might result in an attack.

---

4.   **Unexpected Victim.** The foreseeability criteria have been extended to the question of to whom does the defendant owe a duty.

a.   **Duty owed the plaintiff--**

Palsgraf v. Long Island Railroad Co., 162 N.E. 99 (N.Y. 1928).

Facts. Palsgraf (P) purchased a railroad ticket and stood on a platform of Long Island Railroad's (D's) when a would-be passenger carrying a package attempted to leap aboard a moving train. A train guard pulled the passenger aboard while another guard pushed him from behind, causing his package to dislodge and fall upon the tracks. The package, wrapped in newspaper, contained fireworks that exploded. The shock of the explosion caused some scales at the other end of the platform to fall and strike P. P was awarded damages resulting from her injuries. The Appellate Division affirmed, and D appeals.

Issue. May the defendant's negligence toward a third person be the basis of recovery for injuries to the plaintiff, even though no risk of harm to the plaintiff was foreseeable?

Held. No. Judgment reversed.

♦　　The plaintiff must show a wrong to herself; *i.e.,* a violation of her own right, not merely a wrong to someone else or an unsocial act.

♦　　The reasonably perceivable risk defines the duty to be obeyed. The risk extends to those within the range of reasonable apprehension.

♦　　The purpose of the guard's act was to make the passenger safe. If there was a wrong at all, it was to the safety of the package. There was nothing in the situation to suggest to the most cautious mind that the parcel would spread wreckage through the station.

♦　　Negligence itself is not a tort; it must be negligence in relation to the plaintiff.

Dissent (Andrews, J.). Judgment for P should be affirmed.

♦　　When an act unreasonably threatens the safety of others, the wrongdoer is liable for all proximate consequences regardless of whether they are unforeseeable or unexpected.

♦　　The doctrine of proximate cause is a tool that allows the law to arbitrarily decline to trace a series of events beyond a certain point.

♦　　Due care is a duty imposed on everyone to protect society from unnecessary harm. To say that there is no negligence unless there is a legal duty owed to the plaintiff herself is too narrow a conception. Where there is an unreasonable act, there is negligence.

Comment. This case illustrates the analysis used to determine who is a proper plaintiff in a tort action. To recover, a plaintiff must show that the defendant owed her a duty that was then breached by the defendant.

VI. DEFENSES

A. THE PLAINTIFF'S FAULT

1. **Contributory Negligence.** Contributory negligence is conduct on the part of the plaintiff that contributes, as a legal cause, to the harm she has suffered, and is conduct that falls below the standard to which she must conform. Contributory negligence is much like negligence itself—the criteria are the same—reasonable care for her own safety rather than the safety of others. While the formula for determining negligence and contributory negligence is the same (*see* Judge Learned Hand's formula in *Carroll Towing, supra*), the results are not necessarily the same. The same act may be negligent when done by the defendant, yet not so when done by the plaintiff. The standard of care, as in negligence, is determined by what the reasonable person would have done under the same or similar circumstances.

   a. **Common law rule.** The standard common law rule was that a plaintiff's action for negligence is barred by her own negligent conduct if such conduct is a substantial factor in bringing about her injury. Thus, its effect is to give the defendant a complete defense; *i.e.,* no liability to the defendant.

   b. **Minority rule.** The minority rule was that the plaintiff's minute contribution to her injury is sufficient.

   c. **Burden of proof.** The burden of pleading and proving contributory negligence is on the defendant.

   d. **Distinguish avoidable consequences.** Contributory negligence should be distinguished from "avoidable consequence." If a plaintiff fails to act as a reasonable person in order to mitigate her damages, she will be barred from recovering the damages that could have been avoided. Note that this doctrine is a rule as to damages and not as to liability.

   e. **Limitation to the particular risk.** The defense of contributory negligence is not available to a defendant if the plaintiff's injury did not result from a hazard with respect to which the plaintiff failed to exercise reasonable care. In *Smithwick v. Hall & Upson Co.*, 59 Conn. 261 (1890), the plaintiff negligently failed to heed a warning about an icy platform, but was injured when a wall fell on him. Since the plaintiff's actions were reasonable in regard to the danger that actually caused his injury (the falling wall), the defendant was held liable.

   f. **Injuries intentionally or recklessly caused.** Contributory negligence is not a defense to intentional torts, willful and wanton conduct, or reckless misconduct.

g. **Last clear chance.** This doctrine was promulgated to ameliorate the harsh effects of contributory negligence as a complete defense. It applies where the defendant was negligent and the plaintiff, through her contributory negligence, placed herself in a position of either "helpless" or "inattentive" peril; the defendant must be aware of the plaintiff's situation, under a duty to discover the plaintiff, and able to recognize the plaintiff's peril and avoid injury to the plaintiff. In *Davies v. Mann* (Eng. 1842), a man fettered his donkey and turned it onto a highway where the defendant drove into it with his carriage. The court held that if the defendant could have avoided the animal, the plaintiff could recover notwithstanding the obvious contributory negligence on his part. This case is the origin of the doctrine of last clear chance and reflects the reluctance courts have had to deny recovery on the basis of contributory negligence. Comparative negligence (below) has largely eliminated the use of this doctrine.

h. **Imputed contributory negligence.** Under the theory of imputed negligence, if X is negligent and if there exists a special relationship between X and Y, the negligence of X may be "imputed" or charged to Y, even though Y has had nothing to do with X's conduct, and may even have tried to prevent it. The effect of "imputed negligence" may be either to make Y liable to Z (who has an action against X for negligence, which negligence may be imputed to Y (*e.g.,* in a master (Y)-servant (X) situation)) or to bar recovery by Y against Z where X has been contributorily negligent and such contributory negligence is imputed to Y (*e.g.,* driver (X)-passenger (Y) versus other driver (Z), where both drivers are negligent and Y seeks recovery from Z, who defends on the basis of imputed contributory negligence).

2. **Comparative Negligence.**

a. **Introduction.** Comparative negligence was originally a civil law doctrine, and more widely recognized in Europe than the United States. As late as the 1960s, only a few states in the United States used the doctrine. During the 1970s and early 1980s, comparative negligence became something of a reform movement and gained wider acceptance. Currently, almost all states have adopted a form of comparative negligence.

b. **"Pure" vs. "partial" comparative negligence.** There are two basic types of comparative negligence formulae for assessing liability.

1) **"Pure."** A number of jurisdictions and the Uniform Act have "pure" comparative negligence, which allows a plaintiff to recover a percentage of his damages even if his own negligence exceeds that of the defendant (*e.g.,* if the jury determines that the plaintiff was 90% at fault, he can still recover 10% of his damages).

2) **"Partial."** Other states, however, recognize only "partial" comparative negligence, in that they **deny any recovery** to a plaintiff whose own negligence **equals or exceeds** that of the defendant. This is the so-called "less than" or "49% limit" plan.

    a) **Modification—"50% limit" plan.** Some jurisdictions modify this formula and only deny recovery where a plaintiff's negligence exceeds the defendant's (the so-called "equal to or less than" or "50% limit" plan). Under this approach, if the jury finds that the plaintiff was 50% at fault, the plaintiff can still recover half of his damages.

    b) **Multiple defendants.**

       (1) Where *several* defendants are negligent but are not jointly liable, some states hold that a plaintiff's negligence must be less than that of any defendant. For example, where the jury determines that two defendants acting independently were each one-third at fault, and the plaintiff was one-third at fault, no recovery would be possible in a "49% limit" plan.

       (2) Most courts, however, consider the negligence of multiple defendants in the *aggregate*, permitting a plaintiff to recover something if his fault is less than the combined negligence of the defendants.

    c) **Relevant but inflammatory evidence--**

Fritts v. McKinne, 934 P.2d 371 (Okla. 1996).

Facts. Fritts was injured in an accident when the truck he was in hit a tree at approximately 70 miles per hour and overturned. Fritts had been drinking before the accident, and there is a question as to who was driving. All of Fritts's major facial bones were broken and he suffered impact injury to his chest. Dr. McKinne (D) performed a tracheostomy to allow Fritts to breathe during surgery to repair his face. As D started the tracheostomy, Fritts began to bleed profusely. Fritts lost a major amount of blood, failed to regain consciousness, and died three days later. Fritts's surviving spouse (P) filed a wrongful death suit. D claimed Fritts's artery was in his neck area when it should have been in his chest. D asserted a comparative negligence defense, claiming Fritts caused his injury while driving drunk or was drunk while riding in a vehicle with his friend, who also was drunk. P's motion to exclude evidence of Fritts's drug and alcohol use was denied. The jury found for D and P appeals.

Issue. Did the trial court err in admitting evidence regarding Fritts's history of substance abuse and in allowing the jury to consider comparative negligence, based on the events of the automobile accident, as a basis for reducing or denying recovery on the medical negligence claim?

Held. Yes. Judgment reversed and remanded for a new trial.

♦ P's burden is to establish that D's actions were below the requisite standard of care required and that they resulted in Fritts's death. D argued he did not deviate from the appropriate standard of care, but Fritts's unusual anatomy and the injury to his artery from the accident were the cause of the rupture. D's defense is appropriate. However, we conclude that interjecting the issue of Fritts's possible negligence in the automobile accident diverted the jury's consideration from the relevant medical procedures and directed them to unrelated matters. This was a substantial error.

♦ Patient conduct can be considered under some circumstances; for example, where a patient provides false information to his physician or fails to inform his physician of an important aspect of his medical history. A patient's prior acts may be considered as evidence of contributory negligence. When a patient attempts his own treatment prior to seeing a doctor, the jury may consider whether he was contributorily negligent. Nothing like these examples exists in this case.

♦ Fritts's substance abuse is relevant on the issue of damages. P seeks damages based on future earnings, and Fritts's history of substance abuse may affect his probable life expectancy. However, given the circumstances of this case, such evidence would be extremely inflammatory. The court should order the jury to consider it only as to damages or bifurcate the trial.

―――――――――

c.   **Other issues involving multiple defendants.**

1)   **Introduction.** Joint tortfeasors are persons who either act in concert to cause injury to a plaintiff or act entirely independently but cause a single indivisible injury to a plaintiff. Joint tortfeasors are jointly and severally liable for the damage they cause. Thus, a plaintiff may elect to seek the entire amount from any one of the defendants.

2)   **Satisfaction and release.** An unsatisfied judgment against one of several joint tortfeasors does not bar a plaintiff's action against the others. However, the *satisfaction* of a judgment against one joint tortfeasor extinguishes the cause of action and bars any subsequent suit for a greater or additional amount against any of the others. Many courts formerly reached the same result where a plaintiff had merely *released* one of several joint tortfeasors, regardless of

the sufficiency of compensation paid for the release. Most states now reject the latter rule, requiring that the release specifically waive the right to sue the other joint tortfeasors in order for them to be released.

3) Contribution. At common law, contribution was not allowed between joint tortfeasors; if one satisfied a judgment, she could not recover from the others their per capita share. Today, under most contribution statutes, each joint tortfeasor is responsible for some share of the judgment. In comparative negligence states, contribution is based on each tortfeasor's relative fault.

4) Indemnity. Indemnity is an equitable remedy to prevent unjust enrichment. Whereas contribution involves wrongdoers who are jointly and severally liable and requires each to pay a proportionate share of the judgment, indemnity involves wrongdoers who have unequal degrees of responsibility and requires the one primarily liable to bear the entire burden and compensate the one secondarily liable who was initially compelled to compensate the plaintiff. Some comparative negligence jurisdictions have abolished indemnity based on varying degrees of liability.

B. ASSUMPTION OF RISK

The defense of assumption of risk arises when the plaintiff voluntarily encounters a known danger and, by his conduct, expressly or impliedly consents to take the risk of the danger. In such a case, the defendant will be relieved of responsibility for his negligence.

1. **Not Negligence.** A plaintiff's voluntary assumption of risk need not be a negligent act on his part; *e.g.,* a spectator at a baseball game may be held to assume the risks of flying balls, but it is not negligent to attend a baseball game.

2. **Unreasonable Assumption.** On the other hand, a plaintiff's action may constitute contributory negligence where the plaintiff is unreasonable in assuming the risks of the defendant's conduct.

3. **Knowledge Required.** A plaintiff may be contributorily negligent for failing to discover a danger of which a reasonable person should have been aware. There can be no assumption of risk, however, where the plaintiff had no knowledge or awareness of the particular danger involved.

4. **Must Be Voluntary.** A plaintiff's assumption of risk must be voluntary; if the defendant's acts leave the plaintiff with no reasonable alternative to encountering the danger, there is no assumption of risk.

5. **Rejection Theory.** Writers have consistently attacked "assumption of risk." Some courts have come out rejecting assumption of risk completely by stating that one must find either (i) contributory negligence or (ii) the plaintiff's consent to negligence, which simply means that the defendant owed the plaintiff no duty. Many courts that have adopted comparative negligence have taken this approach.

6. **Exculpatory Agreement Void--**

Dalury v. S-K-I, Ltd., 670 A.2d 795 (Vt. 1995).

Facts. Dalury (P) was injured when he struck a pole that was part of a control maze for a ski lift line owned by S-K-I, Ltd. and others (Ds). P had signed an exculpatory agreement releasing Ds from all liability for negligence, and P's signed photo identification card contained the same release terms. The trial court granted Ds' motion for summary judgment, and P appeals.

Issue. Are exculpatory agreements that require skiers to release ski areas from all liability resulting from negligence void as contrary to public policy?

Held. Yes. Judgment reversed and case remanded.

♦ An exculpatory agreement should be upheld if it is "freely and fairly made," between parties "who are in an equal bargaining position," and "there is no social interest with which it interferes." [Restatement (Second) of Torts §496B comment b]

♦ No single formula will address the relevant public policy concerns in every factual context. Ultimately, "the determination of what constitutes the public interest must be made considering the totality of the circumstances of any given case against the backdrop of current societal expectations."

♦ A business owner has a duty of care to provide safe premises in suitable condition for its customers. A business invitee has a right to assume that aside from obvious dangers, the premises are reasonably safe for purposes for which the invitee is upon them, and that proper precautions have been taken to make them so.

♦ A skier's assumption of risks inherent in skiing does not affect a ski business's duty to warn skiers about risks or correct dangers that, in exercising reasonable prudence under the circumstances, could have been foreseen and rectified.

---

7. **Voluntary Assumption of Risks of Amusements--**

Murphy v. Steeplechase Amusement Co., 166 N.E. 173 (N.Y. 1929).

Facts. Murphy (P) got on an amusement park ride known as the "Flopper." The Flopper had a moving belt that made people fall. P fell and was injured, and he sued Steeplechase Amusement (D) for negligence. P obtained a verdict, and D appeals.

Issue. Was P's decision to get on the Flopper an assumption of risk?

Held. Yes. Judgment reversed.

- ♦ P clearly saw the dangers of the ride. No additional warnings were necessary, since P could observe all risks.

- ♦ The ride was not so dangerous as to require that it be closed.

8. **Comparative Negligence and Assumption of Risk--**

Davenport v. Cotton Hope Plantation Horizontal Property Regime, 508 S.E.2d 565 (S.C. 1998).

Facts. Davenport (P) leases a condominium at Cotton Hope Plantation (D). P's unit is on the third level, approximately five feet from a stairway. For two months, P reported to property management that the lights at the bottom of his stairs were not working. One evening, P fell when he "stepped" on a shadow instead of a step. P sued D and the trial court directed a verdict for D, finding P had assumed the risk, or in the absence of assumption of risk, P was more than 50% negligent. The court of appeals reversed. D appeals.

Issue. Does assumption of risk survive as a complete bar to recovery under the state's modified comparative negligence system?

Held. No. A plaintiff is barred only when the degree of fault arising from the assumption of risk is greater than the defendant's negligence.

- ♦ Currently, to establish the defense of assumption of risk, the plaintiff must: (i) have knowledge of the dangerous condition; (ii) know the condition is dangerous; (iii) appreciate the nature and extent of the danger; and (iv) voluntarily expose himself to the danger.

- ♦ The great majority of courts that have adopted comparative negligence have abolished assumption of risk as an absolute bar to recovery. Many courts distinguish between "express" assumption of risk and "implied" assumption of risk.

♦   Express assumption of risk applies when the parties expressly agree in advance, either in writing or orally, that the plaintiff will relieve the defendant of his legal duty toward the plaintiff. Thus, express assumption of risk remains an absolute defense in an action for negligence.

♦   Primary implied assumption of risk arises when the plaintiff implicitly assumes known or inherent risks, *e.g.*, playing football. Implied assumption of risk is not a true affirmative defense, but instead goes to the initial determination of whether the defendant's legal duty encompasses the risk encountered by the plaintiff. It is merely a part of the initial negligence analysis.

♦   Secondary implied assumption of risk arises when the plaintiff knowingly encounters a risk created by the defendant's negligence. It is a true defense because it is asserted only after the plaintiff establishes a prima facie case of negligence against the defendant. Secondary implied assumption of risk may involve either reasonable or unreasonable conduct on the part of the plaintiff, *e.g.*, a plaintiff running into a burning building to save his hat.

♦   Since express and primary implied assumption of risk are compatible with comparative negligence, we will refer to secondary implied assumption of risk simply as assumption of risk.

♦   It goes against the basis of this state's comparative fault system to require a plaintiff, who is 50% or less at fault, to bear all of the costs of the injury. Accordingly, the defendant's fault in causing an accident is not diminished simply because the plaintiff knowingly assumes a risk. If assumption of risk is retained in its current common law form, a plaintiff would be completely barred from recovery even if his conduct is reasonable or only slightly unreasonable. In our comparative fault system, it would be incongruous to absolve the defendant of all liability based only on whether the plaintiff assumed the risk of injury. Comparative negligence by definition seeks to assess and compare the negligence of both the plaintiff and defendant. This goal would clearly be thwarted by adhering to the common law defense of assumption of risk.

---

9.   The "Firefighter's Rule"--

Levandowski v. Cone, 841 A.2d 208 (Conn. 2004).

Facts. Police officer Levandowski (P) and another officer responded to a complaint about a loud party at a home. The officers approached the home from different sides of the house in order to observe the party. P saw young people playing basketball and heard music and noise. He then heard someone say that the police had arrived and saw cans of what he assumed to be beer being thrown away. Then P saw Cone (D) take some items from a bag in the garage, walk down the driveway while looking over his shoulder, and put some small plastic baggies in his pants. P, believing the baggies contained marijuana, stepped forward, turned his flashlight on D, and asked that D remove the baggies from his pants. Instead, D ran toward the woods. P pursued D, and just as P was about to catch D, P fell off of a ledge onto some rocks. As a result, P sustained severe injuries to his hip and knee, including lacerations, dislocation of the hip, and a 20% permanent disability of his lower right leg. P sued D for injuries negligently caused by D while P was pursuing him on private property. The jury found for P and awarded $65,000 in noneconomic damages and $82,535 in economic damages. D appeals.

Issue. Should the "firefighter's rule" be extended beyond the scope of premises liability so as to bar a police officer from recovering from a negligent tortfeasor who is neither an owner nor a person in control of the premises?

Held. No. Judgment affirmed.

♦ Under the "firefighter's rule," a firefighter or police officer who goes on private property in the exercise of his duties has the status of a licensee, and the property owner owes such person a duty of care that is less than that owed to an ordinary invitee. The landowner owes the firefighter or police officer only the duty not to injure him willfully or wantonly. D argues that the firefighter's rule should be extended to nonpremises liability cases, such as the present case. We do not agree.

♦ When we extended the firefighter's rule to police officers, we did so for three reasons. The first was because of the similar roles of firefighters and police officers and because of landowners' reasonable expectations regarding those two types of public officers. Both enter property at unforeseeable times and under emergency situations, with or without an owner's consent. Only invitees may rely on an implied representation of safety, and it would be unreasonable to require landowners to provide the same standard of care for public officers whose presence the landowners cannot predict. The second reason—a variation on the doctrine of assumption of the risk—recognizes the inherently hazardous nature of the work performed by firefighters and police officers. They enter their professions voluntarily, knowing that they will often confront dangerous situations created by the negligence of the public they serve. The third reason is the avoidance of double taxation upon landowners and the availability of workers' compensation benefits for injured firefighters or police officers.

♦ The firefighter's rule should be confined to claims of premises liability. First, the distinction upon which the rule rests—whether the plaintiff is an invitee or licensee—is a distinction that exists only in claims involving premises liability and a landowner's duty to persons on his land. Second, our legislature has abolished the doctrine of assumption of the risk in negligence actions. To the extent that the firefighter's rule rests on the doctrine of assumption of the risk, it would be inconsistent with the policy of our general tort law to extend the rule beyond its present limits. Third, because a landowner indirectly pays the salaries of police officers and firefighters through taxes, he owes a lesser degree of duty than a defendant who is not a landowner taxpayer. In addition, allowing a plaintiff to recover for a defendant's negligence will tend to lower workers' compensation costs by permitting the plaintiff's employer to recoup those benefits.

♦ We agree with the trial court that it was reasonably foreseeable that P could be injured in pursuing D. P ordered D to stop and D did not; he continued to flee. As P contends, it is common sense that a person fleeing from a police officer who has ordered him to stop should know that an officer in pursuit could be injured while running after him in the dark.

C. PREEMPTION

1. Common Law Tort Action Preempted--

Geier v. American Honda Motor Company, Inc., 529 U.S. 861 (2000).

Facts. Geier, driving a 1987 Honda Accord, was seriously injured when she collided with a tree. P had buckled her shoulder and lap belts, but the car had no airbags. Geier and her parents (Ps) sued American Honda and its affiliates (Ds), alleging negligent and defective design because there was no driver's side airbag. The district court dismissed. The court of appeals dismissed for different reasons. The Supreme Court granted certiorari.

Issue. Does the National Traffic and Motor Safety Act of 1966, when taken together with the relevant regulatory standard, preempt a common law tort action claiming that a car manufacturer, compliant with the standard, ought to have equipped a car with airbags?

Held. Yes. Judgment affirmed.

♦ Under the National Traffic and Motor Vehicle Safety Act of 1966 ("Act"), the United States Department of Transportation promulgated Federal Motor Vehicle Safety Standard ("FMVSS") 208, which, among other matters, required auto manufacturers to equip some, but not all, of their 1987 vehicles with passive restraints. FMVSS 208 gave car manufacturers a choice as to whether to install airbags.

♦ The Act's preemption provision reads: "Whenever a Federal motor vehicle safety standard established under this subchapter is in effect, no State or political subdivision of a State shall have any authority either to establish, or to continue in effect, with respect to any motor vehicle or item of motor vehicle equipment[,] any safety standard applicable to the same aspect of performance of such vehicle or item of equipment which is not identical to the federal standard."

♦   The Act's "saving" clause says that "compliance with" a federal safety standard "does not exempt any person from any liability under common law." Thus, the saving clause assumes that there are common law liability cases to save. Where federal law creates only minimum safety standards, for example, state tort law may operate. The saving clause prevents a broad reading of the express preemption provision that, arguably, might preempt common law tort actions. Such a broad reading would preempt all nonidentical state standards established in tort actions covering the same aspect of performance as an applicable federal standard, even if the federal standard merely established a minimum standard. On that broad reading of the preemption clause little, if any, potential "liability at common law" would remain. We have found no evidence that Congress intended such a broad reading.

♦   Conflict preemption principles are not barred by the saving clause. There is nothing in the clause that suggests saving state tort actions that conflict with federal regulations. The words "compliance" and "does not exempt" sound as if they simply bar a defense that compliance with a federal standard automatically exempts a defendant from state law, whether the federal government meant that standard to be an absolute, or a minimum, requirement. This interpretation does not conflict with the purpose of the saving provision, for it preserves actions that seek to establish greater safety than the minimum safety achieved by a federal regulation intended to provide a floor. Furthermore, we have repeatedly declined to give broad effect to saving clauses that would upset the careful regulatory scheme established by federal law, a concern applicable here. The preemption provision itself favors preemption of state tort suits, while the saving clause disfavors preemption at least some of the time. However, there is nothing in any natural reading of the two provisions that would favor one policy over the other where a jury-imposed safety standard actually conflicts with a federal safety standard.

♦   This lawsuit actually conflicts with FMVSS 208 and the Act itself. FMVSS 208 was a way to give a manufacturer a range of choices among different passive restraint systems that would be gradually introduced, thereby lowering costs, overcoming technical safety problems, encouraging technological development, and winning widespread consumer acceptance. FMVSS sought variety to help develop data on comparative effectiveness, to provide time to overcome safety problems and high costs, and to encourage the development of alternative, cheaper, and safer passive restraint systems, thereby building public confidence necessary to avoid an interlock-type fiasco.

♦   Ps' tort action depends upon their claim that manufacturers had a duty to install an airbag when they manufactured the 1987 Honda Accord. Such a state law by its terms would have required manufacturers of all similar cars to install airbags rather than other passive restraint systems, such as automatic belts or passive interiors. It thereby would have presented an obstacle to the variety and mix of devices that the federal regulation sought.

Dissent (Stevens, Souter, Thomas, Ginsburg, JJ.). The Court has permitted an interim regulation to prevent Ps' proposition that to be safe a car must have an airbag from being addressed. The rule enforced here was not enacted by Congress and was not found in the text of any Executive Order or regulation. It is the product of the Court's interpretation of a commentary accompanying an administrative regulation. We would have preempted tort actions only if they created a "special burden" on the regulatory scheme as envisioned by Congress. There is no such burden here. Ds have not overcome the presumption against preemption in this case.

VII. STRICT LIABILITY

A. TRADITIONAL APPROACH

Certain activities are so dangerous that they involve a serious risk of harm to others despite the use of utmost care to prevent any harm. Strict liability is imposed upon those who engage in such activities. Ultrahazardous activities are those activities abnormal to the area, which necessarily involve a risk to persons, land, or chattels that cannot be eliminated by the use of utmost care. [Restatement of Torts §520]

1. Unnatural Conditions on Land.

a. Principal case--

Fletcher v. Rylands, L.R. 1 Exch. 265 (1866).

Facts. Rylands (D) constructed a reservoir on his land that, when filled with water, burst, causing water to flow into coal mines on Fletcher's (P's) adjoining property. Unknown to D, there were old coal mine shafts under his property, which were discovered by his employees during construction of the reservoir and which weakened the reservoir and permitted the flow of water onto P's property. P sued for damages, and the trial court awarded a verdict in his favor. The Exchequer reversed, and P appeals to the Exchequer Chamber.

Issue. Does a person who brings on his land something that will cause harm to another if it escapes have an absolute duty to prevent its escape?

Held. Yes. Judgment of the trial court affirmed.

♦ A person who brings onto his land anything likely to do mischief if it escapes keeps it at his peril and is prima facie answerable for all damage that is the natural consequence of its escape. He can only excuse himself by showing that the escape was the plaintiff's fault.

♦ In this case, but for D's act, no mischief could have accrued.

♦ This case is distinguishable from traffic and other cases that require proof of a defendant's negligence for recovery. They involve situations where people have subjected themselves to some inevitable risk. Here, there is no ground for saying that P took upon himself any risk arising from the use to which D chose to put his land.

b.   **House of Lords appeal--**

Rylands v. Fletcher, L.R. 3 H.L. 330 (1868).

Facts. Same facts as above. D appeals the affirmance of the trial court by the Exchequer Chamber.

Issue. Is a person who makes a nonnatural use of his land strictly liable for any damages that result to another's property?

Held. Yes. Judgment affirmed.

♦   An owner of land may use the land for any purpose for which it might, in the ordinary course of enjoyment, be used. Thus, if the water had accumulated naturally and run off onto adjoining land, there could be no complaint.

♦   Nevertheless, a landowner who introduces onto the land that which, in its natural condition, was not present, does so at the peril of absolute liability for consequences arising therefrom.

---

c.   **The *Rylands* rule.** The rule of *Rylands* is that one is liable to adjacent landowners when he brings an artificial and unnatural device onto his land, and the unnatural device causes something to escape from the land and harm another's land or property.

2.   **Animals.**

a.   **Trespassing.** The general rule is that the owner of animals that are likely to stray and that do stray onto the land of another is strictly liable for any damage caused by such animals. An exception to this rule was made for domestic pets.

b.   **Wild animals.** The possessor of wild animals is strictly liable for any harm done by the animal if such harm results from its normally dangerous propensities. However, where animals are kept under a public duty, strict liability does not apply; negligence must be shown, although a high degree of care will be required. In *Filburn v. People's Palace & Aquarium Co., Ltd.* (Q.B. Div. 1890), the plaintiff was injured in an attack by the defendant's elephant. The court held that unless an animal is within a class recognized as harmless, either by nature or as so classified by rule of law (*e.g.,* horses, sheep, dogs, etc.), the defendant keeps such animal at his peril and is responsible for any damages caused by it.

    c.   **Known dangerous domestic animals.** If a defendant has knowledge of the dangerous propensities of his animal (*i.e.*, that the animal threatens serious bodily harm or property damage to others), he will be strictly liable for all injuries resulting from that dangerous propensity.

    d.   **"Dog bite" statutes.** "Dog bite" statutes have been enacted in several jurisdictions. Basically, these statutes reversed the common law rule that every dog was entitled to one bite before it became known to be an animal with dangerous propensities. The statutes make an animal's keeper liable for all damage or harm caused by the animal, unless the plaintiff was a trespasser or was committing a tort.

  3.   **Early Adoption of Strict Liability--**

Sullivan v. Dunham, 55 N.E. 923 (N.Y. 1900).

Facts. Two men were conducting blasting operations for Dunham (D). They were directed to dynamite a tree on D's land. The explosion threw a piece of the wood onto a highway, and killed a woman. The deceased's representative, Sullivan (P), sued for the injury. The trial court instructed that negligence need not be proven, and P received a verdict. That verdict was affirmed on appeal, and D appeals further.

Issue. Is strict liability appropriate for injuries caused by blasting?

Held. Yes. Judgment affirmed.

◆   Although D had the right to conduct blasting on his property, the deceased had a right to be on the highway. Her right to safety was greater than D's property right. Here, D's acts were the direct cause of the death. Strict liability will apply for such direct results of a dangerous activity. If the harm had been indirect, such as an injury from shock or concussion from the explosion, negligence would need to be shown.

Comment. The distinction between strict liability for direct injury and negligence for concussion injury has since been abolished in New York.

---

  4.   **Restatement Approaches.** Restatement of Torts sections 519 through 520 recognize strict liability for certain activities.

    a.   **First Restatement.** The Restatement allowed strict liability for ultrahazardous activities, considered to be activities that were not of common usage and whose risks of serious harm could not be eliminated with utmost care.

b. **Second Restatement.** The Restatement (Second) allows strict liability for abnormally dangerous activities. Rather than declaring the elements that must be met, the Second Restatement lists six factors that should be balanced. These factors are:

1) Whether the activity involves a high degree of risk;

2) Whether the gravity of that risk is high;

3) Whether the risk can be eliminated with reasonable care;

4) Whether the activity is not a matter of common usage;

5) Whether the activity is appropriate to the place where it is being carried out; and

6) Whether the value to the community is outweighed by the danger.

c. **Not abnormally dangerous--**

Indiana Harbor Belt Railroad Co. v. American Cyanamid Co., 916 F.2d 1174 (7th Cir. 1990).

Facts. Indiana Harbor Belt Railroad Company (P) sued American Cyanamid Company (D) to recover the costs of decontamination measures ordered by the Illinois Department of Environmental Protection when a railroad tank car containing acrylonitrile leaked and spilled. D had manufactured the chemical and had leased a railroad car to transport it from Louisiana to New Jersey. P, a small switching line, was responsible for switching the railroad car from one line to another. Several hours after the tank car arrived in Chicago, P's employees noticed a leak. It was feared that all 20,000 gallons of the highly toxic and possibly carcinogenic chemical had leaked, and homes in the area were evacuated. Even though only about 4,000 gallons had leaked, P was ordered to undertake decontamination measures that cost $981,022.75. P sued to recover its costs. The trial court granted P summary judgment on its strict liability claim and dismissed P's negligence claim. D appeals and P cross-appeals.

Issue. Should the shipper of a hazardous chemical by rail through a metropolitan area be strictly liable for the consequences of a spill or other accident to the shipment en route?

Held. No. Judgment reversed and case remanded.

♦ With Restatement (Second) section 520 as a basis for application of strict liability here, we have been given no reason for believing that a negligence regime is not perfectly adequate to remedy and deter an accidental spilling of acrylonitrile from rail cars at reasonable cost.

- Acrylonitrile is hazardous in the sense of being both flammable and toxic. It could explode and destroy evidence; however, here, it did not, making it premature to impose strict liability. Moreover, the chemical is not so corrosive or otherwise destructive that it will eat through or otherwise damage a tank car's valves even if they are maintained with due care. There has been no suggestion, therefore, that the leak was caused by the inherent properties of acrylonitrile; rather, it was caused by carelessness.

- Accidents resulting from a lack of care can be prevented by taking care, and when a lack of care can be demonstrated in court, such accidents are deterred adequately by the threat of negligence liability.

- Clearly, the accident here might have been prevented at reasonable cost if the persons who handled the tank car of acrylonitrile had exercised greater care. However, it is difficult to imagine how the accident might have been prevented at reasonable cost by a change in the activity of transporting the chemical. Accordingly, this is not an apt case for imposing strict liability.

---

5. **Defenses.**

   a. **Contributory negligence.** Contributory negligence is not a defense to strict liability unless the plaintiff's negligence was the cause of the ultrahazardous activity.

   b. **Assumption of risk.** Assumption of risk may be asserted as a defense against a plaintiff who voluntarily encounters a known danger and by his conduct expressly or impliedly consents to the risk of the danger.

   c. **Comparative negligence.** Some courts in comparative negligence jurisdictions have been willing to reduce a plaintiff's recovery to reflect the amount that his fault contributed to his injury.

   d. **Injury within the risk created.** For strict liability to be imposed, the injury must have been within the group of risks that made the activity ultrahazardous.

      1) **Different risk.** In *Foster v. Preston Mill Co.*, 44 Wash. 2d 440 (1954), the defendant conducted blasting operations. The plaintiff incurred damage when his minks became frightened by the blasts and killed their kittens. Since the danger of flying debris made the blasting ultrahazardous and since the resulting harm was not from that which makes the activity ultrahazardous, the court did not impose strict liability.

2) **Unforeseeable intervening cause.** Even where the damage is within the foreseeable risk, the majority of courts hold that there is no strict liability if it was brought about by an unforeseeable intervening cause, *e.g.,* an act of God or the intentional acts of third persons.

VIII. LIABILITY FOR DEFECTIVE PRODUCTS

A. INTRODUCTION

1. **Unsafe Products.** Generally, a product can be considered unsafe if it is defective in manufacture (either workmanship or materials) or design, which defect or danger renders it potentially harmful to normal individuals in the foreseeable use of the product.

2. **Common Law.** At early English common law, liability for defective products was grounded in either tort or contract.

    a. **Tort actions.** Originally, the action in tort was in the nature of deceit—an action on the case by the purchaser for breach of an assumed duty.

    b. **Contract actions.** By the beginning of the 19th century, the plaintiff's action gained substantial recognition in contract, but only those injured plaintiffs in "privity of contract" with the manufacturer or supplier of the defective product were permitted a cause of action against them. This cause of action sounding in contract was in assumpsit, either express, implied-in-fact, or implied-in-law, and the recoverable damages were determined by application of the *Hadley v. Baxendale* rules. In 1842, Lord Abinger, in *Winterbottom v. Wright*, 152 Eng. Rep. 402 (1842), rejected the claim against a coach repairman by a passenger injured when the coach collapsed (the repairman had agreed with the owner to keep it in repair), stating that the most absurd and outrageous consequences would result if those not in privity of contract were allowed to sue in contract. Thus, early cases sounding in contract developed the privity of contract theory as a shield to the manufacturer and supplier of a defective product not in privity with the injured plaintiff.

    c. **Privity requirement.** Unless the injured plaintiff was the buyer, no recovery could be had, either in tort or in contract, no matter how negligent the seller's conduct. On the tort side, the early cases generally involved defects known to the seller but undisclosed to the buyer.

    d. **The foreseeable plaintiff.** Gradually, the courts began to make cracks in the privity wall, moving from contracts to torts, and accepting a theory that manufacturers and suppliers of products owe a duty of due care with respect to the condition of the product. Breach of this duty (*i.e.,* supplying the plaintiff with a defective product) was held to be negligence. As the crack widened, the courts began to extend this duty to nonpurchasers. At first, special relationships were required between the purchaser and the injured nonpurchaser (*e.g.,* husband-wife, family members, employer-employee, etc.). Later, the rule was relaxed and, in some instances, unrelated bystanders could be recognized as plaintiffs. Thus, the concept of the foreseeable plaintiff came into play.

e. **Strict liability.** The next step in the development of products liability law, which proceeded to some extent parallel with the development of negligence theory, was a move away from negligence and into the area of strict liability, and in some jurisdictions toward absolute liability (*i.e.,* manufacturers and suppliers are absolutely liable for injuries sustained through use of defective products). The strict liability theory, which at first was applied in cases involving inherently dangerous products (*e.g.,* firearms, poisons, and explosives), was extended into the area of products foreseeably dangerous by reason of the defendant's failure to exercise due care. Today, both the strict liability and negligence theories have become alternative theories upon which injured plaintiffs often rely in stating their cause of action in tort.

f. **Warranty.** While this dual theory approach is common, there is also an increased emphasis being placed on the contract theory of warranty, both express and implied, especially with respect to commercial loss. Part of this trend toward use of warranty as a basis for recovery lies in the fact that the Uniform Commercial Code ("U.C.C.") has now been adopted in the District of Columbia and 49 of the 50 states, and specifically places substantial burdens in the warranty area on manufacturers and suppliers of goods. [*See* U.C.C. §§2-312, 2-314, 2-315]

3. **Intentional Acts as a Basis of Liability.** If a manufacturer or supplier of a chattel sells it with knowledge or with reason to know that it is dangerous or defective, and fails to warn of the danger or defect, it may be liable for a battery to *any* person injured through use or consumption of the product. The requisite intent is established by showing that the injuries suffered were substantially certain to result from use of the chattel in the condition sold by the manufacturer or supplier.

4. **Negligence as a Basis of Liability.**

   a. **Foreseeable risk of harm.** The real breakthrough in providing plaintiff recourse against manufacturers and suppliers of defective products on a negligence theory came in *MacPherson v. Buick Motor Co.*, below.

      1) **Landmark case--**

MacPherson v. Buick Motor Co., 111 N.E. 1050 (N.Y. 1916).

Facts. MacPherson (P) purchased a Buick from a dealer, who had purchased the car from Buick Motor Company (D), the manufacturer. While P was driving the car, a wheel with defective wooden spokes collapsed and P was thrown out and injured. The wheel was not made by D, but was purchased from a subcontractor. Evidence indicated that D could have discovered the defect by reasonable inspection, which was omitted. On a judgment for P, D appeals.

Issue. Is privity between the manufacturer and the plaintiff necessary for the plaintiff to be able to recover against the manufacturer?

Held. No. Judgment affirmed.

♦   If the nature of a product is such that it is reasonably certain to place life and limb in peril when negligently made, it is a thing of danger. If the manufacturer knows or can reasonably foresee that it will be used by persons other than the immediate purchaser (supplier) without new tests, then, irrespective of contract, the manufacturer is under a duty to make it carefully. This holding can be drawn from prior cases involving poisons, explosives, and deadly weapons that had placed a duty on the manufacturer thereof, based on the fact that such products were "implements of destruction" in their normal operation.

♦   The negligence of the wheel manufacturer, such as to constitute an actionable wrong with respect to users of the finished product incorporating the wheel, was a question of proximate cause and remoteness. However, in order for the wheel manufacturer's original negligence to become a cause of the danger, it was necessary for an independent cause to intervene, *i.e.,* the omission of the car manufacturer to fulfill his duty of inspection.

Comment. The rule as originally propounded by the court (Judge Cardozo) in *MacPherson* was as follows: If a reasonable person would have foreseen that the product would create a risk of harm to human life or limb if not carefully made or supplied, the manufacturer and supplier are under a duty to all foreseeable users to exercise reasonable care in the manufacture and supply of the product.

---

b.   **Extensions of the *MacPherson* rule.** The *MacPherson* rule, *supra*, has been further developed to cover the following situations:

(i)   Damage to the product sold resulting from its own defects;

(ii)   Damage to reasonably foreseeable nonusers in the vicinity of the expected use of the product;

(iii)   Damage caused by defects in design as opposed to defects in manufacture;

(iv)   Damage to property in the vicinity of expected use, where the product itself is dangerous to life and limb because it is negligently made;

(v) Liability for products negligently manufactured but posing a foreseeable risk to property only;

(vi) Liability of a processor of a product at an intermediate stage; and

(vii) Liability of those who sell others' products as their own (including dealers, distributors, and any other party in the chain of sale).

1) **Restatement rule.** Restatement rule section 401 places a duty on dealers and distributors to make a reasonable inspection of their products that are inherently dangerous in normal use and to remedy or warn buyers against such defects or dangers. The failure of the dealer to inspect, however, does not relieve the manufacturer of its obligations since the dealer's omissions are considered foreseeable.

2) **Where Restatement does not apply.** However, section 402 of the Restatement does not place such a duty on the dealer where the products are manufactured by others and are not inherently dangerous in normal use. In such cases, the manufacturer is still liable under the *MacPherson* rule, and the dealer may be liable under the theory of warranty or the theory of strict liability. But if the dealer discovers the defect, the common law rule will make the dealer liable to any injured plaintiff who was not warned of the defect prior to the sale. This failure to warn of known defects will operate as an unforeseeable intervening force with respect to the manufacturer's negligence and will relieve it of liability under a negligence theory.

c. **Defenses.** The defenses available to a defendant under a typical negligence action (*e.g.,* contributory negligence, assumption of risk, etc.) may be raised by a defendant in a products liability action grounded in negligence.

5. **Emergence of Liability Without Fault.** Proof of negligence had been required for a tort products liability action. Use of the doctrine of res ipsa loquitur, however, eased the plaintiff's burden of proof.

a. **Prediction of strict liability--**

Escola v. Coca Cola Bottling Co. of Fresno, 150 P.2d 436 (Cal. 1944).

Facts. Escola (P), a waitress, was injured when a Coca Cola bottle "exploded" in her hand. She sued Coca Cola Bottling Company of Fresno (D) for her injuries. The basis of liability was negligence, but lacking evidence of D's specific negligence, P relied upon the doctrine of res ipsa loquitur. The trial court found for P, and the supreme court affirmed.

Issue. Is this case appropriate for res ipsa loquitur?

Held. Yes. Judgment affirmed.

♦ The circumstances of the injury create a presumption of negligence. The injury resulted either from an overcharge of pressurized gas, which could only be the result of D's negligence, or a defect in the bottle. In light of the evidence that the new bottles were not defective, a defective bottle would almost certainly be the result of D's negligence in failing to discover a defective reused bottle.

Concurrence. Manufacturers ought to be absolutely liable for injuries caused to consumers by defective goods. Public policy dictates that manufacturers ought to pay the cost of the injuries they cause. The doctrine of res ipsa loquitur is just an attempt to allege negligence and then allow recovery without proof of negligence. The court should just recognize that a form of strict liability is being used. This strict liability is justified both because of the fairness of placing the cost on the manufacturer and because the consumer is unable to closely inspect modern complex products. The manufacturer can better bear the cost and control quality. There is no reason in law, logic, or public policy to continue to require the consumer to prove fault on the part of the manufacturer.

———————————

6. **Strict Liability.** As stated above, strict liability is liability without fault. The seller is held liable for injuries caused to the plaintiff irrespective of the seller's negligence or even his exercise of all possible care. The rationale of this theory of liability is that the defendant is considered better able to assume the risk of loss through insurance or otherwise than is the innocent consumer.

7. **Restatement View.** Restatement (Second) of Torts section 402A adopted strict liability for product injuries. It required that the product be in a defective condition that was unreasonably dangerous. Users or consumers could recover for physical harm from sellers of the product. However, in 1998, the Restatement Third: Products Liability came into existence and took a different approach. Section 1 provides: "One engaged in the business of selling or otherwise distributing products who sells or distributes a defective product is *subject to liability* for harm to persons or property caused by the defect." Section 2 outlines three types of defects: (i) manufacturing defects, when a product "departs from its intended design"; (ii) design defects, when the "foreseeable risks of harm posed by the product could have been reduced or avoided by the adoption of a reasonable alternative design . . ."; and (iii) inadequate instructions or warnings, "when the foreseeable risks of harm posed by the product could have been reduced or avoided by the provision of reasonable instructions or warnings by the seller or other distributor. . . ."

B. MANUFACTURING DEFECTS

Under a manufacturing defect theory, the essential question is whether the product was flawed or defective because it was not constructed correctly by the manufacturer, without regard to whether the intended design was safe. Such defects result from some mishap in the manufacturing process, improper workmanship, or use of defective materials.

C. DESIGN DEFECTS

1. **Conditions Intended.** The defect in a design case is the result of a condition intended to exist by the manufacturer. The plaintiff claims that a design choice carries a risk of harm in normal use.

2. **Tests Applied.**

   a. **Unreasonably dangerous.** In order to recover, the plaintiff must prove that the design is a defective condition that is unreasonably dangerous (judged by a reasonable consumer standard).

   b. **Consumer expectations.** In *Barker v. Lull Engineering Co.*, 573 P.2d 443 (Cal. 1978), Barker was injured while operating a high-lift loader that had been manufactured by Lull Engineering. Barker alleged that the loader was designed defectively and that he was entitled to strict liability recovery. The trial court instructed that the plaintiff must prove that the product was unreasonably dangerous. After a verdict for the defendant, the judgment was reversed. The court reasoned that California had rejected the unreasonably dangerous language and refused to apply a test based on what a reasonable consumer expected. The consumer must only prove defect. To test whether a product is defective, the court may apply two alternative tests. The failure to perform as an "ordinary consumer expects" may be used, but it is the mere minimum that a product must be. In other words, all products must meet ordinary consumer expectations for safety, or else they are defective. A product may also be defective if its benefits are outweighed by the risk of danger it creates.

   c. **Consumer expectations test rejected--**

Soule v. General Motors Corp., 882 P.2d 298 (Cal. 1994).

Facts. Soule's (P's) ankles were badly injured when her Camaro collided with another vehicle. P sued General Motors (D), claiming that defects in the Camaro allowed its left front wheel to break free, collapse rearward, and mash a floorboard into her. The trial court entered judgment for P, and the court of appeals affirmed. D appeals.

Issue. May a product's design be found defective on grounds that the product's performance fell below the safety expectation of the ordinary consumer if the question of how safely the product should have performed cannot be answered by the common experience of its users?

Held. No. Judgment affirmed.

♦   *Barker v. Lull Engineering Co.* (*supra*) offered two alternative ways to prove a design defect. One permits an inference that the product did not perform as safely as it should have, based on ordinary knowledge. The other determines that the product is defective if its design embodies "excessive preventable danger," *i.e.*, unless the benefits of the design outweigh the risk of danger in using the design.

♦   When the ordinary consumer expectations test is used, expert witnesses may not be used to demonstrate what an ordinary consumer would or should expect. The use of an expert would invade the jury's function.

♦   Instructions based on the ordinary consumer expectations test are not appropriate where the evidence would not support a jury verdict on that theory as a matter of law. Whenever that is so, "the jury must be instructed solely on the alternative risk-benefit theory of design defect."

♦   The crucial question in each case in determining whether the test is applicable is whether circumstances of a product's failure permit the inference that the design of the product performed below legitimate and commonly accepted minimum safety assumptions of its ordinary consumers.

♦   In this case, the jury should have been instructed regarding the risk-benefit theory of design defect. P's theory was one of technical and mechanical detail. An ordinary consumer could not reasonably expect that a vehicle's frame, suspension, or interior would be designed to remain intact in any and all accidents, and ordinary experience would not inform a consumer about how safely the vehicle's design should perform under circumstances such as those present in the instant action.

♦   The trial court's error in instructing the jury on the consumer expectation test was harmless; the consumer expectation theory was never emphasized at any point and the case was tried under the assumption that the alleged design defect was a matter of technical debate.

---

    d.   The crashworthiness doctrine--

Camacho v. Honda Motor Co., Ltd., 741 P.2d 1240 (Colo. 1987), *cert. dismissed*, 485 U.S. 901 (1988).

Facts. In March 1978, Camacho (P) bought a new Honda Hawk motorcycle that was not equipped with crash bars. P suffered severe leg injuries in an accident and sued the parties in the chain of distribution, claiming that the absence of crash bars to protect the legs made the product defective under a strict liability analysis. Depositions supplied by mechanical engineers asserted that effective leg protection devices that would have reduced or completely avoided P's injuries were available in March 1978 and that manufacturers other than Honda Motor Company (D) had made such devices available as optional equipment. The trial court granted D summary judgment. The court of appeals affirmed, and P appeals.

Issue. Is the risk-benefit test the proper test to apply in determining whether a product has a design defect causing it to be in a defective condition that is unreasonably dangerous?

Held. Yes. Judgment reversed and case remanded.

♦ We adopt for this jurisdiction the "crashworthiness" doctrine, under which a motor vehicle manufacturer may be liable in negligence or strict liability for injuries sustained in a motor vehicle accident when a manufacturing or design defect, although not the cause of the accident, caused or enhanced the injuries. This doctrine applies to motorcycle manufacturers as well as automobile manufacturers.

♦ The consumer contemplation test applied by the appeals court is not a satisfactory test. Comment i to section 402A of the Restatement (Second) of Torts states that the article sold must be "dangerous to an extent beyond that which would be contemplated by the ordinary consumer who purchases it, with the ordinary knowledge common to the community as to its characteristics."

♦ This court has adopted the doctrine of strict products liability as set forth in section 402A; however, the principle of products liability contemplated is premised upon the concept of enterprise liability for casting defective products into the stream of commerce. The primary focus must remain upon the nature of the product under all relevant circumstances rather than upon the conduct of either the consumer or the manufacturer. Uncritical rejection of design defect claims in all cases wherein the danger may be open and obvious thus contravenes sound public policy by encouraging design strategies that perpetuate the manufacture of dangerous products.

♦ The factors enumerated in *Ortho Pharmaceutical Corp. v. Heath*, 722 P.2d 410 (Colo. 1986), are applicable to the determination of what constitutes a product that is in a defective, unreasonably dangerous condition. These factors are: (i) the utility of the product to the user and the public; (ii) the safety aspects of the product, the likelihood that it will cause injury, and the probable seriousness of the injury; (iii) the availability of a substitute product that would meet the same need and not be unsafe; (iv) the manufacturer's ability to eliminate the unsafe character of the product without impairing its usefulness or making it too expensive to maintain its utility; (v) the user's ability to avoid danger by the exercise of care in the use of the product; (vi) the user's anticipated awareness of the dangers inherent in the product and their avoidability because of general public knowledge of the obvious condition of the product, or of the existence of suitable warnings or instructions; and (vii) the feasibility, on the manufacturer's part, of spreading the loss by setting the price of the product or carrying liability insurance. By examining and weighing the various interests represented by these factors, a trial court is much more likely to be fair to the interests of both manufacturers and consumers in determining the status of particular products.

Dissent. Because of the nature of the product here, I believe that the appropriate test is the consumer contemplation or consumer expectation test. An ordinary consumer is necessarily aware that motorcycles can be dangerous. P had the choice to purchase other motorcycles by other manufacturers that carried additional safety features.

D. SAFETY INSTRUCTIONS AND WARNINGS

Warnings of risks associated with a product's unintended uses and warnings of dangers that cannot be reasonably reduced by a manufacturer (*e.g.*, side effects of pharmaceuticals) sometimes accompany products. The sufficiency of such warnings has been a common issue before courts.

1. Adequate Warnings--

Hood v. Ryobi America Corporation, 181 F.3d 608 (4th Cir. 1999).

Facts. Hood (P) purchased a fully assembled Ryobi TS-254 miter saw with a 10-inch diameter blade for home repairs. The blade was controlled by a finger trigger on a handle near the top of the blade. Two blade guards shielded almost the entire saw blade. The owner's manual and warnings affixed to the saw warned in several places to keep the guards in place during operation. When P used the saw the day after he purchased it, he removed the guards to saw a piece of wood. He continued to saw with the blade exposed for about 20 minutes. In the middle of a cut, the blade flew off the saw and back toward P. P's left thumb was partially amputated and his right leg was cut. P admits he read the owner's manual and warning labels, but he believed the guards were meant to prevent clothing or fingers from coming into contact with the blade. P claims he was not aware the blade would detach, but Ryobi (D) was. In fact, D had been sued for such an event in the past. P sued D for failure to warn and defective design. The trial court entered summary judgment for D. P appeals.

Issue. Did D provide adequate warnings on its product?

Held. Yes. Judgment affirmed.

♦ P's argument that D's warnings were insufficient because they did not inform the user of the consequences of using the saw without the blade fails. A warning need only be reasonable under the circumstances. A manufacturer need not warn of every conceivable danger.

♦ In determining the adequacy of a warning, we ask whether the benefits of a more detailed warning outweigh the costs of requiring the change.

♦ The cost of changing the labels is not the only consideration. More detail on a label threatens to undermine the usefulness of the warning altogether. Voluminous and technical labels are often not effective.

♦ D's warnings are clear and unequivocal. Two of the seven labels warn of "serious injury." Had the warnings been followed, injury would have been prevented in this case.

♦ The only other incident similar to P's occurred 15 years before P's. P has not shown D's warnings to be insufficient.

Comment. In most cases, adequacy of warning is a matter for the jury. In clear cases, however, it may be a question of law.

---

2. **Learned Intermediary Doctrine--**

Edwards v. Basel Pharmaceuticals, 933 P.2d 298 (1997).

Facts. Edwards's wife (P) filed a wrongful death suit against Basel (D), alleging her husband's death was due to his use of a prescribed medicine, Habitrol nicotine patches, while smoking. P alleged D failed to adequately warn of the effects of an overdose. D responded that it fully warned the prescribing physician of the risks, and further complied with Food and Drug Administration requirements for warning the ultimate user. The warning to the user did not mention the risk of a fatal reaction, but only warned that an overdose might cause the user to faint. The pamphlet provided to physicians prescribing the patch said: "Prostration, hypotension and respiratory failure may ensue with large overdoses. Lethal doses produce convulsions quickly and death follows as a result of peripheral or central respiratory paralysis or, less frequently, cardiac failure." The appeals court certified a question of state law to the state supreme court.

Issue. By complying with the FDA warning requirements, is D protected from liability for inadequate warning by the learned intermediary doctrine, with its attendant shield affording protection to the manufacturer?

Held. No.

♦ Because prescribing physicians were provided with complete warnings, D argues that the "learned intermediary doctrine" bars liability, because the prescribing physicians were given complete warnings regarding the use of the patches.

♦ Our products liability law generally requires a manufacturer to warn consumers of danger associated with the use of its product to the extent the manufacturer knew or should have known of the danger.

♦ Prescription drugs cannot be made safe, but are a benefit despite the risk. Their benefits depend on adequate warnings of their risks.

♦ However, an exception known as the "learned intermediary doctrine" applies in prescription drug and prosthetic implant cases. The manufacturer is not required to warn the ultimate consumer and is shielded from liability if it adequately warns the prescribing physicians of the dangers of the drug. The doctor is viewed as a learned intermediary between the patient and the manufacturer who assesses the medical risks in light of the patient's needs.

♦ The physician has a duty to inform himself of the characteristics of the products involved and to exercise independent judgment in prescribing them and determining what facts should be told to the patient. The patient relies on the physician's judgment.

♦ Prescription drugs can only be obtained by means of a physician's prescription and they are generally monitored by the physician.

♦ There are two exceptions to the learned intermediary doctrine. One involves mass immunizations, because there is no doctor-patient relationship. The other occurs when the Food and Drug Administration mandates that a warning be given directly to the consumer, e.g., in the case of contraceptives.

♦ There is no reason why the second exception should not apply to nicotine patches available by prescription. The FDA has required that prescriptions for nicotine patches be accompanied by warnings to the ultimate consumer as well as to the physician, as is required in the distribution of oral contraceptives and intrauterine devices. D has complied with that mandate.

♦ Courts are split as to whether compliance with the FDA mandate fulfills the manufacturer's legal obligation. The Supreme Court has ruled compliance does not preclude state tort liability. The Court pointed out that a state's police power is not superseded by federal law unless there is a clear and manifest expression to the contrary, and that the Congressional intent is the ultimate touchstone.

♦ The FDA sets minimum standards for drug manufacturers as to design and warnings. Compliance with these minimum standards does not necessarily complete the manufacturer's duty. We are persuaded that, in instances where a trier of fact could reasonably conclude that a manufacturer's compliance with FDA labeling requirements or guidelines did not adequately apprise prescription drug users of inherent risks, the manufacturer should not be shielded from liability by such compliance.

---

3. "Hindsight Analysis" No Longer Applied to Duty to Warn--

Vassallo v. Baxter Healthcare Corporation, 696 N.E.2d 909 (Mass. 1998).

Facts. Vassallo (P) sued Baxter (D) for injuries she claimed she received from breast implants manufactured by a company since bought by D. A jury found for P on her claims of negligence and breach of warranty. D appeals.

Issue. Should our products liability law concerning the implied warranty of merchantability be changed to adopt a "state of the art" standard that conditions a manufacturer's liability on actual or constructive knowledge of the risks?

Held. Yes. Judgment affirmed on negligence count.

♦   We determine that the findings of liability as to the negligence claim is correct and we affirm that portion of the decision.

♦   Our current products liability law presumes a manufacturer was fully informed of all risks associated with the product at issue, regardless of the state of the art at the time of the sale, and amounts to strict liability for failure to warn of these risks. This is based on the public policy that a defective product, unreasonably dangerous because of inadequate warnings, is unfit for its intended use regardless of the absence of fault on the defendant's part.

♦   We are among a minority of states that apply a "hindsight analysis" to the duty to warn. The majority of states follow the Restatement (Second) of Torts, section 402A comment j (1965), which states that "the seller is required to give warning against [a danger], if he has knowledge, or by the application of reasonable, developed human skill and foresight should have knowledge, of the . . . danger." This principle was reaffirmed by the Restatement (Third) of Torts: Products Liability, section 2(c) (1998). Risks that are unforeseeable cannot be warned against. A seller is charged with knowledge of what reasonable testing would reveal.

♦   We revise our law to state a defendant will not be held liable under an implied warranty of merchantability for failure to warn or provide instructions about risks that were not reasonably foreseeable at the time of sale or could not have been discovered by way of reasonable testing prior to marketing the product. A manufacturer will be held to the standard of knowledge of an expert in the appropriate field, and will remain subject to a continuing duty to warn (at least purchasers) of risks discovered following the sale of the product at issue.

E. DEFENSES

In jurisdictions where a plaintiff's negligence completely bars his recovery, contributory negligence, in the form of failure to exercise reasonable care to discover the defect, is no defense where the action is one based in strict liability. But where the user discovers the danger and nevertheless proceeds unreasonably, comparative fault may be applied. Contributory negligence is always a defense in an action based on negligence.

1. Conduct Beyond Failure to Discover or Guard Against a Defect--

General Motors Corporation v. Sanchez, 997 S.W.2d 584 (Tx. 1999).

Facts. Sanchez, Jr. left his home to feed heifers. The ranch foreman found Sanchez's lifeless body the next morning. There were no witnesses, but it appeared Sanchez's 1990 Chevy pickup had rolled backward with the driver's side door open. Sanchez was pinned to the open corral gate in the angle between the open door and the cab of the truck. Sanchez bled to death from a deep laceration in his right upper arm. The Sanchez family, his wife, and his estate (Ps) sued General Motors (D) and the dealership from which the truck had been purchased for negligence, products liability, and gross negligence based on a defect in the truck's transmission and transmission-control linkage. Circumstantial evidence presented at trial supported the theory that Sanchez drove his truck into the corral and stopped to close the gate. He mis-shifted into what he thought was Park, but what was actually an intermediate, "perched" position between Park and Reverse where the transmission was in "hydraulic neutral." The gear shifted into Reverse as Sanchez walked away, rolled back and slammed against him, pinning him. D theorized Sanchez left the truck in Reverse or in Neutral. The jury found for Ps, but found Sanchez was 50% responsible. The trial court did not take the responsibility finding into account and awarded Ps $8.5 million in actual and punitive damages. The appeals court affirmed. D appeals.

Issue. Is a consumer's conduct, other than the mere failure to discover or guard against a product defect, subject to comparative responsibility?

Held. Yes. Court of appeals reversed; judgment for Ps with actual damages, as reduced by the jury's comparative responsibility finding (50%).

♦ D does not dispute the transmission may have mis-shifted. Ps and D agree all transmissions can mis-shift. An expert's testimony indicated, however, there was a safer alternative design. There was sufficient evidence to support the jury's finding of a design defect.

♦ Based on the statutory comparative negligence system in effect at the time, we have previously held that a plaintiff's failure to discover or guard against a product defect is not a defense to strict liability. Later, the legislature changed the statute from comparative negligence to comparative responsibility. Under comparative responsibility, a claimant's recovery is reduced by the percentage of responsibility attributed to him by the jury. Strict liability suits were included in the new statute.

♦ Under the new statute, the percentage of responsibility is determined from a party's "negligent act or omission, . . . [or] by other conduct or activity violative of the applicable legal standard." Thus, the new statute applies to a party's failure to use ordinary care.

♦ Prior to the new statute, a consumer had no duty to discover or guard against a product defect; the new statute does not impose a new duty on consumers.

♦ Comment n of section 402A of the Restatement (Second), which imposed no duty on a plaintiff's failure to discover a defect or guard against its existence, was not carried forward to the Restatement (Third), section 17(a), which provides "a plaintiff's conduct should be considered to reduce a damages recovery if it fails to conform to applicable standards of care…." Comment d provides, however, that when this claim is made, "there must be evidence that the plaintiff's conduct in failing to discover a defect, did, in fact, fail to meet a standard of reasonable care."

♦ We find that the duty to discover and guard against defects would defeat the purpose of strict liability. Conduct other than this, however, is subject to comparative responsibility.

♦ The truck owners' manual provided safety measures and Sanchez's father testified that Sanchez probably read the whole manual. Ps' experts testified Sanchez did not perform any of the safety measures provided in the manual and that any one would have prevented the accident (*i.e.*, place the truck in Park; set the parking brake; turn off the engine). This is sufficient evidence to support the jury's negligence finding.

――――――――――

2. **Misuse.** If the plaintiff misuses the product or engages in an abnormal use that was not foreseeable, the defendant will not be held liable, even under a strict liability theory.

    a. **When is a use abnormal?** The use becomes abnormal when the plaintiff fails to follow the defendant's directions and instructions.

b. Modification--

Jones v. Ryobi, Ltd., 37 F.3d 423 (8th Cir. 1994).

Facts. Jones's (P's) hand was injured by an offset duplicator, a type of printing press, manufactured by Ryobi (D). The machine had been delivered equipped with a plastic safety guard and an electrical interlock switch that automatically shut off the machine if the guard was opened. Sometime after the press was delivered to P's employer, someone removed the guard and disabled the switch to allow the press to run without the guard. The modification was a common practice in the printing industry because it increased production by saving a few seconds in the duplication process. While P was using the machine, she caught her hand in the press's moving parts and it was crushed. P brought a products liability action against D. The trial court granted judgment as a matter of law for D, and P appeals.

Issues.

(i)   To recover in strict liability for defective design under Missouri law, must P prove that she was injured as a direct result of a defect that existed at the time the product was sold?

(ii)   Does P have the burden to show that the product had not been modified to create the defect that could have proximately caused her injury?

Held. (i) Yes. (ii) Yes. Judgment affirmed.

♦   If a third party makes a modification that renders an otherwise safe product unsafe, the seller of the product is not liable for resulting injuries even if the modification is foreseeable.

♦   While it is true that D provided tools for the general maintenance of the offset duplicator that could also be used to remove the guard, D was not responsible for the guard's removal. A third party removed the guard.

♦   P's employer knew that the guard was missing and the switch disabled, but did not follow the advice of P's distributor to repair the disabled safety features. For this reason, P's distributor's service work on the press did not extend the distributor's liability for injuries due to defects that were not present when the press was sold.

Dissent. P's expert witness supported the inference that the press was not safe as originally manufactured. Furthermore, the fact that the overwhelming majority of all machines in the industry have their guards removed after the machines are delivered is evidence that the machine was incapable of operating efficiently according to industry standards.

c. **Foreseeable misuse.** Where an unusual or abnormal use should be anticipated by the defendant (*e.g.,* when a sailor walking over containers used for transoceanic shipping was injured when he fell through a defective container, it was abnormal but foreseeable), strict liability may apply.

d. **No substantial modification defense in failure to warn case--**

Liriano v. Hobart Corp., 700 N.E.2d 303 (N.Y. 1998).

Facts. Liriano (P), 17, a grocery store employee, was operating a commercial meat grinder, manufactured by Hobart (D). The safety guard on the grinder had been removed. P lost his hand and lower forearm after his hand was caught in the grinder. The grinder carried no warning labels, nor were warnings provided to indicate it was dangerous to operate the machine without the safety guard. A year after the grinder was manufactured, D became aware that purchasers were removing the safety guard, and D began issuing warnings regarding removal. P sued D for defective product design and failure to warn. D impleaded the grocery store ("Super") as a third-party defendant, seeking indemnification and/or contribution. The trial court dismissed all of P's claims except those based on failure to warn. The jury determined that D's failure to warn was the proximate cause of P's injuries and apportioned liability 5% to Hobart and 95% to Super. On partial retrial, limited to the extent of P's responsibility, the jury assigned him 33-1/3% of the responsibility. D and Super appealed. The Second Circuit appeals court certified the following question to the state court.

Issue. Can manufacturer liability exist under a failure to warn theory in cases in which the substantial modification defense would preclude liability under a design defect theory?

Held. Yes.

♦ A manufacturer has a duty to warn against latent dangers resulting from foreseeable uses of its product of which it knew or should have known, and to warn of the dangers of reasonably foreseeable unintended uses. However, if the product has been purposefully manufactured to allow use without a safety feature, a plaintiff may recover for injuries suffered as a result of removing the safety feature.

♦ In *Robinson v. Reed-Prentice Division of Package Machine Co.*, 403 N.E.2d 440 (N.Y. 1980), we held that a manufacturer is not liable for injuries caused by substantial alterations to the product by a third party that render the product defective or unsafe. The rationale underlying our decision is to protect manufacturers from having to design a product that is impossible to abuse, or from having to track their product through every possible user to assure one will not adapt the product to its own unique purpose. Factoring into the design equation all post-sale modifications would be impossible and would result in imposing on manufacturers absolute liability for all product-related injuries.

- These concerns discussed in *Robinson* are not as strongly involved in the context of a duty to warn. In a duty to warn case, the focus is on the foreseeability of the risk and the adequacy and effectiveness of any warning. Placing a warning on a product about the danger of foreseeable modifications is not as burdensome as designing a perfectly safe product.

- We have held that a manufacturer may be liable for failing to warn against the dangers of foreseeable misuse of its product, and we see no material distinction between foreseeable misuse and foreseeable alteration.

- We are not requiring manufacturers to warn against obvious dangers. Whether a danger is open and obvious is most often a question for the jury, but may be decided by the court when only one conclusion can be drawn from the facts.

F. BEYOND PRODUCTS?

1. **Seller of Goods.** The Restatement requires that the defendant be a seller of goods in order for strict liability to attach. Providers of services may only be held liable for negligence.

2. **Provider of Service--**

Royer v. Catholic Medical Center, 741 A.2d 74 (N.H. 1999).

Facts. Royer (P) underwent total knee replacement surgery at Catholic Medical Center (D). The prosthetic knee provided by D was found to be defective, and P underwent a second operation in which the prosthesis was removed, and a second prosthesis inserted. P sued Dow Corning, which filed for federal bankruptcy, and P filed a second writ against D, alleging that D was strictly liable because it had sold a defective prosthesis that was in an unreasonably dangerous condition. D's motion to dismiss was granted. P appeals.

Issue. Is a health care provider that supplies a defective prosthesis in the course of delivering health care services a "seller" of prosthetic devices?

Held. No. Judgment affirmed.

- In this state, strict liability is determined by the legislature and by common law to the extent the legislature has not seen fit to change the court's determination. The lack of privity between the buyer and manufacturer, the difficulty of proving negligence in a situation involving mass production, and the ability of the manufacturer to spread risk among consumers are the underlying reasons for development of strict liability.

♦ We recognize limits to the doctrine. Architects and building contractors render a service and we have excluded them from strict liability. Similarly, health care providers render a service, and the provision of a prosthetic device is incidental to that service.

♦ D is not "engaged in the business of selling" prosthetic knees. Under the Restatement (Second) of Torts, §402(A), if a defendant merely provides a service, there is no liability absent proof of a violation of a legal duty.

G. THE INTERSECTION OF TORT AND CONTRACT

1. Economic Harm.

a. **Pure economic loss.** Using tort theories in order to recover damages when the only loss is purely economic is difficult (see Chapter IV). Courts have generally been reluctant to allow consumers to use strict products liability as a basis for recovery when the only loss suffered is an economic loss. Section 402A of the Restatement (Second) of Torts indicates that such recovery is to be limited to "physical harm . . . caused to the ultimate user or consumer, or to his property."

b. **Damage to product itself.** When the defect in the product causes the product itself to be damaged and additional economic loss to be suffered but no other harm is caused, the courts are split as to the applicability of strict products liability.

1) **Recovery of loss.** In *Santor v. A & M Karagheusian, Inc.*, 207 A.2d 305 (N.J. 1965), a product was defective and of a lesser value than it should have been. Although no additional harm was threatened, the court allowed recovery for the defective product under strict liability.

2) **Recovery denied.** In *Seely v. White Motor Co.*, 403 P.2d 145 (Cal. 1965), a product was defective but it only damaged itself. The court refused to extend strict liability coverage to such a case. This case is recognized as the majority rule.

3) **Application in admiralty law--**

East River Steamship Corp. v. Transamerica Delaval, Inc., 476 U.S. 858 (1986).

Facts. East River Steamship (P) chartered ships with turbines made by Transamerica Delaval (D). The turbines proved defective, had to be repaired, and thus caused an economic loss. P sued D for the loss, basing the action on both negligence and strict liability theories. The trial court granted D's motion for summary judgment, and the court of appeals affirmed. The Supreme Court granted certiorari.

Issue. Can P recover in strict liability for a defective product when the only loss is the purely economic loss of damage to the product itself?

Held. No. Judgment affirmed.

♦ Admiralty law adopts the principles used in products liability cases.

♦ Tort theories are designed to protect the injured party from dangerous conditions that could harm the plaintiff or his property. Where the loss is of the product itself, the loss can more properly be covered by a bargained-for exchange. Contract remedies, specifically here the warranty rights, are the appropriate method of handling such problems.

Comment. The Court in this case adopted the position in *Seely*, *supra*, and rejected the position of *Santor*, *supra*.

---

2. **Personal Injury and the Uniform Commercial Code.**

   a. **Warranty as a basis of liability.** As stated above, a products liability action can be based in contract upon breach of warranty. The "warranty" upon which the plaintiff will rely will generally be a statement or representation, either express or implied, made by the seller (or attributed to him) with respect to the character, quality, function, performance, reliability, or other matter of the item sold.

      1) **Cause of action.** If a plaintiff brings his cause of action on a warranty theory, he must show:

         a) The existence of the warranty;

         b) Breach of that warranty (*i.e.*, sale of the product in a condition that does not comply with the warranty); and

         c) Injury proximately caused by reason of the warranty defect in the product. With respect to this last element, if, for example, a warranty states that a widget has five coats of waterproof paint and in fact it has only one coat, the fact that this warranty is breached will not give a plaintiff a cause of action for physical injuries suffered as a result of some mechanism unrelated to the warranty (although the plaintiff would have a breach of contract action for contract damages based on the failure of the widget to comply with the express warranty).

2) **Privity.** In the past, courts considered an action for breach of warranty as a contracts action and required privity of contract between the plaintiff and defendant as a precondition to a finding of liability. However, this notion and the concept of privity have been stretched by the courts and in some instances entirely discarded or modified by statute.

3) **Express warranties.** An express warranty is an affirmation of fact or promise made by the seller about the product sold, which acts as an inducement to the purchaser to buy the product. U.C.C. section 2-213 provides that an express warranty can be created by such an affirmation of fact or promise, any description of the product that is made part of the basis of the sale transaction, or furnishing a sample or model where the product is represented to conform to such sample or model. This U.C.C. section further provides that the words "guarantee" or "warranty" need not appear anywhere in the transaction for such a warranty to arise. The affirmation of fact or promise may be expressly included in the contract by written representations or oral statements made by the supplier, or by a salesperson, through advertising, or otherwise. The courts have made an exception for statements of opinion or "puffing language"; however, the risk that such a statement may be construed by the courts as an express warranty is on the seller, and the tendency has been to find that such statements are warranties where such a construction is reasonable.

4) **Implied warranties.** Implied warranties are creatures of the law and become part of a sales transaction by operation of law rather than by the acts or agreements of the parties. Until adoption of the U.C.C., the principal statute giving buyers implied warranties was the Uniform Sales Act ("U.S.A."), originally drafted in 1905. The U.S.A. provisions, however, were designed to apply only between the seller and his immediate buyer. The U.C.C., while specifically applicable only to the sale of "goods," followed in general the U.S.A.'s "privity" format in sections 2-314 and 2-315, but attempted in one version of section 2-318 to create rights in remote purchasers and any "natural person who may reasonably be expected to use, consume, or be affected by the goods and who is injured in person by breach of the warranty." This version has not been widely adopted, although some states have adopted similar, even more encompassing consumer legislation. [*See, e.g.*, Cal. Civ. Code §§1790 *et seq.*]

    a) **Merchantability—U.C.C. section 2-314.** When goods are supplied by a merchant who deals in goods of that description, the law implies a warranty in the sale transaction that the goods are of fair average quality and reasonably fit for the general purposes for which they were sold.

b) **Fitness for particular purpose—U.C.C. section 2-315.** When goods are supplied by a seller who knows or has reason to know that the buyer is purchasing the goods for a particular purpose and is relying on the seller's skill or judgment in selecting the goods, the law implies a warranty in the sales transaction that the goods are suitable or fit for the special purpose of the buyer. Fitness of the goods for general purposes will not satisfy this warranty.

c) **State consumer protection.** Some states have expanded the U.C.C. warranties in cases where the transaction involves consumer goods. Typical of such expanded protection is the California consumer protection legislation, which includes within the implied warranty of merchantability attached to the consumer goods the warranty that the goods are free from defects in workmanship and materials, and are adequately contained, packaged, and labeled and conform to the representations on the label. [Cal. Civ. Code §1791]

IX. TRESPASS AND NUISANCE

A. TRESPASS

Every unauthorized entry of a person or thing on land in the possession of another is a trespass. The basis of the tort is the right of another to the exclusive possession of land.

1. **The Prima Facie Case.** A plaintiff's prima facie case consists of the following elements:

    a.   An act by the defendant;

    b.   An invasion of land in possession of the plaintiff;

    c.   The intent of the defendant; and

    d.   A causal relationship.

2. **Possession.** For purposes of trespass to land, "possession" means occupancy of the land with intent to control it and to exclude others. The possession that is sufficient to entitle a plaintiff to bring an action for trespass may be actual or constructive (*i.e.,* land in the custody of a person responsible to the plaintiff, *e.g.,* employee, agent, etc.). It has been argued that one who has an immediate right to possession, although never having made actual entry on the land, has a right to maintain an action for trespass if the act of trespass occurs after the creation of the right to possession. Note that an owner of land may commit a trespass on her own land if the right to exclusive possession has been transferred to another (as under a lease).

3. **Intent and Damages.**

    a.   **Common law.** At common law, the important factor in determining liability was an unauthorized entry on the land of another. The plaintiff did not need to prove damages. However, the intent of the defendant to commit the trespass was determined only on the basis of whether the act forming the basis of liability was voluntary. For example, if, without her consent, the defendant was pushed by a third party into the plaintiff's store and caused damage, she would not be held liable for a trespass since she did not act voluntarily. As with other intentional torts, there was no requirement that the defendant's "intent" be malicious or intentionally harmful.

    b.   **Present authority.** Under the majority rule, if the defendant intends to be on the land of the plaintiff (whether the defendant's presence is based upon mistake, ignorance as to the ownership or boundary, claim of right, or some other matter), she is liable for trespass. The common law rule that the plaintiff need prove no damages or actual harm to the land continues to apply. Since the gist of the tort is interference with the right to possession, it is considered immaterial that the defendant's acts were intended but did not benefit the land (*i.e.,* the defendant entered and constructed fences and made other improvements). In addition to the liability for intentional trespass, present authority recognizes liability for harm done to the land of another that results from negligence or an ultrahazardous activity, such as blasting, even though unintentional. However, such actions are prosecuted on the basis of negligence or tort and, unlike intentional trespass, require proof of some actual damages.

4.   **Invasion of Land--**

Martin v. Reynolds Metals Co., 342 P.2d 790 (Or. 1959), *cert. denied,* 362 U.S. 918 (1960).

Facts. Martin (P) sued Reynolds Metals Company (D) for damages to his farm. D had emitted fluoride compounds in the air and did substantial injury to P's property. P claimed that it was a trespass, making the six-year statute of limitations applicable. D claimed that it was a nuisance, making the two-year limit applicable. The trial court characterized the act as a trespass and allowed recovery for 1951 through 1955. D appeals.

Issue. Is the invasion of one's property by airborne fluorides a trespass?

Held. Yes. Judgment affirmed.

♦   Trespass is the invasion of one's land that disrupts the right to possession. Nuisance is a disruption of use and enjoyment. One act by D can be both.

♦   The "invading" particles in the case are too small to be seen but they do exist. These particles did invade the exclusive possession of P.

B. NUISANCE

"Nuisance" refers to interference by the defendant with a right of the plaintiff to the use or enjoyment of property. Nuisances are types of damage or harm. It is best considered as a field of liability rather than as a particular tort. The utility of the defendant's activity versus harm to the plaintiff's interests is the key to nuisance. Each possessor of land is privileged to use her own property or to conduct her own affairs at the expense of some harm to her neighbors; if the use is "unreasonable," it will constitute a nuisance.

1. **Kinds of Nuisance.** There are two kinds of nuisances.

   a. **Public nuisance.** "Public nuisance" refers to an act or omission that obstructs or causes inconvenience or damage to the public in the exercise of rights common to all citizens.

   b. **Private nuisance.** "Private nuisance" refers to an unreasonable and substantial interference with the use or enjoyment of an individual's property interest in land. It is distinguished from trespass in that it does not require a physical entry upon a plaintiff's premises. It follows from the principle that everyone should use her property so as not to injure the property of another.

2. **Basis of Liability.**

   a. **Three bases.** Liability can rest on any of three bases:

      1) Intentional conduct;

      2) Negligence; or

      3) Strict liability.

   b. **Substantial interference.** There must be a substantial interference with the use and enjoyment of land that would be offensive to a reasonable person of ordinary sensibilities.

   c. **Locality.** The nature of the locality becomes an important factor here. The courts must determine what is a reasonable use within the context of the custom of the community.

3. **Judicial Zoning--**

Boomer v. Atlantic Cement Co., 257 N.E.2d 870 (N.Y. 1970).

Facts. The residences of Boomer and others (Ps) suffered damages from dirt, smoke, and vibrations emanating from Atlantic Cement's (D's) large cement plant. Although the trial court found that D maintained a nuisance that substantially damaged Ps' properties, the court failed to issue the injunction for which Ps had brought the action because of the relatively small damage suffered in comparison with the value of D's operation. The trial court did award damages for injuries up to the time of trial, and also determined the amount of permanent damages for the guidance of the parties in a settlement. The appellate court affirmed, and Ps appeal.

Issue. When a business is so operated as to be a nuisance that substantially injures nearby residents, and when the value of the business operation is far more than the relatively small damages suffered, may permanent damages be awarded in lieu of an injunction?

Held. Yes. Lower court ordered to grant an injunction, which shall be vacated upon payment of permanent damages.

♦ Permanent damages may be awarded in lieu of an injunction where the value of the activities sought to be enjoined is disproportionate to the relatively small damage caused thereby.

♦ Permanent damages are fair because they fully recompense the damaged property owner while at the same time they provide an incentive to the business to abate the nuisance and avoid suits by others.

♦ The granting of a short-term grace period in which to solve the problem prior to issuance of an injunction is impractical and will lead to requests for extensions. Furthermore, it puts the burden for correction of an industry-wide problem on one private enterprise.

Dissent. An injunction should be granted to take effect 18 months hence unless the nuisance is abated. In permitting the injunction to become inoperative upon the payment of permanent damages, the majority is licensing a continuing wrong. The incentive to eliminate the wrong is alleviated by the majority's holding. The holding of the majority imposes a servitude upon Ps' lands without their consent and is unconstitutional.

Comments.

♦ If a statutory ordinance is in effect, it governs; in its absence, courts such as this one must resort to what is sometimes referred to as "judicial zoning." This case exemplifies judicial zoning.

♦ The "unreasonableness" issue in a nuisance action can be handled at the remedy level as well. That is, if the plaintiff asks for an injunction but the value of the defendant's activity is great, the court (as in this case) may deny the injunction and permit the defendant to pay past damages plus future damages (for permanent injury to the plaintiff's interest).

---

4. **Defenses to Nuisance Actions.** The defenses available to the defendant are dependent upon whether her conduct has been intentional or negligent, or whether she is deemed strictly liable for the interference.

    a. **Contributory negligence.** Contributory negligence is available only in situations where the nuisance is based on the negligent acts of the defendant.

    b. **Assumption of risk.** Assumption of risk is available in situations where the nuisance is based on the negligent conduct of the defendant and where the nuisance is based on strict liability.

5. **Remedies.** An injured plaintiff may bring an action to recover damages or to enjoin further interferences by the defendant with the plaintiff's protected interest, or both. Also available to the injured plaintiff in some jurisdictions is the privilege of self-help to abate the nuisance. The plaintiff must use only reasonable force to abate the nuisance; such force, under the prevailing rule, does not include the infliction of bodily harm on anyone.

X. DAMAGES AND INSURANCE

A. DAMAGES

1.   **Purpose.** Damages are the sum of money that may be recovered in the courts by a plaintiff who has suffered damage (*i.e.,* loss, detriment, or injury), whether to person, property, or rights, through the conduct of the defendant.

2.   **Nominal Damages.** Nominal damages equal a small sum of money awarded to a plaintiff for a technical invasion of her rights (*i.e.,* no substantial loss or injury) in order to make the judgment a matter of record, so that prescriptive rights can be avoided and to cover at least part of the costs of bringing the action.

3.   **Compensatory Damages.** Compensatory damages equal the sum of money deemed the equivalent of the full loss or harm suffered by the plaintiff (*i.e.,* to compensate the plaintiff for the wrong suffered).

4.   **Punitive (Exemplary) Damages.** Punitive damages equal the sum of money over and above what will compensate the plaintiff fully for the loss suffered. The purpose of punitive damages is to punish the defendant and to make an example to others in instances where the defendant's conduct is of an aggravated nature (*e.g.,* intent to injure, willful and wanton misconduct, or gross disregard of the consequences).

5.   **Personal Injuries.** If the plaintiff suffers personal injuries, she is entitled to recover a sum that will fairly and adequately compensate her for all injuries that are the direct and proximate result of the defendant's conduct. This can include, among other things, physical and mental pain; future loss of earnings; and reasonable expenses incurred in treatment of the injury, including doctor, hospital, and nursing care expenses. Of course, the damages that the plaintiff is expected to suffer in the future must be proven with reasonable certainty.

6.   **Jury Decision--**

Seffert v. Los Angeles Transit Lines, 364 P.2d 337 (Cal. 1961).

Facts. Seffert (P) was entering a bus operated by Los Angeles Transit Lines (D) when she was injured. The bus door closed on her foot, she was knocked to the pavement, and she was then dragged a short distance. Her injuries included permanent disfigurement to her foot, permanent crippling, and permanent pain. P has had nine operations, including several skin grafts. P's foot may ultimately have to be amputated. P proved $53,903.75 in medical expenses and loss of earnings. P also asked for $134,000 for pain and suffering. D claimed that these amounts were excessive. The jury awarded P the total amount requested, and D appeals.

Issue. Can the court reduce the jury's damage award?

Held. No. Judgment affirmed.

♦ The amount of the award is ordinarily a decision for the jury. When an award is characterized as excessive, it is reduced only when the court is convinced that it is so large that it shocks the conscience and appears to be the result of passion or prejudice. Although this award is high, it is not excessive.

Dissent. The award of pain and suffering damages is excessive here. The attorney used a "per diem" argument for this element. He argued that P should be awarded a certain amount for each day from the time of the accident to the day of trial. In addition, he argued that she should receive a net amount for each year of her life. This argument misleads the jury.

Comment. It is up to the jury to estimate future pain and suffering and the amount that will properly compensate the plaintiff. Often, counsel for the plaintiff will use a "per diem" argument, such as "the plaintiff's pain and suffering should be compensated at the rate of one penny per second," because such small amounts seem rather trivial to the jury. However, arguing damages on a unit-of-time basis has been prohibited by a minority of courts because it tends to deceive the unwary. (In the example, one penny per second equals $315,360 per year.)

---

7. Loss of Enjoyment of Life--

McDougald v. Garber, 538 N.E.2d 372 (N.Y. 1989).

Facts. Emma McDougald (P) underwent a Cesarean section and tubal ligation performed by Garber (D) as the surgeon, and Armengol and Kulkarni (Ds) provided anesthesia. During surgery, P suffered oxygen deprivation that resulted in severe brain damage and left her in a permanent comatose condition. A jury found all Ds liable and awarded damages for pain and suffering, loss of the pleasures and pursuits of life, lost earnings, and the cost of custodial and nursing care. The trial judge reduced the awards.

Issues.

(i) Can there be recovery for conscious pain and suffering if the plaintiff is incapable of experiencing pain or appreciating her condition?

(ii) Should loss of enjoyment of life be considered a category of damages separate from pain and suffering?

Held. (i) Yes. (ii) No. New trial on the issue of nonpecuniary damages.

- ◆   Damages for nonpecuniary losses are among those that can be awarded as compensation to the victim. This aspect of damages, however, stands on less certain ground than does an award for pecuniary damages. An economic loss can be compensated in kind by an economic gain. For noneconomic losses, however, a monetary award may provide a measure of solace for the condition created.

- ◆   An award of damages for loss of enjoyment of life to a person whose injuries preclude any awareness of the loss does not serve a compensatory purpose. In such circumstances, the award has no meaning or utility to the injured person. Cognitive awareness is a prerequisite to recovery for loss of enjoyment of life.

- ◆   We do not agree that awards for pain and suffering and loss of enjoyment of life should be treated separately. These awards are not amenable to analytical precision. The trial advocate's art is a sufficient guarantee that none of P's losses will be ignored by a jury.

Dissent. Loss of enjoyment of life is an objective damage item, conceptually distinct from conscious pain and suffering. While the victim's "emotional response" and "frustration and anguish" are elements of the award for pain and suffering, the "limitation of life's activities" and the "inability to participate in activities" are recoverable under loss of enjoyment.

---

8.   The Collateral Source Rule--

Arambula v. Wells, 72 Cal. App. 4th 1006, 85 Cal. Rptr. 2d 584 (1999).

Facts. Arambula (P) was injured in a rear-end automobile accident caused by Wells (D). P was unable to work because of his injuries, but the family-owned company continued to pay P his $2,800 weekly salary. P sued D for negligence and for damages including loss of earnings. P testified that his brother, who owned 70% of the company, "wished" to be reimbursed for P's wages, but he had not promised to do so. D admitted fault. The case went to trial on causation and damages. D's motion to exclude evidence of P's lost wages claim was granted. The trial judge instructed the jury not to award damages for lost earnings. P appeals.

Issue. Under the collateral source rule, can a plaintiff's recovery include lost earnings, even though wages were paid by an employer with no obligation of reimbursement?

Held. Yes. Case remanded to determine amount of lost wages.

- The trial judge based his ruling on dicta in a footnote in the leading case, *Helfend v. Southern California Rapid Transit District*, 465 P.2d 61 (Cal. 1970). He denied lost earnings "because his employer paid for the time he was off without any requirement to do so and there was no agreement by plaintiff to refund same."

- The collateral source rule permits plaintiffs in personal injury actions to recover full damages even though they have received compensation for their injuries from "collateral sources" such as medical insurance. The underlying theory is that tortfeasors should not receive a windfall from those who have purchased insurance, or secured pension or disability benefits. *Helfend* did not comment on any payments other than insurance.

- Existing California law (prior to *Helfend*) made no special distinction for purely gratuitous collateral benefits. Courts have held the collateral source rule applies to wages paid by an employer, and that whether treatment was paid for pursuant to contract or gratuitously, a cause of action to recover the reasonable value of such treatment was not defeated.

- Many post-*Helfend* decisions have allowed plaintiffs to recover the costs of gratuitous medical care as an element of their damages, even without any contractual right to reimbursement.

- The majority of jurisdictions are in accord with application of the collateral source rule to gratuitous payments and services. Furthermore, public policy encourages citizens not only to purchase insurance, but to provide private charitable assistance. If we permit a tortfeasor to mitigate damages because of a charitable gift, the plaintiff would be in a worse position than had nothing been done. The law favors gifts for charitable purposes.

---

9. **Appropriate Cases for Punitive Damages.** Because punitive damages are intended to punish the defendant and make an example of him, they may be allowed in a suit for battery, where the defendant intended to injure the plaintiff. They may be allowed in certain cases for defamation, malicious prosecution, misrepresentation, and products liability cases. Punitive damages are not allowed for negligent conduct, although some states permit such damages where the defendant has engaged in reckless conduct, such as drunk driving.

   a. **Driving under influence of alcohol--**

Taylor v. Superior Court, 598 P.2d 854 (Cal. 1979).

Facts. Taylor (P) sued Stille for injuries suffered in an auto accident. Part of the complaint sought punitive damages. These damages were based on allegations that Stille was intoxicated while driving, had a habit of driving while intoxicated, had arrests and accidents for driving while intoxicated, and was facing "driving while intoxicated" charges when this accident occurred. The trial court dismissed the punitive damages claim, and P seeks a writ of mandamus to require the judge to reinstate the claim.

Issue. Are punitive damages available in a negligence case?

Held. Yes. Writ issued.

♦ Stille's actions represent a disregard for the safety of others. Because of the extreme risks involved and the need to deter this type of conduct, punitive damages are appropriate.

Concurrence. Although this case is appropriate for punitive damages, not all "driving while intoxicated" cases would be. This driver had repeated instances of this type. This case, at least, creates a jury question as to whether punitive damages should be awarded.

Dissent. Punitive damages should not be allowed in driving under the influence of alcohol cases. These damages are intended to act as a deterrent, and they will not do so in these cases.

---

b.   **Excessive punitive damages--**

State Farm Mutual Automobile Insurance Co. v. Campbell, 538 U.S. 408 (2003).

Facts. Campbell (P) attempted to pass six vans on a two-lane highway in Utah. To avoid a head-on collision, a second driver swerved onto the shoulder, lost control, and collided with a third vehicle, permanently disabling the other driver and killing himself. P's insurer, State Farm (D), contested liability to the estate of the deceased driver and to the disabled driver and declined to settle for the policy limits of $50,000 ($25,000 per claimant). D also ignored its investigator's advice and took the case to trial, assuring P that his assets were safe and that D would represent his interests. The jury found P 100% at fault, and a judgment was rendered against P for $185,849. D refused to cover the $135,849 in excess of the policy limits or post a bond to allow P to appeal. P then hired his own counsel and appealed, but P's appeal was denied. D then paid the entire judgment. P, however, filed the complaint in this case against D for bad faith, fraud, and intentional infliction of emotional distress. D's decision not to settle was found to be unreasonable. Also, D's decision to take the underlying case to trial was described in evidence introduced by P to be part of D's nationwide scheme to cap payments on claims company wide—a Performance, Planning, and Review ("PP&R")

policy. Over D's objection, the trial judge allowed evidence of D's practices nation-wide to determine whether D's conduct was intentional and sufficiently egregious to warrant punitive damages. Much of the evidence the trial court allowed in concerned D's business practices over 20 years in numerous states and bore no relation to third-party auto insurance claims like that underlying P's complaint against D. Following trial, the jury awarded P $2.6 million in compensatory damages and $145 million in punitive damages. The trial court reduced the awards to $1 million and $25 million, respectively, and both parties appealed. The Utah Supreme Court reinstated the $145 million punitive damages award, relying in part on D's PP&R policy. The Supreme Court granted certiorari.

Issue. Is an award of $145 million in punitive damages excessive and in violation of the Fourteenth Amendment's Due Process Clause if the award was not proportionate to the wrongful conduct, the plaintiff was awarded compensatory damages of $1 million, and the civil penalty for a comparable case was $10,000?

Held. Yes. Judgment reversed and case remanded.

♦ Punitive damages are aimed at deterrence and retribution. Although states have discretion over the imposition of punitive damages, there are constitutional limitations on these awards. The Due Process Clause prohibits the imposition of grossly excessive and arbitrary punishments on tortfeasors.

♦ Courts reviewing punitive damages awards must consider: (i) the degree of reprehensibility of the defendant's misconduct; (ii) the disparity between the harm suffered by the plaintiff and the punitive damages award; and (iii) the difference between the punitive damages awarded by the jury and the civil penalties authorized or imposed in comparable cases.

♦ While D's conduct was indeed reprehensible, the trial court and the state supreme court improperly used this case as a platform to expose D's nationwide operations and to punish and deter conduct that bore no relation to P's harm. A defendant should be punished for conduct that harmed the plaintiff, not for being an unsavory individual or business.

♦ We decline to impose a ratio that a punitive damages award cannot exceed. However, awards exceeding a single-digit ratio between punitive and compensatory damages are less likely to satisfy due process. The punishment must be reasonable and proportionate to the compensatory damages and to the amount of harm to the plaintiff. There is a presumption against an award with a 145-to-1 ratio. The $1 million award for 18 months of emotional distress was complete compensation for P.

♦ The wealth of a defendant does not justify an unconstitutional punitive damages award. State Farm's assets bear no relation to the actual harm sustained by P.

- The civil sanction imposed under Utah state law for cases comparable to this case is a $10,000 fine for fraud. This amount is dwarfed by the $145 million in punitive damages awarded here.

- The punitive damages award of $145 million was neither reasonable nor proportionate to the wrong committed and was an irrational and arbitrary deprivation of D's property.

Dissent (Scalia, J.). The Due Process Clause provides no substantive protections against "excessive" or "unreasonable" awards of punitive damages.

Dissent (Thomas, J.). The Constitution does not constrain the size of awards of punitive damages.

Dissent (Ginsburg, J.). Although the large award in this case indicates why damage-capping legislation may be proper, this does not justify the Court's substitution of its judgment for that of Utah's decisionmakers. Also, it is significant that the trial evidence established that State Farm's policies were reprehensible and its behavior was egregious and malicious. When this Court first began overriding state court punitive damages awards, it did so moderately. It no longer exhibits such respect and restraint.

B. INTRODUCTION TO INSURANCE

1. **Types of Insurance.** All insurance is designed to cover risks of loss. Through either the accumulation of a reserve fund or a spreading of the risk among many people, a contract of insurance agrees to pay, should a loss occur. The loss may be one incurred by the insured (first-party insurance) or caused by the insured (third-party insurance).

    a. **First-party insurance.** First-party insurance covers losses that the insured incurs personally. It usually includes life insurance, fire insurance, or medical insurance.

    b. **Third-party insurance.** Third-party insurance covers losses that the insured may have caused to others. Liability insurance is an example of this type.

2. **Coverage of Loss.** Loss insurance is a first-party insurance. The insured seeks coverage for injuries that she personally incurred. There is no requirement of seeking recovery elsewhere.

3. **Collateral Source Rule.** In most states, a party is entitled to recover the full amount of her damages without any deduction for benefits that she may have received from sources "collateral" to the tortfeasor. These collateral sources may, of course, include insurance payments. Recent legislation in some states

has permitted deductions for collateral benefits in certain cases (*e.g.,* medical malpractice actions).

4. Subrogation--

Frost v. Porter Leasing Corp., 436 N.E.2d 387 (Mass. 1982).

Facts. Frost (P) was injured in an accident and sued Porter Leasing Corporation (D) for his injuries. While the action was pending, P's insurer paid $22,700 for medical treatment. P settled with D for $250,000. The insurer sought to recover the $22,700 it had paid P. The trial court allowed the insurer to recover, and P appeals.

Issue. Does the right to subrogation exist in the absence of a contract provision for it?

Held. No. Judgment reversed.

- ◆ Subrogation is the right that one who is secondarily liable has to succeed to the claims of the injured party against the primarily liable party once the secondary party has paid the injured party. Although the right to subrogation may be specifically stated in a contract of insurance, it may also be implied.

- ◆ Subrogation is not implied in all insurance contracts, but depends upon the type of coverage. Generally, subrogation is implied in property insurance but not in personal insurance contracts.

- ◆ It is unlikely that P will receive a windfall. Although the medical expenses were paid twice, other expenses were probably not compensated at all.

Concurrence. There is no problem with subrogation in medical insurance. The amounts are clearly determined and, in fairness, P should not receive double recovery. In this case, however, P had no notice of the possibility of subrogation.

---

5. Present Third-Party Liability Insurance System. At present, most car owners carry insurance against whatever liability they may incur to third parties in connection with the operation of their vehicles (known as "third-party" insurance). Such insurance is also carried for homeowners liability, products liability, and malpractice liability, and the same principles apply.

a. Coverage--

Lalomia v. Bankers & Shippers Insurance Co., 35 A.D.2d 114, 312 N.Y.S.2d 1018 (1970).

Facts. Michael Maddock (a 12-year-old boy) and Lalomia were killed in an accident involving a motorized bicycle owned by Maddock's father, Daniel. Lalomia's estate (P) sued Maddock's estate and Daniel Maddock (Ds) for the injury. Several insurance policies had been issued, and this action seeks a declaratory judgment specifying which policy should cover this accident.

Issue. Do any of the policies cover the accident?

Held. Yes. Judgment entered accordingly.

♦ Bankers Insurance had issued automobile policies to Daniel Maddock. These, however, only covered "private passenger automobiles" and did not cover motor-driven bicycles.

♦ Insurance Company of North America had issued a homeowner's policy to Daniel Maddock that covered operation of vehicles. Since Daniel Maddock was negligent in allowing his son to operate a vehicle, this insurer is liable for the father's negligence.

♦ Liberty had issued an automobile policy to Lalomia that included an uninsured motorist provision. Since no other policy covers the son's negligence, this provision is applicable. Therefore, this insurer is also liable.

---

b. **General operation of the third-party insurance system.** When an accident covered by third-party insurance occurs, the defendant's insurance carrier investigates the claims of the injured party and pays all the costs of defending any lawsuit that is filed.

1) **Insurance carrier's role in lawsuit.** The suit is defended in the name of the insured defendant (rather than in the name of the insurance company), and the jury generally is not told whether the defendant is insured.

a) **Direct action against insurer.** Most liability insurance policies insure a defendant only against liability established by a judgment in a legal action. Therefore, until a judgment is returned, most states provide that the injured party has no direct action against the defendant's insurance company. (A very few states are contra by statute.)

b) **After judgment.** Once a judgment is returned, however, the plaintiff is treated as a third-party beneficiary of the defendant's insurance company's promise to pay any judgment against the defendant, and hence can sue the defendant's insurer directly if it fails to discharge the judgment against the defendant.

  2) **Effect of intentional or "wanton and reckless" conduct.** Most liability insurance policies cover only negligent conduct by the defendant. Hence, in cases where the plaintiff alleges that the defendant was acting intentionally, or "wantonly and recklessly" (usually in an attempt to claim punitive damages), the defendant's insurance carrier may refuse to defend. Alternatively, the insurance carrier may defend with a "reservation of rights," meaning that it pays the costs of defense but reserves the right to refuse to pay any judgment that is returned against the defendant if the jury finds the defendant's conduct intentional, or "wanton and reckless."

  c. **Insured's duty of "cooperation."** An express or implied provision of every liability insurance contract is that the insured party will "cooperate" with the insurer, so that if the defendant acts collusively with the plaintiff, fails to testify when required, etc., the defendant's insurance carrier may be able to deny coverage as to any judgment against the defendant.

  d. **Insurer's duty of "good faith" re settlement.** Every liability insurance policy has a maximum limit—*e.g.,* $25,000 for injury to any one person—and should a judgment be returned that exceeds the limit, the defendant is personally liable for the excess. Hence, courts today recognize that an insurance company owes at least a duty of good faith to its insured to attempt to settle any claims against the defendant within the policy limits (so as to avoid the risk of the defendant being held personally responsible for satisfying part of the judgment). The question is often phrased as whether the insurer would have settled if the policy had no limits.

  1) **Effect of insurer's breach of duty.** If the insurance carrier fails to make a "good faith" effort to settle within the policy limits, it may be held liable for the full amount of any judgment subsequently returned against the defendant (including the excess over policy limits).

  a) **Bad faith action fails--**

Pavia v. State Farm Mutual Automobile Insurance Co., 626 N.E.2d 24 (N.Y. 1993).

Facts. Pavia (P), an injured passenger in Rosato's vehicle, was assigned all causes of action that the Rosatos might have against State Farm Insurance (D) through executing an agreement, which included a covenant whereby P would not execute any excess portion of the judgment against the Rosatos. P sued D, alleging D's bad faith failure to accept a settlement offer made by P's counsel in an underlying personal injury action. P's counsel had demanded the full $100,000 policy limit within 30 days. D failed to respond in time, and D's subsequent offer of $100,000 in settlement was rejected as "too late." The original personal injury award was reduced to $3,880,000 by the court of appeals. After trial on the bad faith claim, the trial court entered an "excess judgment" award for P in the amount of $4,688,030. The court of appeals affirmed, and D appeals.

Issue. Was D's failure to respond to P's time-restricted demand for a settlement at a time when the insured's liability was under investigation enough to establish a prima facie case of bad faith?

Held. No. Judgment reversed.

♦ To establish a prima facie case of an insurer's bad faith, a plaintiff must show that the conduct of the insurer constituted "gross disregard" of the insured's interests; *i.e.,* "a deliberate or reckless failure to place on equal footing the interests of its insured with its own interests when considering a settlement offer." A plaintiff must show that the insurer "engaged in a pattern of behavior evincing a conscious or knowing indifference to the probability that an insured would be held personally accountable for a large judgment if the settlement offer . . . were not accepted."

♦ It is a prerequisite for a bad faith action that the plaintiff prove that a demand for settlement was made.

♦ That an offer of settlement was made and not accepted, however, is not dispositive of an insurer's bad faith. A plaintiff must show that the insured lost a real opportunity to settle a claim during a time "when all serious doubts about the insured's liability were removed."

♦ In determining bad faith, the court must consider (i) a plaintiff's likelihood of success on the issue of liability, (ii) the potential magnitude of damages, (iii) the financial burden each party may incur as a result of refusing to settle, (iv) the insurer's failure to investigate properly the claim and any defenses, (v) information the insurer had access to at the time the settlement demand was made, and (vi) the insured's fault in delaying or ending settlement negotiations by misrepresenting the facts.

♦ In this case, D's failure to respond to the settlement demand while the insured's liability was under investigation is insufficient to establish a prima facie case of bad faith. "Permitting an injured plaintiff's chosen timetable for settlement to govern the bad faith inquiry would promote the customary manufacturing of bad faith claims, especially where an insured of meager means is covered by a policy which could finance only a fraction of the damages in a serious personal injury case."

2) **Insured may assign its claim against the insurer.** It is further recognized that the defendant's cause of action against her insurance company for failing to make a "good faith" effort to settle is assignable. Hence, where the plaintiff recovers a judgment in excess of the defendant's insurance limits, the defendant (in order to avoid personal liability for the excess) will usually assign to the plaintiff her cause of action against her insurance company.

3) **Bad faith breach of contract not necessary in most cases.** The "good faith" rule is essentially a "reasonableness" requirement; it does not mean that the insurer is liable for an excess judgment only if it acted in bad faith. Thus, for example, it has been held that the insurer has a duty to use due care to attempt to settle within policy limits whenever there is a substantial likelihood of a recovery exceeding those limits. Unreasonable failure to settle under these circumstances is at the insurer's risk of liability for the whole amount of any judgment against the defendant, regardless of whether "bad faith" is shown.

4) **Strict liability.** Other courts have suggested the adoption of a strict liability standard, making the insurer liable for *every* judgment above policy limits if it fails to offer settlement within those limits.

XI. A SURVEY OF ALTERNATIVES

A. TORT REFORM

As the number of tort claims has risen, there has been a significant increase in damages amounts awarded. These increases have prompted tort reform to address concerns in such areas as medical malpractice and products liability and such problems as those involved with non-economic damages, punitive damages, and insurance premiums. For example, the medical profession and liability insurers for the medical profession have claimed that there is a major crisis in medical malpractice, and most states have passed some type of legislation in reaction to the crisis. However, there has been no uniform or systematic approach to dealing with it. Nevertheless, there are some common forms of relief, such as caps on the amount of recovery.

B. OCCUPATIONAL INJURIES—WORKERS' COMPENSATION

1. **Introduction.** Employer liability for employees injured at work was the field in which liability insurance first developed. Shortly thereafter, legislation was passed (now every state has such a system) to provide employer contributions to a state fund to compensate injured employees, regardless of fault (known as "workers' compensation" statutes). Benefits are limited in amount and duration. In most states, employers can insure against these risks or employees may choose to be governed by traditional fault principles.

2. **Scope of Coverage.** Workers' compensation covers accidents "arising out of and in the course of employment." Typically, workers' compensation is the sole remedy an employee has against his employer. Furthermore, accidents occurring in commuting to and from work are not covered (the "coming and going" rule).

3. **Compensation Benefits.**

   a. **Statutory.** All workers' compensation benefits have a statutory basis. The statutes typically set a formula for the determination of the allowable benefit.

   b. **Amounts.** Using the formula to determine the amount of recovery requires reference to the statutes of the jurisdiction involved. Most states, however, consider the seriousness of the injury, expected length of incapacity, and average weekly wage of the worker. This provides lost wages. States also set a maximum amount allowable.

4. Exclusive Remedy—Policy Grounds. The workers' compensation statutes provide prompt, certain recovery for injured workers. The worker does not have to prove fault and does not risk losing benefits due to contributory negligence, assumption of risk, or other defenses. The employer gains the benefit that the compensation benefits are limited in amount and are generally the exclusive remedy available to the injured employee.

C. "NO-FAULT" AUTO INSURANCE

About half of the states have adopted statutes changing the handling of auto accident claims through "no-fault" insurance plans.

1. Advantages to Adopting "No-Fault" Plans. Eliminating "fault" as the basis for liability in auto accident cases alleviates the following objectionable features of negligence actions:

    a. "All or nothing" recoveries. In "all or nothing" recoveries, the plaintiff gets nothing unless he can convince the jury that the defendant was "at fault"; likewise, where the defendant can convince the jury that the plaintiff was contributorily negligent or had assumed the risk (prior to states adopting comparative negligence standards), the plaintiff gets nothing.

    b. Delays and expenses of litigation. Proving "fault" requires litigation with attendant expenses and attorneys' fees for both parties. Until a judgment is returned (or settlement made), an injured plaintiff gets nothing (even though it is in the interim that he needs help the most); and the increasing burden of such litigation has congested court calendars so that plaintiffs frequently have to wait years for a trial.

    c. Inaccurate compensation. There has also been concern that the settlement process has led to the overcompensation of small cases and the undercompensation of large cases.

    d. Rising cost of insurance. Insurance premiums have soared due to the costs of litigation and high verdicts.

2. Operation of Proposed "No-Fault" Plans. Although the plans enacted vary considerably, the following are the essential provisions:

    a. Mandatory insurance. All car owners are required to obtain (and keep in effect) insurance covering claims arising out of the operation of their cars. Failure to do so usually results in forfeiture of automobile registration and/or driver's license. This policy would cover both liability and no-fault claims.

    b. Scope of coverage. The insurance extends to all claims arising out of operation of any motor vehicle, without regard to fault. Generally, this includes claims allowed under traditional tort concepts, as well as certain claims not presently allowed; *e.g.,* claims by an injured "guest" in an auto and by the driver who hurts himself by his own fault. However, the insurance does ***not*** apply to claims arising out of defects in the vehicle itself (*i.e.,* products liability claims, discussed *supra*).

c. **Claims handled on "first-party" basis.** Any driver injured in an automobile accident would make a claim against his own insurer (*i.e.,* the policy covering the car that the injured party was riding in), so that in the typical two-car crash, the occupants of each car would claim against the insurance covering that car.

1) **Compare—"third-party" system.** In contrast, under the present "third-party" insurance system, the injured party usually makes a claim against the insurer of the other car. The "third-party" procedure would be retained only where the accident is not covered by first-party insurance; *e.g.,* a pedestrian injured by an automobile would still make a claim against the insurer covering the car that struck him. (Under a few plans, however, if the pedestrian owned a car, he would claim against his own insurer.)

2) **Procedure for claims.** Since "fault" would be immaterial, the claims procedure is relatively simple; any disagreement between the policyholder and his insurance company as to the amount recoverable (*see infra*) is subject to arbitration.

d. **Damages recoverable.** None of the major plans provide insurance coverage for pain and suffering or disfigurement. Coverage is limited to economic losses (*e.g.,* lost wages, medical bills, etc.). However, the plans vary considerably as to the amount of such coverage.

3. **Impact of "No-Fault" Plans—Curtailment of Tort Litigation.** The plans vary concerning the extent to which traditional negligence actions (with traditional "fault" principles) would still be permitted.

a. **"Pure" no-fault.** A few proposals would abolish tort actions altogether (*e.g.,* the American Insurance Association proposal). However, no state has adopted such a plan.

b. **"Partial" no-fault.** All existing plans currently allow at least certain actions.

1) Under some plans, tort actions can still be maintained in all but relatively minor cases; for example, a plaintiff can sue for pain and suffering whenever the medical expenses exceed $500, or where any permanent or disabling injury (*e.g.,* a bone fracture) is involved.

2) Under other plans, however, only severe tort cases could ever be pursued in court; *e.g.,* a tort action could be maintained for economic losses not covered by the injured party's own insurance, and for general damages in excess of $5,000, but ***only if*** the accident caused death, permanent injury or disfigurement, or inability to work for more than six consecutive months.

D. OTHER NO-FAULT SYSTEMS

1. **Reasons for Expansion.** With the initial success of automobile no-fault insurance, suggestions have been made to use the principles in other areas.

2. **Defective Products.** Use of a form of no-fault liability has been suggested for the products liability area. It has been suggested that an "enterprise" could be liable for all injuries caused.

3. **Medical Malpractice.** If no-fault coverage were enacted for medical malpractice, several benefits would be gained. Also, while patients would not have to prove fault, they would give up other tort recovery.

E. COMPREHENSIVE NO-FAULT

1. **New Zealand.** The New Zealand Compensation Act provides a complete no-fault scheme. All personal injuries due to accidents are covered by insurance. Most tort claims in New Zealand, therefore, have been abolished.

2. **Social Insurance.**

   a. **Basic purpose.** Welfare programs are designed to compensate people who fall within specific criteria. The plans are not necessarily intended to cover accident victims, but such victims may fit within the scheme.

   b. **Available funds.** The funds available may take several forms. Recipients may be entitled to cash or benefits in kind.

XII. INTENTIONAL HARM

A. BASIC DOCTRINE

1. Intent.

    a. Introduction. One of the major classifications of tort liability is liability based on the intent of the defendant. However, what is meant by intent is not only the desire to bring about the physical results, but also the knowledge or belief that certain results are substantially certain to follow from the actor's conduct.

        1) Need not be malicious. The intent forming the basis of tort liability need not be immoral, malicious, or hostile; instead, it need only be an intent to affect a legally protected interest in a way that will not be permitted by law.

        2) Objective standard. The subjective knowledge or belief on the part of the actor that certain results are substantially certain to follow from his conduct is determined on an objective rather than a subjective basis. That is, actual knowledge or belief, or lack thereof, on the part of the defendant is immaterial if a reasonable person in the position of the defendant would have believed that certain results were substantially certain to follow from the conduct of the defendant. Of course, the external, objective standard must have certain subjective inputs based upon the position of the defendant; *e.g.,* age, physical abilities, mental capacity, special skills, etc.; and it is on the basis of the theoretical reasonable person who possesses the same characteristics as the defendant that knowledge or belief for purposes of tort liability is determined.

    b. Substantial certainty--

Garratt v. Dailey, 279 P.2d 1091 (Wash. 1955).

Facts. Garratt (P) alleged that Dailey (D) had *deliberately* pulled a chair out from under her as she was sitting down, causing her to fall and fracture her hip. D, five years old, claimed that he had moved the chair so that he could sit in it himself, and, upon noticing that P was about to sit down, tried in vain to move the chair back in time. On remand, the court found that when D moved the chair, he knew with substantial certainty that P would attempt to sit down where the chair had been. P appeals from a decision denying P recovery of damages for an alleged assault and battery.

Issues.

(i)   In an action for assault and battery, may the defendant be held liable if he did not subjectively intend to cause the resultant harm but knew with substantial certainty that his actions would likely cause it?

(ii)   Can a minor be held liable for an intentional tort?

Held. (i) Yes. (ii) Yes. Judgment reversed and case remanded.

♦   Battery is the intentional infliction of a harmful or offensive bodily contact upon another.

♦   An "act" is deemed to be intentional if it is done either with the subjective purpose of causing the contact or the apprehension thereof, or with the knowledge that such contact or apprehension is ***substantially certain to result*** therefrom.

♦   Since the court found on remand that D knew with substantial certainty that P would attempt to sit where the chair had been located, he had the requisite intent to be liable for battery.

♦   When a minor has committed a tort with force, he is liable to be proceeded against as any other person would be.

Comment. Intentional conduct is an act that a reasonable person in the defendant's position would know is substantially certain to lead to the damage of another's legally protected interests.

———————

    c.   **Intentional acts by children.** Children are charged with what is expected of them considering their age, experience, intelligence, etc. They are liable only for what they are capable of, considering the foregoing factors. If they are capable of knowledge of the consequences of an act, they may be held liable for these consequences.

    d.   **Transferred intent.** The old common law form of action called "trespass" gave rise to five modern actions: battery, assault, false imprisonment, trespass to land, and trespass to chattels. Under the doctrine of transferred intent, if the defendant acts intending to cause one of these harms to X, the defendant will be liable on an intentional tort theory if any of the harms occurs to X, or even if they occur to another person entirely (*i.e.,* the plaintiff). This is true even if the plaintiff is unexpected and the type of harm is unexpected.

  2.   **Assault.** The basic elements of an assault case are as follows:

a. **Act by the defendant.** This element of the tort is satisfied by some volitional, external movement of the defendant. This would preclude an unconscious act, or a movement made by a person under the influence of drugs. This requirement also eliminates any purely reflex action by the defendant.

1) **Words alone are usually not sufficient to create this tort.** There must be an apprehension of immediate offensive touching by the plaintiff before there can be an assault. Words alone usually will not be sufficient to create the apprehension of the imminent touching; *i.e.,* unless there is some act or action that indicates the present ability and intention to do personal violence, there is no assault.

b. **Intent.** The defendant must have intended to inflict a harm on the plaintiff or put her in fear of an immediate harmful or offensive touching. This can be established under the "transfer of intent theory" (*i.e.,* A intends to injure B, but C is injured instead; the intent to injure B is transferred to C).

c. **Apprehension.** The actions of the defendant must actually put the plaintiff in apprehension of an imminent harmful or offensive touching. The standard laid down for this test is not subjective (*i.e.,* was the plaintiff apprehensive?) but is based on what a reasonable person in the plaintiff's shoes might have thought (*i.e.,* would a reasonable person have been apprehensive?).

d. **Causation.** The plaintiff's apprehension must have been caused by the defendant's actions.

e. **Damages.** It is not necessary to prove actual damages to sustain a prima facie case for assault. If the case is otherwise made out, the plaintiff can recover nominal damages.

3. **Battery.** The elements necessary to establish the tort of battery are as follows:

a. **Act by the defendant.** Like an action for assault, there must be a volitional act by the defendant that causes the plaintiff's injury.

b. **Intent.** The act done by the defendant must have been done with the requisite intent to commit the harmful or offensive touching.

1) **Test.** The general test used to determine intent is whether the defendant acted with the desire to cause, or substantially knew that his actions would cause, harm or offense. Since this test is founded on the defendant's desire or what he believed would be the consequences of his actions, the test is entirely subjective.

c. **Harmful or offensive touching.** The defendant's action must result in the infliction of a harmful or offensive touching to the plaintiff or something that is so closely associated with the plaintiff as to be tantamount to a touching of the plaintiff. A harmful touching is one that inflicts any pain or injury, while an offensive touching is one that offends a reasonable person's sense of personal dignity.

d. **Causation.** The defendant's action must be the legal cause of or be the force that puts in motion the force that results in the plaintiff's injury.

e. **Damages.** As with assault, it is not necessary to prove actual damages. An award of damages is based on the commission of a harmful or offensive touching. The plaintiff can receive compensatory damages for all damages directly caused by the touching as well as for all consequential damages. Punitive damages are also recoverable when it appears that the defendant was motivated to intentionally harm the plaintiff.

f. **Illustration of assault and battery--**

Picard v. Barry Pontiac-Buick, Inc., 654 A.2d 690 (R.I. 1995).

Facts. Picard (P) sued Barry Pontiac-Buick (D) for assault and battery. P was upset with the service she received during a brake inspection at D. P later returned with a camera and argued with D's service worker. D's service worker testified that he had never touched P but only pointed at her and placed his index finger on P's camera while P was attempting to photograph the service worker as he tested P's brakes. P contended that the worker "lunged at her and spun her around," injuring her back. The trial court found for P, and D appeals.

Issues.

(i)   Did P establish a reasonable apprehension of injury necessary for a prima facie case of assault?

(ii) Was the service worker's contact with P's camera sufficient to constitute battery?

(iii) Were the damages awarded P excessive as a matter of law?

Held. (i) Yes. (ii) Yes. (iii) Yes. Judgment affirmed in part and reversed in part, and case remanded.

♦   P testified that she was frightened when she was approached by the service worker. The service worker admitted approaching P, and the photograph taken by P showed the service worker pointing his finger at P. These factors show that P had a reasonable apprehension of imminent bodily harm.

- P's camera was attached to or identified with P's body; it was clutched in P's hand. D's intentional "offensive contact with an object attached to . . . [P's] body was sufficient to constitute a battery."

- The incident was characterized as a slight touching by all witnesses except P, whose testimony was inconsistent. P's medical disabilities predated the incident and there was no competent medical evidence of causation. P was not entitled to punitive damages as there was no proof of malice or bad faith.

---

g.   No battery--

Wishnatsky v. Huey, 584 N.W.2d 859 (N.D. 1998).

Facts. While Huey (D), an assistant attorney general, was engaged in conversation in a colleague's office, Wishnatsky (P), a paralegal, without knocking or announcing his entry, attempted to enter the office. D pushed the door closed, thereby knocking P back into the hall. P reentered the office and D left. P sued D for battery. D's motion for summary judgment of dismissal was granted. P's motion to alter the judgment was denied and P appeals.

Issue. Did the trial court err in granting summary judgment because P's evidence satisfied the elements of a battery claim?

Held. No. Judgment affirmed.

- Originally, battery meant the infliction of physical injury. In a crowded world, however, there is much personal contact. The Restatement (Second) of Torts has balanced the inevitable and the unwanted contacts. Section 19 provides that an actor is subject to liability for battery if he "acts intending to cause a harmful or offensive contact with the person of the other or a third person, or an imminent apprehension of such a contact, and . . . an offensive contact with the person of the other directly or indirectly results."

- Conduct is offensive if it "offends a reasonable sense of personal dignity" of an ordinary person. It is contact "unwarranted by the social usages prevalent at the time and place at which it is inflicted."

- P's affidavit indicated he was a born-again Christian who cultivated holiness in his life and that he was "very sensitive to evil spirits and . . . greatly disturbed by the demonic. . . ."

- Evidence here showed D closed the door opened by P; the bodily contact was incidental. D was rude and abrupt, but his conduct would not be offensive to a reasonable sense of personal dignity.

4. **False Imprisonment.** "False imprisonment" is the total obstruction and detention of the plaintiff, of which she is aware, within boundaries and for any length of time, with intent by the defendant to obstruct or detain the plaintiff or another, and without privilege or consent. The plaintiff's prima facie case includes the following elements:

(i) Act by the defendant;

(ii) Obstruction or detention of the plaintiff;

(iii) Intent; and

(iv) Causal relationship.

For liability to attach, there must be an absence of consent and of privilege.

a. **Plaintiff compelled to remain--**

Lopez v. Winchell's Donut House, 466 N.E.2d 1309 (Ill. 1984).

Facts. Lopez (P) was employed as a clerk in Winchell's Donut House's (D's) donut shop for about three years. On April 9, 1981, at 4:30 p.m., Cesario phoned P and asked her to come to the shop. Upon P's arrival, Cesario asked her to accompany him into the baking room at the rear of the store, where Bell was also present. P was asked to sit down and the door was latched. P testified at a deposition that the two men told her they had proof that spotters had purchased donuts from P and that her register had not shown the sale. After being refused her request to see the "proof," P stated she was "too upset" to respond to the question of how long the alleged "shorting" had been going on. P stated that D's employees never directly threatened to fire her, that they made no threats during the interrogation, that at no time did she fear for her safety or refuse to answer any question put to her, and that there was never a point in the interrogation where she asked to leave and was prevented from doing so. D moved for and was granted summary judgment. P appeals.

Issue. Did the trial court err in granting summary judgment because there exists a genuine issue of material fact?

Held. No. Judgment affirmed.

♦ P asserts that she felt compelled to stay in the room to protest her innocence and protect her reputation. In order for a false imprisonment to be present, there must be actual or legal intent to restrain. Restatement (Second) of Torts lists the following as ways in which an action may bring about confinement: (i) actual or apparent physical barriers; (ii) overpowering physical force or submission to physical force; (iii) threats of physical force; (iv) other duress; and (v) asserted legal authority.

♦ It is essential that the confinement be against P's will. If a person voluntarily consents to confinement, there can be no false imprisonment. Moral pressure is not enough.

---

5. **Intentional Infliction of Emotional Distress.**

    a. **Introduction—the cause of action.** The tort of intentional infliction of emotional distress is characterized by physical injury or severe mental suffering by the plaintiff resulting from emotional disturbance (without physical impact), caused by highly aggravated words or acts of the defendant, done with intent to cause mental suffering or with reckless disregard that such is likely to result from such words or acts, and without consent or privilege.

        1) The words or acts must be extreme and outrageous, exceeding all socially acceptable standards, and must cause injury of a serious kind to the plaintiff.

        2) Today, however, most courts have abandoned the requirement that there be some physical injury manifestations from the emotional disturbance caused by the defendant. On the other hand, the law recognizes that humans must occasionally "blow off steam," and ordinarily defendants are not liable for mere insults that may cause emotional disturbance.

    b. **No physical damage or bodily harm required--**

Womack v. Eldridge, 210 S.E.2d 145 (Va. 1974).

Facts. Eldridge (D), who was in the business of investigating cases for attorneys, deceitfully obtained a photograph of Womack (P), a coach at Skateland. The photo was used at Seifert's trial for sexually molesting young boys. At the preliminary hearing, Seifert's attorney showed P's photo to the two young boys, who said P was not the person who molested them. P's photo did not resemble Seifert, and the only excuse given by D for having taken the picture was that P was at Skateland when Seifert was arrested; the offenses alleged against Seifert did not occur at Skateland. The Commonwealth's attorney directed a detective to go to P's home and bring him to court; P came voluntarily and testified he had not molested any children and knew nothing about Seifert. P was questioned several times thereafter, was summoned to appear before the grand jury, and was summoned to appear several times at Seifert's trial because of continuances. P testified that he suffered great shock, distress, and great anxiety as to what people would think of him and feared he would be accused of molesting boys. P was unable to sleep and while testifying became emotional and incoherent. The jury returned a verdict for P for $45,000, which the trial court set aside. P was granted a writ of error.

Issue. Is one who by extreme and outrageous conduct intentionally or recklessly causes severe emotional distress to another subject to liability for such emotional distress absent bodily injury?

Held. Yes. Judgment reversed.

♦   Courts are not in accord on this issue; however, most have allowed recovery in recent years when the act was intentional and the wrongdoer desired the emotional distress or knew or should have known it was likely to result.

♦   We adopt the view that a cause of action will lie for emotional distress, unaccompanied by physical injury, provided that: (i) the conduct was reckless or intentional; (ii) the conduct was outrageous and intolerable in that it offends against generally accepted standards of decency and morality; (iii) there was a causal connection between the wrongdoer's conduct and the emotional distress; and (iv) the emotional distress was severe.

---

c.   **Traditional objections to mental distress as a basis of tort liability.** Mental distress was recognized as an element of damages in early assault cases. However, it was not until relatively recent times (about 1900) that the intentional infliction of mental distress, without any other accompanying tort (such as assault), gained recognition as a separate basis for finding tort liability. The relatively slow development of the law to recognize the plaintiff's peace of mind as a legally protected interest has been due to the following objections:

(i)   The character of the injury suffered in mental distress is difficult to determine; you cannot see mental anguish, whereas it is easy to see a broken arm, an unlawful restraint, etc.

(ii)   The damages resulting from mental distress are of a subtle and speculative nature (*e.g.*, peculiar, variable, hard to assess, etc.).

(iii)   Mental distress lends itself to fictitious claims.

(iv)   Recognition of the basis of liability will open a floodgate of litigation.

(v)   Permitting recovery for mental distress will encourage perjury, either through overstating the facts or fabrication.

Notwithstanding the objections cited above, the law seems to be moving toward an expansion of the circumstances under which liability for the infliction of mental distress will be found.

d.   Substance over form--

McDermott v. Reynolds, 530 S.E.2d 902 (Va. 2000).

Facts. McDermott (P) received a telephone call from a woman informing him that she had just followed her husband, Reynolds (D), and P's wife to a motel. The McDermotts had been married for 18 years and had three children. P confronted D and demanded he cease the adulterous relationship. Instead, D "flaunted it outwardly." P sued D for intentional infliction of emotional distress. P filed a motion for judgment. D demurred. The trial court sustained the demurrer and dismissed. P appeals.

Issue. Is an action for intentional infliction of emotional distress barred when the conduct alleged would support an action for alienation of affection, a cause of action specifically prohibited by statute?

Held. Yes. Judgment affirmed.

♦   Code section 8.01-220, provides: "Notwithstanding any other provision of law to the contrary, no civil action shall lie or be maintained in this Commonwealth for alienation of affection, ..."

♦   While the Code does not mention the tort of intentional infliction of emotional distress, it does encompass many types of conduct unrelated to the causes of action specified in the statute. With this statute, the legislature sought to abolish common law actions seeking damages for a particular type of conduct, regardless of the name applied to the conduct. The conduct at issue here is exactly the type the Code excluded from civil liability.

♦   P has pleaded the elements of an emotional distress claim, but it is the nature of the action, not the form that permits recovery. The basis of P's claim is D had an open and notorious adulterous affair with P's wife.

e.   Public figures and First Amendment limitations--

Hustler Magazine, Inc. v. Falwell, 485 U.S. 46 (1988).

Facts. Falwell (P), a nationally known minister, sued Hustler Magazine (D) as a result of an ad parody in D's November 1983 issue that played on the sexual double entendre of the general subject of "first times." The ad portrayed an alleged "interview" with P in which P states that his "first time" was during a drunken incestuous rendezvous with his mother in an outhouse. P brought an action for libel, invasion of privacy, and intentional infliction of emotional distress. The district court granted a directed verdict for D on the invasion of privacy claim. The jury found against P on the libel claim and for P on the emotional distress claim. D's motion for judgment notwithstanding the verdict was denied. The Fourth Circuit affirmed the judgment against D, and D appeals.

Issue. May a public figure receive damages for emotional harm caused by the publication of an ad parody offensive to him and gross and repugnant in the eyes of most?

Held. No. Judgment reversed.

♦ P would have us find that a state's interest in protecting public figures from emotional distress is sufficient to deny First Amendment protection to speech that is patently offensive and intended to inflict emotional injury, even when that speech could not reasonably have been interpreted as stating actual facts about the public figure involved. We decline to do so.

♦ We have consistently ruled that a public figure may hold a speaker liable for the damage to reputation caused by publication of a defamatory falsehood, but only if the statement was made "with knowledge that it was false or with reckless disregard of whether it was false or not." P argues that a different standard should apply because the state seeks to prevent not reputational damage, but the severe emotional distress suffered by the person who is the subject of an offensive publication. P's view is that as long as the utterance was intended to inflict emotional distress, was outrageous, and did in fact inflict severe emotional distress, it is of no constitutional import whether the statement was fact or opinion, or true or false. It is the intent to cause injury that is the gravamen of the tort, and the state's interest in preventing emotional harm simply outweighs whatever interest a speaker may have in speech of this type.

♦ We have held in *Garrison v. Louisiana*, 379 U.S. 64 (1964), that "even when a speaker or writer is motivated by hatred or ill-will, his expression [is] protected by the First Amendment: Debate on public issues will not be uninhibited if the speaker must run the risk that it will be proved in court that he spoke out of hatred; even if he did speak out of hatred, utterances honestly believed contribute to the free interchange of ideas and the ascertainment of truth." Therefore, while a bad motive may be deemed controlling for purposes of tort liability in other areas of the law, we think that the First Amendment prohibits such a result in the area of public debate about public figures.

♦ We conclude that public figures and officials, in order to recover for the tort of intentional infliction of emotional distress by reasons of publications such as the one here, must show that the publication contains a false statement of fact made with actual malice, *i.e.*, with knowledge of the falsity of the statement or with reckless disregard as to whether or not it was true.

Concurrence (White, J.). The judgment below cannot be squared with the First Amendment.

———————————

6. **Defenses and Privileges.**

a. **Consent.** Consent of the plaintiff or the existence of a privilege in the defendant will exonerate the defendant from liability for an act which, on its face, would otherwise give rise to tort liability. Of course, the burden is on the defendant to plead and prove the existence of a privilege or consent.

1) **The general rule of consent.** Under the general rule, consent by the plaintiff to an act that would otherwise give rise to tort liability will act as a bar to an action based on such act. However, the consent must be effective to act as a bar. Problems often arise as to whether the plaintiff has in fact given consent and whether the plaintiff has the capacity to give consent.

2) **Manifestation of consent.** Consent may be express or implied. When the plaintiff, by words or conduct, intentionally indicates that she is willing to permit an invasion of her rights by the defendant, there is *express consent. Implied consent*, on the other hand, may be either implied-in-fact, as when the plaintiff acts in such a way as would be understood by a reasonable person to be consent to invasion of her rights by the defendant, or implied-in-law, as where circumstances are such as to create the privilege in the defendant to invade the plaintiff's rights without liability (*e.g.*, a doctor rendering emergency medical care to an unconscious person).

3) **Mistake of fact.** The plaintiff's mistake as to the nature of the defendant's conduct will vitiate the plaintiff's apparent consent. For example, if a plaintiff submits to a body massage under the mistaken belief that the defendant is treating an illness and that the massage is a necessary part of the treatment, the plaintiff will not be deemed to have consented to the defendant's offered indecent familiarities. Similarly, a person who accepts and eats candy poisoned by the defendant, without knowledge of the poison, does not consent to be poisoned by the defendant.

4) **Mistake of law.** Consent is ineffective if given under a mistake of law, *e.g.*, submitting to arrest under the belief that an arrest warrant is valid, when in fact it is not.

5) **Fraud.** Consent procured by fraud is ineffective. However, fraud as to a collateral matter does not vitiate consent; *e.g.*, if a plaintiff

consents to sexual intercourse with the defendant in return for a $10 bill offered by the defendant, which is counterfeit, the consent is not negated if it is otherwise effective.

6) **Duress.** Consent given in response to physical force or threats thereof against the plaintiff or a member of her family will be ineffective.

7) **Unlawful acts.** There is a split of authority concerning whether a voluntary participant to an unlawful act can be deemed to have "consented" thereto for the purpose of barring a subsequent action against a fellow participant for damages.

8) **Prize fighting--**

Hart v. Geysel, 294 P. 570 (Wash. 1930).

Facts. Hart (P), administrator of Cartwright's estate, brought an action on Cartwright's behalf. Cartwright died as the result of a blow received in a prize fight. A statute made the fight illegal. The trial court granted D's demurrer to the complaint and dismissed. P appeals.

Issue. Can an action be maintained for wrongful death when the encounter, though unlawful, was entered into with the consent of both parties?

Held. No. Judgment affirmed.

- Prize fighting is unlawful, and one who engages in it is guilty of a gross misdemeanor.

- The majority rule imposes liability for physical injury where the parties engage in mutual combat in anger. This rule is followed where the parties use deadly weapons.

- The minority rule provides that parties who engage in mutual combat in anger will be denied relief in a civil action in the absence of excessive force or malicious intent to do serious injury. This rule is followed in fistfights.

- Here, there are no facts showing anger, malicious intent to injure, or excessive force. They do not contain the anger required by the minority rule.

- We do not adopt either rule. We hold that one who engages in prize fighting, even though prohibited by law, and sustains an injury, should not have a right to recover any damages that he may sustain as the result of the combat, which he expressly consented to and engaged in as a matter of business or sport.

♦ To enforce the criminal statute against prize fighting, it is not necessary to reward the one who got the worst of the encounter at the expense of his more fortunate opponent.

---

b. **Self-defense.** One may be privileged to use force in his own self-defense if such force appears reasonably necessary for protection.

1) **Nondeadly force.** Nondeadly force (not likely to cause death or serious bodily harm) may be used in self-defense if the actor reasonably believes he will be caused immediate harm by the other person's conduct. The force used by the actor must be reasonable under the circumstances, and cannot go beyond the necessity of the situation. There is generally no duty to retreat or comply with the demands of the aggressor.

2) **Deadly force.** Deadly force (likely to cause death or serious bodily harm) may be used in self-defense if the actor reasonably believes that the other person's conduct will result in either death or serious bodily harm to the actor. Under the modern trend, the actor has a duty to retreat before using deadly force, except if the actor is in his own home (or, in a few jurisdictions, place of business), or if retreating would be dangerous, or if the actor is attempting a valid arrest.

3) **Retaliation.** There is no right to retaliate. When the danger has passed, the privilege of self-defense expires.

4) **Excessive force.** When an actor uses excessive force in asserting his privilege of self-defense, the other party then has the privilege of protecting himself against the degree of force being exerted by the actor.

5) **Reasonable force.** Whether force is reasonable is determined on an objective basis; *i.e.,* the amount of force that would have been used by a reasonable person under the same or similar circumstances.

6) **Mistake--**

Courvoisier v. Raymond, 47 P. 284 (Colo. 1896).

Facts. Courvoisier (D),who slept in a room above his jewelry store, was awakened in the night by men who were attempting to break in. Armed with a revolver, D ejected two men from the premises and, finding others outside who threw stones at him and his building, he fired shots in the air to disburse them. The shots attracted Raymond (P), a deputy sheriff, to the scene. P attempted to approach D. Thinking P to be one of the rioters, D shot him. P sued for damages. The jury was instructed to bring a verdict for P if they found that P was not assaulting D when D shot him. D appeals the judgment for P of $3,143.

Issue. Where the circumstances are such as to lead a reasonable person to believe his life is in danger, is that person justified in using force against another whom he mistakenly believes to be part of the danger?

Held. Yes. Judgment for P is reversed.

♦   The jury instruction had the effect of eliminating the circumstances created by the rioters from consideration by the jury.

♦   If D would have been justified in shooting one of the rioters who approached D as P did, and if D actually mistook P, then the circumstances might have justified D's action.

♦   A person may be justified in using force not only against those who actually endanger his life but also against those whom a reasonable person in the same circumstances would believe endanger his life.

---

c.   **Defense of property.** One is privileged to use only that force *reasonably* necessary to defend one's property. Deadly force generally can only be used in defense of one's dwelling, and many courts further restrict its use to situations where the invasion appears to threaten death or serious bodily harm (*i.e.,* tying it into another privilege—self-defense or defense of others).

1)   **Mechanical devices (mantraps)--**

Katko v. Briney, 183 N.W.2d 657 (Iowa 1971).

Facts. Katko (P) entered the Brineys' (Ds') farmhouse, which was boarded up and posted with "no trespassing" signs, to look for and steal old bottles and jars. Ds lived far away and had set a shotgun (mantrap) in the bedroom to shoot whoever opened the door because Ds' farm building had been broken into before. There was no posted notice of the mantrap. P was shot as he entered the room and most of his leg was blown off. The jury awarded P actual and punitive damages. Ds appeal.

Issue. May a landowner lawfully set a spring gun against possible trespassers?

Held. No. Judgment affirmed.

♦ A landowner cannot mechanically do what he could not do in person. The value of life outweighs that of the interest of the landowner; he has no right to use force likely to kill or inflict serious harm, unless self-defense or another privilege is involved.

Dissent. I see no reason for liability as a matter of law for a case such as this where an owner is trying to protect all his life's possessions and installed a device only as a warning to thieves.

Comment. The same rule applies to vicious dogs.

---

d. **Recovery of property.** Under Restatement (Second) of Torts sections 101 through 106, one is privileged to use reasonable force to recapture chattels if he is entitled to immediate possession, return has been demanded and refused, he is in "fresh pursuit" (*i.e.,* he has been reasonably diligent in discovering his loss and in attempting to recover the chattel), the person from whom the recapture is effected is the wrongdoer, and the force used is reasonable under the circumstances.

e. **Necessity.**

1) **Public necessity.** One is privileged to enter land or interfere with chattels of another if it is reasonably necessary or if it reasonably appears necessary to avert a public disaster. To invoke the privilege, the following is required: (i) an immediate and imperative necessity and not just one that is expedient or utilitarian; and (ii) an act that is in good faith, for the public good. The privilege is conditional, and it disappears when the act becomes unreasonable under the existing circumstances. The rationale behind this privilege is that when peril threatens the whole community or so many people that there is public interest involved, one has a complete defense or privilege to act to protect the public interest. A defendant is not liable for any damage or destruction to the land or chattels involved, as long as this was done in the proper exercise of the privilege.

2) **Private necessity.** When there is no public interest involved and the defendant acts to protect his own interest, he is not liable for the technical tort and the landowner has no privilege to expel him.

a) **Damages--**

Vincent v. Lake Erie Transportation Co., 124 N.W. 221 (Minn. 1910).

Facts. Lake Erie Transportation Company (D), following Vincent's (P's) instruction, moored its boat to P's wharf so that P's cargo could be unloaded. During unloading, a storm arose that prevented the boat from leaving the dock. The storm threw the boat against the dock and damaged the wharf. P sued D to recover for damages. D appeals an order denying the motion for judgment notwithstanding the verdict.

Issue. May one who is forced by necessity to use the property of another do so without liability for injury to the property caused by his use?

Held. No. Judgment affirmed.

♦ The ship's master exercised ordinary prudence and care in keeping the ship moored during the storm.

♦ In so doing, he deliberately protected the ship at the expense of the wharf.

♦ The damage to the wharf did not result from an act of God or an unavoidable accident, but rather from circumstances within D's control.

♦ Having deliberately availed himself of P's property, as the storm gave D the right to do, D was liable for injury inflicted by his actions.

Dissent. Judgment for P should be reversed. The master exercised due care and the injury to the dock was an inevitable accident. The owner of the dock who had entered into contractual relations with the owner of the vessel should bear the loss.

B. GOVERNMENT LIABILITY

1. Federal Civil Rights Action.

a. **Civil rights torts.** The problem of official violation of civil rights has confronted the courts for years. These rights are now protected by statute in most cases, but the scope of protection is determined by the courts. 42 U.S.C. section 1983 imputes liability to any person who, under color of law, deprives another of his civil rights.

b. **Beyond the scope of the search warrant--**

Wilson v. Layne, 526 U.S. 603 (1999).

Facts. In "Operation Gunsmoke," United States Marshals together with state and local police worked to apprehend dangerous, armed criminals wanted for violent felonies. The Wilsons' (Ps') son, Dominic, was a target of the operation. The address listed on warrants for Dominic's arrest was actually his parents' home. The warrants did not mention media presence or assistance. The Gunsmoke team of United States Marshals and local police officers assembled to execute the warrants was accompanied by a reporter and a photographer, invited as part of a ride-along policy. Ps were in bed when the officers and media representatives entered their home at 6:45 a.m. Dressed only in briefs, Mr. Wilson ran into the living room, and, seeing men in street clothes with guns in his living room, he angrily demanded that they state their business, and repeatedly cursed the officers. Mistaking him for Dominic, the officers subdued him on the floor. Mrs.Wilson, in only a nightgown, observed her husband being restrained by the armed officers. After the protective sweep was completed, the officers learned that Dominic was not in the house, and they left. During the incident, the photographer took numerous pictures. The reporter was also present. Neither was involved in the execution of the arrest warrant. The photographs were never published. Ps sued the law enforcement officials (Ds) personally, claiming the officers' actions in bringing members of the media to observe and record the attempted execution of the arrest warrant violated their Fourth Amendment rights. The district court denied Ds' motion for summary judgment on the basis of qualified immunity. On interlocutory appeal, the appeals court reversed but declined to decide whether the actions of the police violated the Fourth Amendment. Recognizing a split among the circuits on this issue, the Supreme Court granted certiorari.

Issues.

(i)   Is the accompaniment of law enforcement authorities by media personnel, during the execution of an arrest warrant in a home, a violation of the homeowner's Fourth Amendment protection against unlawful search and seizure?

(ii)   Are the officers entitled to the defense of qualified immunity?

Held. (i) Yes. (ii) Yes. Judgment affirmed.

♦   Under statutory and common law, a plaintiff may seek money damages from government officials who have violated his Fourth Amendment rights. Government officials performing discretionary functions have a qualified immunity so long as their conduct does not violate clearly established statutory or constitutional rights.

♦   Here, the officers had a warrant and were entitled to enter Ps' home. However, in *Horton v. California*, 496 U.S. 128 (1990), we held "[i]f the scope of the search exceeds that permitted by the terms of a validly issued warrant or the character of the relevant exception from the warrant requirement, the subsequent seizure is unconstitutional without more." The presence of reporters inside the home was not related to the objectives of the authorized intrusion. The media representatives did not assist the police and were not present for any reason related to the justification for police entry into the home.

♦   Ds' arguments that officers should have discretion to decide when media would further law enforcement and that the presence of media would foster good public relations bear no relation to the constitutional justification for the police intrusion into a home in order to execute a felony arrest warrant. The argument that a third-party presence minimizes police abuse and protects suspects can be addressed by the police videotaping home entries themselves. Here, the reporters were working on their own story; it was the newspaper that kept the photographs, not the police.

♦ Since the police action in this case violated the petitioners' Fourth Amendment rights, we now must decide whether this right was clearly established at the time of the search. The objective legal reasonableness of an action determines whether an official protected by qualified immunity may be held personally liable for an allegedly unlawful official action. This reasonableness is assessed in light of clearly established legal rules at the time of the action.

♦ "Clearly established" for purposes of qualified immunity means that "[t]he contours of the right must be sufficiently clear that a reasonable official would understand that what he is doing violates that right. This is not to say that an official action is protected by qualified immunity unless the very action in question has previously been held unlawful, but it is to say that in the light of pre-existing law the unlawfulness must be apparent." The right must be specifically defined. Here, we must determine whether a "reasonable officer could have believed that bringing members of the media into a home during the execution of an arrest warrant was lawful, in light of clearly established law and the information the officers possessed."

♦ The constitutional question presented by this case is not open and shut. There was a warrant for entry. Media coverage serves an important public purpose. It is not obvious from general Fourth Amendment principles that the officers violated the Fourth Amendment. Media ride-alongs were common practice and there were no judicial opinions in Ds' jurisdiction holding this practice illegal. The law on third-party entry into homes was not clearly established at the time of this incident.

Concurrence and dissent (Stevens, J.). The homeowners' right to protection against this type of trespass was clearly established.

Comment. Operation Gunsmoke ultimately resulted in over 3,000 arrests in 40 metropolitan areas.

---

2. **Federal Officials.** Federal officials may be held liable for torts, but the judgment may be of little value. The individual official may well be unable to pay a substantial judgment. In addition, some officials may have immunities for acts done under their official duties.

XIII. DEFAMATION

A. COMMON LAW BACKGROUND

1. **Introduction.** At common law, every element of the prima facie case of defamation was based on strict liability except that of publication. Publication had to be intentional or negligent. Substantial changes in the proof requirements have occurred due to modern constitutional decisions. This chapter is organized to present the common law principles first, with the impact of the constitutional decisions later. The common law elements are the following:

    a. The matter published must be capable of a defamatory meaning.

    b. It must be understood as referring to the plaintiff.

    c. It must be understood in a sense defamatory of the plaintiff.

    d. There must be a publication.

    e. There must be causation.

    f. There must be damages.

2. **Publication.** In order to hold the defendant liable, the plaintiff must show either that the defamatory matter was intentionally communicated by the defendant to some third person who understood it, or that the communication to the third person was made through the defendant's failure to exercise due care (*i.e.,* done negligently).

3. **Defamatory Meaning--**

Romaine v. Kallinger, 537 A.2d 284 (N.J. 1988).

Facts. This case involves a passage in a nonfiction book that alludes to Randi Romaine (P) having knowledge of a junkie. P brought a claim for libel against the publisher and author (Ds). The trial court granted Ds' motion for summary judgment, and the appellate court affirmed. P appeals.

Issue. Is the statement at issue reasonably susceptible to a defamatory meaning?

Held. No. Judgment affirmed.

♦ A defamatory statement is one that is false and "injurious to the reputation of another;" exposes another person to "hatred, contempt, or ridicule;" or subjects another person to "a loss of the good will and confidence" in which she is held by others. [*See* Lears v. Green, 24 N.J. 239 (1975)]

♦   The question is one to be decided first by the court according to the fair and natural meaning that will be given it by reasonable persons of ordinary intelligence.

♦   When a statement is capable of being assigned more than one meaning, whether it is defamatory is to be resolved by the trier of fact. Certain statements denote such defamatory meaning that they are considered defamatory as a matter of law, as with the false attribution of criminality.

♦   We concur with the courts below that only the most contorted reading of the offending language could lead to the conclusion that it accuses P of illegal drug use or criminal associations. The reasonable meaning of the critical sentence, "Maria was eager for news from Randi about a junkie they both know who was doing time in prison," is that both women shared sympathy and compassion, not any predilection toward or involvement in criminal drug activity.

---

4.   **Imputation of Homosexuality--**

Matherson v. Marchello, 100 A.D.2d 233, 473 N.Y.S.2d 998 (1984).

Facts. During an interview with a singing group called "The Good Rats" (Ds) on WBAB, a discussion ensued about an establishment called the "OBI," where the Rats were no longer permitted to play. A Rat said that this was because "we used to fool around with his [Matherson's] wife" and "somebody started messing around with his boyfriend." The Mathersons (Ps) sued the group, the individuals in the group, and their record company (Ds), alleging that these remarks were defamatory. The lower court granted Ds' motion to dismiss, and Ps appeal.

Issue. Are the allegedly defamatory statements actionable?

Held. Yes. Judgment reversed.

♦   Unless we can say as a matter of law that the statements could not have had a defamatory connotation, it is a question for the jury to decide whether they did.

♦   The first remark about Mrs. Matherson is clearly libelous; it could have been interpreted to mean that Mrs. Matherson was having an affair with one of the Ds.

♦   The second comment, Ps contend, constitutes an imputation of homosexuality. Ds do not deny such a reading and claim that many public officials have acknowledged their homosexuality, thus removing any social stigma attached to such an allegation.

♦   We disagree. Despite the fact that an increasing number of homosexuals are publicly expressing pride in their status, the potential and probable harm of a false charge of homosexuality in terms of social and economic impact cannot be ignored. On the facts of this case, where Ps are husband and wife, we find that the imputation of homosexuality is "reasonably susceptible of a defamatory connotation."

———————

5.   **"Of and Concerning" Plaintiff.**

   a.   **Identification required.** One of the basic elements of defamation is that the statement be "of and concerning" the plaintiff. If the plaintiff is clearly identified in the statement, such as having her name mentioned, proof of this element is easy. When additional facts are necessary to indicate that the plaintiff is the one intended, this additional area of proof is referred to as "colloquium."

   b.   **Group libel.** When a defamatory statement attacks members of a group generally, it is difficult for any one member of the group to seek a remedy. In order for any one member of such a group to recover, certain requirements must ordinarily be met. First, the statement must be understood to include all or, in some cases, most of the people in a group. It would be difficult, for example, for a member of a group to recover if the statement included only "some" or "a few" of the group. Success would be more likely for the plaintiff, however, if the statement referred to "all" of the group. Secondly, the size of the group must be small. As the size of the defamed group increases, there is less chance for any one member of the group to recover. For example, a defamatory statement about "all lawyers" would not be the basis for a claim by any one lawyer.

6.   **Strict Liability and Damages.**

   a.   **Libel.** "Libel" is defamation usually appearing in some written or printed form; *i.e.,* reduced to some permanent, physical embodiment such as in newspapers, a letter, etc.

   b.   **Slander.** "Slander" is usually oral defamation—representations to the ear rather than to the eye. The principal character of slander is that it is in a less physical form. Defamation in the form of slander is not actionable without a showing of special damages, unless the defamation is of a class that the law deems to be actionable per se. Special damages are usually a pecuniary loss. (*See* the section on slander per se, *infra*, for a description of the four slander per se categories and the difference between general and special damages.)

    c.   **Difficult cases.** In some cases, it is very difficult to determine whether the publication is slander or libel. For example, the defamations contained on an audiotape or videotape seem to contain elements of each.

        1)   **Factors considered.** In these cases, the courts usually consider the following factors:

            a)   The permanency or nonpermanency of form;

            b)   The area of dissemination; and

            c)   Whether the publication is deliberate or premeditated.

        2)   **Restatement.** Restatement (Second) of Torts, section 568A provides that "broadcasting of defamatory matter by means of radio or television is libel, whether or not it is read from a script."

    d.   **Libel—damages.** At common law, proof of special damages was not required for an action in libel. The plaintiff could recover damages without proof of those pecuniary losses. A minority of jurisdictions, however, distinguish between libel per se and libel per quod.

        1)   Libel per se is a libel that is defamatory on its face and needs no special damages.

        2)   Libel per quod is not defamatory on its face and requires proof of special damages in order for any recovery to be allowed.

        3)   A few cases apply the damage rules of slander (*supra*) if the statement is libel per quod.

    e.   **Special damages not required--**

Matherson v. Marchello, 100 A.D.2d 233, 473 N.Y.S.2d 998 (1984).

Facts. [*See* same case, *supra*] In the defamation action, the Mathersons (Ps) pleaded humiliation, injury to the marriage, lost customers, and loss of business opportunity. The trial court dismissed the action for a failure to plead special damages, and Ps appeal.

Issue. Did this action require the pleading of special damages?

Held. No. Judgment reversed and complaint reinstated.

♦ If the action were one of slander, it would require pleading of special damages. It would appear, since the words were spoken, that it was slander. The true test, however, concerns the capacity for harm. The broadcast of statements over radio has wide dissemination and a certain permanence that gives it a greater capacity for harm. Such statements, therefore, will be treated as libel.

♦ Although it is libel, if it is not defamatory on its face, it will be considered libel per quod and still require the pleading of special damages. In this case, the statement concerning "fooling around" with his wife clearly implies that the wife was having an affair and is libelous on its face. The statement concerning his "boyfriend" implies homosexual conduct and is still libelous on its face in our society.

---

f.   Slander—damages.

   1)   Actual damages. Care must be used in reviewing the damage principles applicable to libel and slander. The constitutional decisions (*infra*) now require proof of actual damages in many defamation cases in order to recover damages.

   2)   Nominal damages. At common law, proof of a libel or a slander per se would, in the absence of proof of damages, entitle the plaintiff to at least nominal damages.

   3)   Compensatory damages. Compensatory damages are of two types:

   a)   General. General damages are available where the words are actionable per se and the plaintiff prevails. At common law, these were presumed to be the natural or probable consequences of the defendant's conduct, and the plaintiff did not need to prove actual damages. Under modern constitutional decisions, however, the plaintiff must prove actual damages in many cases.

   b)   Special. Special damages must be alleged in the pleadings and proved by the evidence. These damages are usually to recover pecuniary losses and had to be proven at common law for an action in slander to lie.

   4)   Punitive damages. Punitive damages are given only when claimed in the pleadings and the evidence shows actual malice.

g.   Slander per se—damages. Special damages do not have to be proved for an action in slander in four (and only four) situations:

1) Where the defendant charges that the plaintiff has committed a serious, morally reprehensible crime, or that the plaintiff has been incarcerated for such a crime;

2) Where the defendant imputes to the plaintiff a presently existing, loathsome, communicable disease (venereal disease, leprosy, etc., but not tuberculosis or insanity);

3) Where the defendant imputes to the plaintiff conduct, characteristics, etc., incompatible with the proper performance of the plaintiff's business, trade, office, or profession; and

4) Where the defendant imputes unchastity to a female plaintiff.

h. **Statement of character--**

Liberman v. Gelstein, 605 N.E.2d 344 (N.Y. 1992).

Facts. Liberman (P), a landlord, sued tenant Gelstein (D), who is alleged in P's cause of action to have asked a member of the tenants' board of governors "which cop is on the take from Liberman." Furthermore, D is alleged in P's fifth cause of action to have said in the presence of employees of the building that P tried to punch him, screamed at D's wife and daughter, called D's daughter a slut, and threatened to kill D and his family. The trial court dismissed both causes of action. The court of appeals affirmed, and P appeals.

Issues.

(i) Are both statements slander per se?

(ii) Does D's alleged settlement in the fifth cause of action fall within the "trade, business, or profession" exception to the special damages rule?

Held. (i) No. (ii) No. Judgment affirmed.

♦ Slander is generally not actionable unless a plaintiff has suffered special damages (*i.e.,* "the loss of something having economic or pecuniary value"). Since P has not claimed special damages, P's slander claims cannot be sustained unless they fall into one of the rule's exceptions. [*See* g., *supra*]

♦ If a plaintiff is accused of criminal conduct, the seriousness of the charged crime is taken into consideration. Here, D's statement does charge a serious crime—bribery—and is actionable without the need to establish special harm, absent any privilege (*i.e.,* it is slander per se). In this case, however, the statement is privileged. [*See* Liberman, *infra*]

♦ Harassment, however, is a relatively minor offense and, therefore, an accusation of harassment is not slanderous per se.

♦   D's alleged statements in the fifth cause of action were unrelated to P's status as a landlord, and therefore, were not actionable under the "trade, business, or profession" exception. That exception is limited to "defamation of a kind incompatible with the proper conduct of the business, trade, profession, or office itself." The statement must refer to a matter important for that purpose, rather than simply reflect upon a plaintiff's character or characteristics.

---

7. **Defenses.**

    a. **Truth.** At common law, truth was an absolute defense. The defendant could avoid liability by proving that the statements sued on were true. Modern constitutional decisions still recognize that truth defeats liability, but the burden of proof on that issue has changed. In order to recover in these cases, the plaintiff must now prove that the statements were false.

    b. **Privileges.** Although a statement may be defamatory, a defendant may escape liability by proving that she had a privilege to speak. These privileges are in the nature of true defenses and must be pleaded and proved by the defendant. The privileges are creations of public policy and are usually intended to protect some important public interest. These public interests may include protecting the rights of people in certain positions to speak or protecting the rights of people in certain relationships to exchange information. It is important to note that privileges may be either absolute or qualified.

        1) **Absolute privileges.** Absolute privileges are a complete defense to any action for publication of a defamation. They are not affected by the showing of malice, excessive publication, or abuse.

            a) **Governmental privileges.**

                (1) **Judicial.** Witnesses, attorneys, judges, jurors, and the parties in an action are privileged to utter defamations that have some relevancy to the matter at hand.

                (2) **Legislative.** All federal and state legislative members are absolutely privileged to utter defamations while on the floor or in committee. The utterances need not be relevant.

                (3) **Executive.** Top cabinet-grade executives of state or federal government are absolutely privileged. This includes the President, Cabinet officers, and department heads. Relevancy is a requirement, however.

  b) **Domestic privilege.** A spouse may utter defamations of third persons to the other spouse. Some courts extend this privilege to utterances among members of the immediate family.

 2) **Qualified privileges.** Under certain conditions, a speaker may have a qualified privilege to speak. Although privileged to speak, the defense may be lost if the statements were the result of excessive publication. By this, the court usually means either revealing more information than necessary or telling more people than necessary. Some courts have indicated that the privilege may be lost by a showing of malice. There is, however, a split on this issue and little uniformity. Some courts hold the privilege lost under this concept by a showing of ill will, while others require proof that the statement was made when the speaker knew that the statement was false or had no reasonable belief in the truth of the statement. These qualified privileges may arise in one of several ways.

  a) **Protect personal interest.** Where the speaker seeks to protect some interest personal to herself, the statements may be privileged.

  b) **Common interest.** Where the speaker seeks to protect some interest common to her and the listener, the statement may be privileged.

  c) **Third-party interest.** Where the speaker seeks to protect some interest of the listener or some other third party, the statement may be privileged.

  d) **Other.** Other qualified privileges exist for such activities as credit reporting or fair comment on newsworthy events.

 3) **"Common interest privilege"--**

Liberman v. Gelstein, 605 N.E.2d 344 (N.Y. 1992).

Facts. [*See* same case, *supra*]

Issue. Does D's alleged statement in the second cause of action fall within the "common interest privilege?"

Held. Yes. Judgment affirmed.

♦ One conditional, or "qualified," privileged communication is one that is made to a person upon a subject of mutual interest. The underlying rationale is to foster the flow of information between persons sharing a common interest.

- Both D and his fellow tenant to whom he made the statement were members of the governing body of the association formed to protect the interests of the tenants, and P's bribing of police so that P's cars could have spaces in the front of the building would be contrary to the tenants' interests. Accordingly, the statement bore a conditional privilege.

- Were P able to show either that D's statement was made with knowledge that it was false or with reckless disregard of whether or not it was false, or was made with spite or ill will, the conditional privilege could be defeated. D admitted that he did not know whether the bribery charge was true, but there was no indication that D was "highly aware" that it was probably false. D did harbor ill will toward P, but D made the statement to a fellow association member so that the member could investigate the matter in order to determine whether there was truth to the bribery allegations.

---

4) Public proceedings--

Medico v. Time, Inc., 643 F.2d 134 (3d Cir. 1981), *cert. denied*, 454 U.S. 836 (1981).

Facts. Time (D) published a story that appeared to summarize FBI reports indicating that Medico (P) was a member of organized crime. The trial court granted D's motion for summary judgment on the basis that the story was "fair comment" and was therefore privileged. P appeals.

Issue. Was D's report privileged?

Held. Yes. Judgment affirmed.

- D's report was a fair and accurate summary of the FBI report.

- This privilege usually requires that the report be of a public proceeding. The purpose of such a requirement is to allow the public to review public activities and be informed of those events. The report of the FBI information meets those criteria.

---

   c.   **Consent.** Although rarely raised, consent is a defense to an action for defamation. It may arise where a plaintiff asks that a third party be sent information and the third party receives a defamatory report.

d. **Retraction statutes.** Many jurisdictions provide statutes that allow the defendant to retract defamatory statements. If these statutes are followed, the publisher will not be liable for general damages, although special damages may still be recovered upon sufficient proof.

1) **Retraction statute defined narrowly--**

Burnett v. National Enquirer, Inc., 144 Cal. App. 3d 991, 193 Cal. Rptr. 206 (1983).

Facts. On March 2, 1976, National Enquirer, Inc. (D) published a gossip item about Carol Burnett (P), stating that P had had a loud argument with Henry Kissinger in a Washington restaurant, and then "became boisterous, disturbing other guests." P's attorney demanded a retraction, and D retracted on April 8, 1976. P was dissatisfied with D's retraction and filed a complaint for libel. A jury trial resulted in an award of $300,000 compensatory damages and $1.3 million in punitive damages. D appeals.

Issue. Is D a "newspaper" within the contemplation of section 48(a) of the Civil Code of California and therefore protected by the damages limitations of this statute?

Held. No. Judgment affirmed.

♦ The statute's major rationale is to protect publications that are "not generally in a position adequately to guard against publication of material which is untrue." The element of time is significant here and the protection of the statute is limited to those who engage in the immediate dissemination of news and who cannot always check their sources for accuracy and inadvertent publication errors.

♦ To justify the expanded barrier against libel damages, a publication should be characterized as a "newspaper" only if the constraints of time, as a function of the production requirements of the publication, dictate that result. D does not fall into the newspaper classification.

e. **Right of reply.** Some jurisdictions have passed statutes that require a media defendant to give plaintiffs the right to reply. Although upheld as they apply to television, these statutes have been held unconstitutional when applied to newspapers.

f. **Internet service provider immunity--**

Carafano v. Metrosplash.com, Inc., 339 F.3d 1119 (9th Cir. 2003).

Facts. Carafano (P) is a popular actress who uses the stage name Chase Masterson. In 1999, Matchmaker.com, a commercial Internet dating service, accepted a trial personal profile from an unknown person and posted it on its website. The profile was that of P and included pictures of P, her home address, and an e-mail address that provided her telephone number. Also, the profile was sexually suggestive and was without P's knowledge, consent, or permission. As a result of the posting, P received numerous phone calls, voicemail messages, written letters, e-mail, and a highly threatening and sexually explicit fax that also threatened her son. Feeling unsafe in her home, P stayed in hotels or away from Los Angeles for several months. P initially sued Matchmaker and its corporate successors (Ds) in California state court for defamation and other claims. Ds removed the case to federal district court. The court rejected Ds' claim that it was immune under 47 U.S.C. section 230(c)(1) from liability for publishing false or defamatory material, finding that D had provided part of the profile content. However, the court also rejected P's claims on other grounds and granted Ds' motion for summary judgment. P appeals.

Issue. Is a commercial Internet dating service immune from liability for publishing defamatory material if the information was provided by another party?

Held. Yes. Judgment affirmed.

♦ Under 47 U.S.C. section 230(c)(1), an interactive computer service, which D is, qualifies for immunity as long as it does not also function as an information content provider for the portion of the statement or publication at issue. Because of the statutory exemption, Internet publishers are treated differently from publishers in print, television, and radio. The provision was enacted to promote the free exchange of information and ideas over the Internet and to encourage voluntary monitoring for offensive or obscene material.

♦ Although D provided questions from which the unknown party provided the content in the form of answers and essays, D cannot be considered an "information content provider" under the statute because no profile has any content until a user actually creates it. D simply transmits information unaltered to profile viewers and so is immune from liability.

B. CONSTITUTIONAL LIMITATIONS ON DEFAMATION

1. **Basis of Liability.** Since 1964, the tort of defamation is no longer always a strict liability action. If the plaintiff is a public figure, it must be proved that the defendant knew that the statement was false or recklessly disregarded truth or falsity. If the plaintiff is a private figure and the matter is one of public concern, at least negligence must be proved.

   a. **Public officials--**

New York Times Co. v. Sullivan, 376 U.S. 254 (1964).

Facts. New York Times Company (D) published an advertisement that criticized the action of officials in Montgomery, Alabama, with regard to their treatment of civil rights workers. The advertisement stated that the treatment violated constitutional rights of blacks through intimidation and violence. It was uncontroverted that many facts asserted in the advertisement were false. Commissioner Sullivan (P) was responsible for the police department. P sued D, and the trial court awarded P $500,000 in damages. The trial court held that a false publication is libelous per se if it injures an official in his public office or imputes misconduct to his office. The award was sustained by the Alabama Supreme Court, and D appeals.

Issues.

(i)   May a public official recover damages for a defamatory falsehood relating to his official conduct if he does not prove that the statement was made with actual malice?

(ii)   May an impersonal criticism of a governmental operation be the basis for a libel suit brought by the public official responsible for the operation?

Held. (i) No. (ii) No. Judgment reversed.

♦   The constitutional guarantees of free speech and press require a federal rule that prohibits a public official from recovering damages for defamation unless the statements were made with actual malice.

♦   The advertisement was an expression of protest on a major public issue and hence clearly qualifies for First Amendment protection.

♦   Protection of statements made in the exercise of a First Amendment freedom has never depended upon the truth of the statement.

♦   Injury to official reputation affords no more excuse for repressing otherwise free speech than does factual error.

♦   The fact that the Alabama law allows the defense of truth does not save the law from unconstitutionality. A rule compelling a critic of official conduct to guarantee the truth of his statements on pain of a libel judgment imposes self-censorship and a dampening of free choice.

♦   The rule created by this case is analogous to that which protects federal officials from libel suits for their nonmalicious statements about private citizens.

♦   "Actual malice" means with knowledge that the statement is false or making the statement with a reckless disregard of the truth or falsity. P's case lacks proof of actual malice.

- ◆ Prosecutions for libel of the government cannot be brought even by an official who insists that they are a reflection on his conduct.

- ◆ There was no reference to P in the advertisement either by name or position, and there was no basis suggested at trial to justify P's belief that he was personally attacked by references in the advertisement to the police.

Concurrence (Black, Douglas, JJ.). The First and Fourteenth Amendments do not merely "delimit" a state's power to award damages to "a public official" for libel but completely prohibit a state from exercising such power. D had an unlimited, unqualified constitutional right to publish the advertisement. Furthermore, the First Amendment leaves people and the press free to criticize officials with impunity.

Concurrence (Goldberg, Douglas, JJ.). The First and Fourteenth Amendments give citizens and the press an absolute, unconditional privilege to criticize official conduct with impunity, despite the harm that might flow from its abuse.

Comment. This case holds, in effect, that the news media (and probably private citizens) can defame public persons as long as the publication occurs without the defendant's knowledge that the statement is false and without reckless disregard of the truth by the defendant.

---

b. **Private plaintiffs--**

Gertz v. Robert Welch, Inc., 418 U.S. 323 (1974).

Facts. Gertz (P), a reputable attorney, represented the family of a youth who had been shot and killed by a police officer in a civil action against the officer. Robert Welch, Inc. (D) published an article in its magazine (*American Opinion*), accusing P of participation in a Communist conspiracy against the police, and membership in two Marxist organizations. P sued D for libel, and the trial court directed a verdict on the liability issue in P's favor because the statements were admittedly false and libelous per se. The jury returned a verdict of $50,000, but the trial judge entered a judgment notwithstanding the verdict for D on the ground that the article was about a matter of public interest and protected by the *New York Times* rule, *supra*, absent a showing of actual malice. An appeals court affirmed, and P appeals.

Issues.

(i) Is there a constitutional privilege to publish defamatory falsehoods about an individual who is neither a public official nor a public figure?

(ii) May a private individual who sues for defamation be awarded punitive damages when liability is not based on knowledge of falsity or reckless disregard of the truth?

Held. (i) No. (ii) No. Judgment reversed and case remanded.

♦   An erroneous statement of fact is not worthy of constitutional protection but it is inevitable in free debate. Some falsehoods must be protected in order to protect important speech and avoid media self-censorship that results when the media are required to guarantee the accuracy of their factual assertions.

♦   Nevertheless, there is a legitimate state interest underlying the law of libel, which is the compensation of the victims of defamation.

♦   The balance of freedom of speech and the state's interest in protecting its citizens from libel requires that a different rule be applied to private individuals than that stated in *New York Times*.

♦   A private individual does not have the access to the media that is available to public officials and public figures to contradict the libel and minimize its impact.

♦   Public officials and public figures, by their involvement in public affairs, accept the risk of close public scrutiny. Private individuals who are defamed are thus more deserving of recovery.

♦   So long as they do not impose liability without fault, the states may define the appropriate standard of liability for defamation of a private individual.

♦   P, although he had been active in civic and professional organizations, was not a public figure. He had not sought public notoriety. Furthermore, he never discussed the case with the media.

♦   Because of the competing interest of the First Amendment, state remedies for defamation must only compensate the actual injury, unless actual malice is proven.

♦   States may not presume damages in this type of case. Actual injury must be shown by competent evidence.

♦   The awarding of punitive damages must necessarily be carefully limited; otherwise, juries have the power to punish the expression of unpopular views.

Concurrence (Blackmun, J.). A definite ruling in this area of the law is needed, so I join the majority.

Dissent (Burger, C.J.). A lawyer who takes on an unpopular case should not automatically become fair game for the press. Limits on punitive damages allow that to occur.

Dissent (Douglas, J.). The rights of free press and free speech are absolute rights. As has been previously held, the right is applied to the states not through the Due Process Clause of the Fourteenth Amendment (which would allow state governments the power to regulate the right of free press), but through the Fourteenth Amendment generally. The state here is interfering with that right. The subject matter ("Communist plots") is of public interest.

Dissent (Brennan, J.).

♦ There is a profound national commitment to free press and free speech. The majority opinion would have chilling effects on those rights.

♦ The public figure test is a legal fiction that should be discarded. The key to the public involvement aspect of the *New York Times* case is, "Is the event one of public interest?" If it is, then the person involved in it is a public figure.

Dissent (White, J.).

♦ The right of the ordinary citizen to recover for damage to his reputation has been almost exclusively the domain of the state courts. The majority opinion federalizes these important aspects of these defamation laws. These sweeping changes ignore the past court history of defamation.

♦ The private person should not have to bear the heavy burden of proving that his reputation has actually been injured (damages should be presumed).

♦ The majority is overly concerned with the potential for immoderate damage assessments by juries. Appellate courts can protect against that.

♦ The Court wrongly rejects the punitive damages (express malice) test in favor of a test requiring a plaintiff to show intentional falsehood or wrongful disregard ("actual malice"). There is nothing so constitutionally wrong with requiring a publisher to adhere to those standards of care ordinarily followed in the publishing industry.

♦ The *New York Times* doctrine is appropriate for public figures, but it should not be stretched to cover the private person. Accountability is not forbidden by the First Amendment. People have the right to have their reputations protected by the states (Ninth and Tenth Amendments).

Comment. This case created the following rules: Liability without fault cannot be imposed on the news media defendant. A plaintiff must prove that the publisher either knew the statement was false or was at least negligent in ascertaining the truth. In addition, in order to recover damages, actual damages must be proved. Only if actual malice can be shown can damages be presumed.

---

c. **Public-private distinction.** As noted above, the proper basis of liability in a defamation case depends on a determination of whether the plaintiff is a public or private figure. If the plaintiff is a public figure, actual malice is the appropriate standard. If the plaintiff is a private figure, at least negligence is required.

1) **Test to apply.** The courts have developed two tests to determine whether a plaintiff is a public figure:

   a) A plaintiff is a public figure for all purposes if that plaintiff has assumed a role of special prominence in the affairs of society.

   b) A plaintiff is a public figure for the limited purposes being reported if that party thrust herself to the forefront of a particular public controversy in order to influence the resolution of the issues involved.

2) **Identifying a public figure--**

Wells v. Liddy, 186 F.3d. 505 (4th Cir. 1999).

Facts. It is commonly believed that the burglars involved in the Watergate break-in at the Democratic National Committee ("DNC") in June 1972 were trying to replace malfunctioning listening devices that had previously been installed illegally. Wells (P) worked for the Executive Director of the Association of State Democratic Chairmen, whose phone was tapped. P's calls on that phone were also tapped, and a key to P's desk was found in the burglars' possession when they were arrested. P was subpoenaed to testify before a grand jury and before the Senate Select Committee that investigated the break-in. Liddy (D) was counsel to the Committee to Reelect the President, and, as a result of the break-in, he was convicted and jailed. Two books were published about the events that tied the break-in to the DNC arranging for call girls for visiting dignitaries. One book asserted that photographs were locked in P's desk drawer. D agreed with the theory and repeated it during two public appearances, during a radio show, and on a web site for Accuracy in Media. P filed a defamation action against D. The court granted D's motion for summary judgment and found for D. P appeals.

Issue. Is P an involuntary public figure who must prove actual malice by clear and convincing evidence?

Held. No. Judgment reversed and remanded.

♦ *Gertz v. Robert Welch, Inc.*, 418 U.S. 323 (1974) created three types of public figures: (i) "involuntary public figures," who become public figures through no purposeful action of their own; (ii) "all-purpose public figures," who achieve such pervasive fame or notoriety that they become public figures for all purposes and in all contexts; and (iii) "limited-purpose public figures," who voluntarily inject themselves into a particular public controversy and thereby become public figures for a limited range of issues.

- Clear and convincing proof that a defamatory statement was made with knowledge of its falsity or reckless disregard for the truth is required for a public figure to recover for defamation. After *Gertz*, the level of a defendant's fault that must be proved by private figures to recover compensatory damages in defamation actions is left to the states.

- We have developed a five-factor test to determine whether a plaintiff is a limited-purpose public figure. In order to classify a plaintiff as a limited-purpose public figure, the defendant must prove that: (i) the plaintiff has access to channels of effective communication; (ii) the plaintiff voluntarily assumed a role of special prominence in the public controversy; (iii) the plaintiff sought to influence the resolution or outcome of the controversy; (iv) the controversy existed prior to the publication of the defamatory statement; and (v) the plaintiff retained public-figure status at the time of the alleged defamation. We look at the nature and extent of a plaintiff's participation in the incident giving rise to the defamation.

- D argues that because P was interviewed by the FBI, mentioned in the newspaper, subpoenaed to testify before the grand jury, and called before the Senate, the five-part test is satisfied. P also published a letter to the editor in a newspaper, spoke to a reporter on the 20th anniversary of the break-in for an article that appeared in the Washington Post, spoke to the BBC, was named in a television broadcast entitled "The Key to Watergate" and a Geraldo Rivera documentary "Now It Can Be Told," and spoke to an historian, James Rosen. While this shows P has access to channels of effective communication, we conclude D has failed to show that P has voluntarily assumed a role of special prominence in the public controversy.

- P was unwillingly dragged into the controversy when a crime was committed at her workplace and later investigated. P's discussions with the FBI, response to the grand jury subpoena, and appearance before the Senate committee were compelled by law. Even if P were involved in the crime, precedent advises that a person who engages in criminal conduct does not automatically become a public figure.

- There is no evidence that P had any voluntary interaction with the authors of the books that advanced the prostitution-related theory. In fact, the books revealed the name of the sole source of the theory. P did not seek a prominent role in the Watergate controversy as a result of being named in the books.

- In examining P's media contacts, the letter to the editor in response to a book review of *Secret Agenda*, which named P as a figure involved in arranging dates with prostitutes, falls within the category of self-help and reasonable response to reputation-injuring statements. As for P's three other media contacts, P served as a witness to history in response to requests. P did not "thrust herself to the forefront of [a public] controversy" or attempt to influence the merits of a controversy. D has not met the five-factor test. P is not a limited-purpose public figure.

♦ We do not find that P is an involuntary public figure as the district court did. Based on *Dameron v. Washington Magazine, Inc.*, 779 F.2d 736 (D.C. Cir. 1985), the district court determined that P was an involuntary public figure because she had the "misfortune" of being "drawn by a series of events into the Watergate controversy." "Misfortune" is only one aspect of the considerations that should be weighed before concluding that an individual is an involuntary public figure. *Gertz* cautions that involuntary public figures "must be exceedingly rare."

♦ *Gertz*, the only Supreme Court case to mention the concept of involuntary public figure, provided two reasons for concluding that public figure status must be the determinative inquiry in the balance of interests between the plaintiff and the First Amendment in a defamation case. First, the public figure can take better advantage of the free press and has an easier time resorting to self-help because notoriety guarantees better access to the media and channels of communication. Second, the public figure has taken actions through which she has voluntarily assumed the risk of publicity.

♦ We believe that to prove that a plaintiff is an involuntary public figure the defendant must demonstrate that the plaintiff has become a central figure in a significant public controversy and that the allegedly defamatory statement has arisen in the course of discourse regarding the public matter. A plaintiff is a central figure if she has been the regular focus of media reports on the controversy. A significant public controversy is one that touches upon serious issues relating to, for example, community values, historical events, governmental or political activity, arts, education, or public safety. Also, although an involuntary public figure may not have sought to publicize her views on the relevant controversy, she must have nonetheless assumed the risk of publicity, taken some action, or failed to take action when action was required, in circumstances in which a reasonable person would understand that publicity would likely inhere. Unlike the limited-purpose public figure, an involuntary public figure need not have specifically taken action through which she has voluntarily sought a primary role in the controversy to influence the outcome of debate on the matter.

♦ P is not an involuntary public figure. There are few published reports that name her. Since the publication of the call-girl theory, she has been a minor figure.

♦ P is a private figure. She need not prove actual malice to recover compensatory damages under the applicable law.

---

2. The Defendant as Commentator.

a. Fact or opinion.
At common law, there was a simple distinction that had to be made in defamation actions. The plaintiff's claim could only

be based on a defamatory *fact*; it could not be based on an ***opinion***. In the constitutional cases, this idea was carried forward by refusing to allow recovery for statements of opinion. It is difficult, however, to determine what is fact and what is opinion.

b. No constitutionally protected opinion--

Milkovich v. Lorain Journal Co., 497 U.S. 1 (1990).

Facts. Milkovich (P) was coach of a high school wrestling team that was involved in 1974 in a brawl with a competing team and placed on probation by the Ohio High School Athletic Association ("OHSAA"). Parents of some team members sued to enjoin OHSAA from enforcing the probation. At a court hearing, P and the school superintendent denied that P had incited the brawl. A sports columnist wrote a column indicating that P had lied under oath, thereby preventing the team from receiving just punishment. P and the superintendent sued the newspaper (D) separately. After 15 years of litigation, the Ohio Court of Appeals held that the column was constitutionally protected opinion and granted D's motion for summary judgment. The Ohio Supreme Court dismissed, and the United States Supreme Court granted certiorari.

Issue. Is there a First Amendment-based protection for defamatory statements categorized as "opinion"?

Held. No. Judgment of the Ohio Court of Appeals reversed.

♦ An expression of "opinion" may often imply an assertion of objective fact.

♦ *Philadelphia Newspapers, Inc. v. Hepps*, 475 U.S. 767 (1986), stands for the proposition that a statement on matters of public concern must be provable as false before there can be liability under the state defamation law, at least in situations where a media defendant is involved. *Hepps* ensures that a statement of opinion relating to matters of public concern that does not contain a provably false factual connotation will receive full constitutional protection.

♦ The *Bresler-Letter Carriers-Falwell* line of cases provide protection for statements that cannot "reasonably [be] interpreted as stating actual facts about an individual," providing assurance that public debate will not suffer for lack of "rhetorical hyperbole."

♦ We are not persuaded that an additional separate constitutional privilege for "opinion" is required. The dispositive question in this case then is whether a reasonable factfinder could conclude that statements in D's column imply that P perjured himself. We think the answer is yes. The language in the article is not the loose, figurative, hyperbolic language that would "negate the impression that the writer was seriously maintaining [that P] committed the crime of perjury." Also, the connotation that P committed perjury is sufficiently factual to being proved true or false; "unlike a subjective assertion, the averred defamatory language is an articulation of an objectively verifiable event."

Dissent (Brennan, Marshall, JJ.). The challenged statements cannot reasonably be interpreted as either stating or implying defamatory facts about P.

---

c.   **Provably false fact--**

Flamm v. American Association of University Women, 201 F.3d 144 (2nd Cir. 2000).

Facts. The American Association of University Women ("AAUW") and the AAUW Legal Advocacy Fund (Ds) are non-profit corporations dedicated to improving educational opportunities for women and girls. Ds maintain a referral service of attorneys and other professionals willing to consult with women who have brought or are considering bringing gender discrimination actions. Ds compile a directory of the participating attorneys and professionals, listing names, contact information, and a short blurb about each person. Ds distributed copies of the directory to the people listed in it, to members, and to any others requesting a copy. It is not clear how the directory was compiled, but two entries included the notation "not reached in survey." Some of the entries appear to include statements made by the person listed. Of the approximately 275 entries in the directory, only P's contained a negative comment. Following Flamm's (P's) name, address, and telephone numbers, the directory states: "Mr. Flamm handles sex discrimination cases in the area of pay equity, harassment, and promotion. *Note: At least one plaintiff has described Flamm as an 'ambulance chaser' with interest only in 'slam dunk cases.'*" P sued Ds, alleging libel per se. The district court granted Ds' motion to dismiss. P appeals.

Issue. Is the statement challenged by P a non-actionable opinion and, as such, protected by either the United States Constitution or the New York Constitution?

Held. No. Judgment vacated and remanded.

♦   In *Gertz v. Robert Welch, Inc.*, 418 U.S. 323 (1974), the Supreme Court stated: "Under the First Amendment there is no such thing as a false idea. However pernicious an opinion may seem, we depend for its correction not on the conscience of judges and juries but on the competition of other ideas." *Gertz* is understood to have extended an "absolute constitutional protection" to opinions. Later, the Court disclaimed "an additional separate constitutional privilege for 'opinion' under the First Amendment. (See *Milkovich v. Lorain Journal Co.*, 497 U.S. 1 (1990)) The New York appeals court based its opinion on the New York Constitution.

- *Milkovich* held that before liability can be established in defamation suits against media defendants, a statement that involves a matter of public concern must be provable as false. The court did not address whether the same rules apply in suits against nonmedia defendants.

- The distinctions found in the law of defamation—between matters of public and private concern, between media and nonmedia defendants, and between public officials or public figures and private plaintiffs—were enunciated in an attempt to balance "the State's interest in compensating private individuals for injury to their reputation against the First Amendment interest in protecting . . . expression."

- In *Dun & Bradstreet v. Greenmoss Builders*, 472 U.S. 749 (1985), a majority of justices agreed that the *Gertz* rule requiring a showing of actual malice to support recovery of presumed or punitive damages does not apply to cases involving matters of only private concern. The First Amendment's basic protection extends to matters of general public importance. We agree with the plurality and concurring opinions in *Dun & Bradstreet* that a distinction drawn according to whether the defendant is a member of the media or not is untenable. In a suit by a private plaintiff involving a matter of public concern, we hold that allegedly defamatory statements must be provably false, and the plaintiff must bear the burden of proving falsity, at least in cases where the statements were directed towards a public audience with an interest in that concern.

- This approach balances the state interest in compensating private individuals for wrongful injury to reputation, which is significantly weaker when the factfinding process is unable to resolve conclusively whether the speech is true or false, with First Amendment interest in protecting free expression. This interest is advanced by requiring private plaintiffs to prove the falsity of allegedly defamatory statements involving matters of public concern, especially when the challenged statements are directed towards a public audience with an interest in that concern.

- We look at the content, form, and context of a given statement, as revealed by the whole record, to determine whether a publication addresses a matter of public concern. Ds' efforts to fight gender discrimination is a matter of public concern as is the allegation that P, an attorney specializing in the field, engages in the unethical solicitation of victims, particularly when made public in Ds publication. The directory was mailed to hundreds of P's peers, to other professionals, and to others interested in gender discrimination. This distribution was clearly intended to influence public discourse and affect the public. To survive the motion to dismiss, P must have shown that a reasonable person could find that the challenged statement alleges or implies a provably false fact, and P has done that.

- We must determine whether the description of P as an "ambulance chaser" reasonably implies that he has engaged in unethical solicitation, and if so, whether this is capable of being proven false. Ds admit the term "ambulance chaser" is provable as true or false when understood literally to accuse a lawyer of the unethical or criminal behavior of solicitation. The directory states facts in all respects. Its purpose is to provide referral to qualified attorneys and professionals to assist victims of gender discrimination. Seeing negative comments about one attorney, a reader of the directory would probably look elsewhere, particularly here, where the note about P is highlighted in italics, suggesting that it warrants special attention and consideration. Because there is nothing in the directory to suggest otherwise, a reasonable reader is more likely to treat P's description as fact.

♦ Ds' contention that "with interest only in 'slam dunk cases'" is slang and cannot be read literally, therefore suggesting that the entire statement amounts to a purely subjective judgment, has little merit. If there is any merit in Ds' argument, it cannot be said that it would be unreasonable to conclude otherwise. The description of P can be interpreted to mean an attorney who improperly solicits clients and then takes only easy cases.

♦ We hold that the challenged statement is reasonably susceptible to the defamatory meaning imputed to it and a jury must decide whether it was likely to be understood by the reader in a defamatory sense. The case is not entitled to dismissal under the First Amendment.

♦ New York courts consider three factors when distinguishing actionable fact from non-actionable opinion. Examining the overall context in which the assertions were made, and whether a reasonable reader would believe the challenged statements were factual, the courts looks at: (i) whether the specific language in issue has a precise meaning, which is readily understood; (ii) whether the statements are capable of being proven true or false; and (iii) whether either the full context of the communication in which the statement appears or the broader social context and surrounding circumstances are such as to signal readers or listeners that what is being read or heard is likely to be opinion, not fact. These criteria apply to media and nonmedia.

♦ Here, a reputable professional organization has prepared a fact-laden national directory, nearly 70 pages in length, that purports to list "attorneys and other specialists" willing to consult with women involved in higher education who are seeking redress for sex-based discrimination. Names, addresses, phone numbers, and, generally, a short statement of the person's area of interest or expertise are provided. In this context, the reader would be less skeptical and more willing to conclude that the directory stated or implied facts.

3.   **The Press as Repeater.**

a. **Common law.** Repeating a libel at common law would make the repeater of the statement as liable as was the original speaker. Certain privileges arose, however, to protect the repeater under certain circumstances. Ordinarily, this privilege existed to allow the report of information gained from public proceedings or from governmental sources. Recent decisions have indicated that the protection for freedom of speech and press found in the First Amendment may grant a constitutional privilege for the repeating of matters of public concern.

b. **Neutral reportage privilege--**

Khawar v. Globe International, Inc., 965 P.2d 696 (Cal. 1999), *cert. denied*, 526 U.S. 1114 (1999).

Facts. Robert Morrow ("Morrow") published a book about the murder of Robert Kennedy ("the Morrow book") that alleged that Kennedy's assassin was not Sirhan Sirhan, but a man named Ali Ahmand. The Morrow book contained four photographs of a young man the book identified as Ali Ahmand standing in a group of people around Kennedy at the Ambassador Hotel in Los Angeles shortly before Kennedy was assassinated. Khawar (P) alleged he was the person in the photographs, and not Ahmand. Globe International, Inc. (D), in its tabloid newspaper, *Globe,* carried a front-page headline, which read "Iranian secret police killed Bobby Kennedy," and summarized the Morrow book's allegations. The article included a photograph from the Morrow book. The individuals' images were enlarged and an arrow was added pointing to one of the men (P) and identifying him as the assassin. P sued D, alleging the book's accusation, repeated in the *Globe* article, that he had assassinated Kennedy was false and defamatory and had caused him substantial injury. Three months later, P's father sued. These two actions were consolidated. After the other parties settled, a jury trial followed. The evidence showed that at the time of the assassination, P was a Pakistani citizen and a free-lance photojournalist working on assignment. He stood on the podium near Kennedy so that a friend could photograph him with Kennedy, and so that he could photograph Kennedy. He knew the photos would be publicized. P was questioned but never considered a suspect. When the *Globe* article was published, 21 years later, P was a naturalized United States citizen living with family in California, where he owned and operated a farm. His father had also become a naturalized United States citizen and settled in California. After reading the article, P became very frightened for his and his family's safety. He received threatening telephone calls and he and his children received death threats, and his home and his son's car were vandalized. He was interviewed by a local television station about the article. The trial court granted D's motion for nonsuit as to P's father on the ground that the allegedly defamatory statements were not "of and concerning" him. As to P, the jury returned, among others, these special verdicts: (i) the *Globe* article contained statements about P that were false and defamatory; (ii) D published the article negligently and with malice or oppression; (iii) with respect to Kennedy's assassination, P was a private rather than a public figure; and (iv) the *Globe* article was a neutral and accurate report of the Morrow book. The parties had previously agreed that the jury's findings on the last two issues would be advisory only. The jury awarded P $100,000 for injury to his reputation, $400,000 for emotional distress, $175,000 in presumed damages, and, after a separate punitive damages phase, $500,000 in punitive damages. The trial court reviewed the verdicts that were deemed advisory and determined as a matter of law that (i) the *Globe* article was ***not*** an accurate and neutral report of the statements and charges made in the Morrow book (thus disagreeing with and rejecting the jury's advisory special verdict); and (ii) with respect to the events in question, P was a private and not a public figure (thus agreeing with and adopting the jury's advisory special verdict). The trial court's finding that the *Globe* article was not an accurate and neutral report of the Morrow book was apparently based on the court's subsidiary finding that although P could be identified from the photograph of him that appeared in the *Globe* article, which included an arrow pointing directly at P, it was impossible to identify P from the smaller, darker, and less distinct image of him, without an arrow, that appeared in the Morrow book. Based upon its findings that P was not named in and could not be identified from the photographs in the Morrow book, the trial court vacated Morrow's default and ultimately entered judgment in his favor. The court granted judgment on the special verdicts for P and against D in the amount of $1,175,000. The appeals court affirmed the judgment, concluding that P was not a public figure, that California had not adopted a neutral reportage privilege for private figures, and that the evidence supported the trial court's findings of negligence and actual malice. The state supreme court granted D's petition for review.

Issues.

(i)   When a published book places a person at the center of a public controversy, is that person an involuntary public figure for the limited purpose of a media report about that book and that controversy?

(ii)   Does the First Amendment to the federal Constitution mandate a privilege for a media defendant's publication of a neutral and accurate report about a controversial book's allegations regarding matters of public concern?

(iii)   Does the evidence support the jury's special verdict finding of actual malice?

(iv)   Does the evidence support the jury's special verdict finding of negligence?

Held. (i) No. (ii) No. (iii) Yes. (iv) Yes. Judgment affirmed.

◆   The malice requirement was imposed on defamation actions by public figures and public officials because they have media access enabling them to effectively defend their reputations in the public arena; and, by injecting themselves into public controversies, they may fairly be said to have voluntarily invited comment and criticism. [*Gertz (supra)*] The Supreme Court has indicated also that purposeful activity may not be essential for public figure characterization, but it has not stated or implied that it would be proper for a court to characterize an individual as a public figure where there is proof that the individual had neither engaged in purposeful activity inviting criticism nor acquired substantial media access in relation to the controversy at issue. We infer from *Gertz* that one may become an involuntary public figure if he, despite never having voluntarily engaged the public's attention in an attempt to influence the outcome of a public controversy, nonetheless has acquired such public prominence in relation to the controversy as to permit media access sufficient to effectively counter media-published defamatory statements.

♦ There is no evidence P acquired sufficient media access in relation to the assassination or book to effectively counter the defamatory falsehoods in the *Globe* article. After the assassination and before the Morrow book was published, P was not asked for an interview. He was not a suspect; he did not testify; and his views on the assassination were never published.

♦ California has adopted the common law regarding one who republishes a defamatory statement; the republisher is deemed thereby to have adopted the defamatory statement and may be held liable, together with the person who originated the statement, for resulting injury to the reputation of the defamation victim.

♦ *Edwards v. National Audubon Society, Inc.*, 556 F.2d 113 (2d Cir. 1977), *cert. denied*, 434 U.S. 1002, provided an exception to the republication rule that is known as the neutral reportage privilege. The *Edwards* court defined the privilege: "[W]hen a *responsible, prominent organization . . .* makes serious charges against a *public figure*, the First Amendment protects the *accurate and disinterested reporting* of those charges, regardless of the reporter's private views regarding their validity."

♦ The significant informational value to the public of defamatory allegations regarding an existing public controversy, regardless of their truth, is the theory underlying the privilege. The character of the controversy is revealed, its nature, viciousness, and intensity. Regarding republication of a false and defamatory accusation, proponents of the privilege urge that the "accusation should be deemed neither defamatory nor false if the report accurately relates the accusation, makes it clear that the republisher does not espouse or concur in the accusation, and provides enough additional information (including, where practical, the response of the defamed person) to allow the readers to draw their own conclusions about the truth of the accusation."

♦ Neither the Supreme Court nor we have ever addressed this privilege. States and commentators are divided. D's argument that the privilege should be applied to P because he is a public figure fails because we have determined that P is a private figure. D next argues the privilege should extend to private figures.

♦ Some commentators argue that republication of accusations made against private figures is never protected by the neutral reportage privilege regardless of the public's interest in knowing that prominent individuals have made charges against a private figure because recognition of an absolute privilege for the republication of those charges would be inconsistent with the United States

Supreme Court's insistence on the need for balancing the First Amendment interest in promoting the broad dissemination of information relevant to public controversies against the reputation interests of private figures. If the scope of the privilege were to include defamations of private figures, a neutral reportage route out of liability could emasculate the *Gertz* distinction between private and public figure plaintiffs. We agree. Such accusations can destroy the accused's reputation and are rarely informative. The private individual has not voluntarily elected to encounter an increased risk of defamation and may lack sufficient media access to counter the accusations. Furthermore, a defamation action may be an inadequate remedy. It is costly, and the source of the defamation may be insolvent or unable to respond to the charges. We do not decide or imply here that the neutral reportage privilege exists as to republished defamations about public figures; we hold only that the appeals court did not err when it determined that in California there is no neutral reportage privilege extending to reports regarding private figures.

♦ As a private figure, P was not required to prove actual malice, only negligence to recover damages. Because P sought punitive damages, the issue of actual malice was presented to the jury. When the finding of actual malice is based on republication, it may be upheld where the informant's veracity or accuracy is clearly doubtful and the republisher does not interview obvious witnesses who could have confirmed or disproved the allegations, or review relevant sources.

♦ Here, there were obvious reasons to doubt the accuracy of the allegations. During the intense investigation of the assassination, massive amounts of evidence pointed to Sirhan as lone assassin. He was charged and it was undisputed that he fired the fatal shot. He was convicted of first degree murder. The assertion that P had killed Kennedy was highly improbable. There is no evidence that attempts were made to verify the accuracy of the claim. There was no evidence that D was aware of facts that would justify unquestioning reliance on Morrow's improbable accusations. We agree with the appeals court that the evidence shows D purposefully avoided the truth.

C. PROPOSALS FOR REFORM

1. **Need for Reform.** Plaintiffs claim a need for reform in order to protect themselves from defamatory statements. They claim that the constitutional protections have given the press the right to defame freely without fear of being held responsible. Although defendants have avoided liability in most actions, they also seek reform. The cost of defending actions is high.

2. **Reform Proposals.** Reform proposals have taken two forms. Suggestions have centered around either the need for retraction statutes or the need for declaratory relief.

a. **Retraction.** Proposals for retraction statutes usually have several specific suggestions. These statutes would require the plaintiff to request a correction in order to activate the statute. Once the correction request is made, the defendant should make a correction in a timely and conspicuous manner. Ordinarily, the plaintiff will be encouraged to make the request because failure to do so will limit the damages recoverable. Defendants will be encouraged to make the correction because compliance will mitigate damages.

b. **Declaratory relief.** This proposal allows the plaintiff to seek a declaratory judgment that the statements were false. Damage recovery would continue to be limited by the constitutional standards. The burden of proof in the case would be by clear and convincing evidence.

XIV. PROTECTING PRIVACY

A. INVASION OF PRIVACY

1. **Introduction.** The focus of this tort is not injury to reputation, but interference with the "right to be let alone" that results in injury to feelings, without regard to any effect on property, business, or reputation. Most states recognize this tort by case law, and some do by statute; a few states do not recognize it at all.

2. **The Prima Facie Case.**

   a. **Introduction.** The elements of the cause of action are the following:

      1) **Act by the defendant.** The act may consist of words or any type of affirmative conduct.

      2) **Serious and unreasonable invasion of the plaintiff's privacy.** This is the crux of most invasion of privacy suits.

      3) **Intent, negligence, or strict liability.** Most invasion of privacy suits involve intentional acts, but this is not essential. Liability may be imposed for negligent invasions and, at common law, even for invasions based on strict liability. Constitutional privileges may affect this element of the case.

      4) **Causation.** Both actual and proximate causation must be proved.

      5) **Damages.**

   b. **Types of action.** There are four types of actionable invasions of privacy:

      1) Unreasonable publicity given to another's private life (public disclosure);

      2) Publicity that unreasonably places another in a false light before the public (false light);

      3) Appropriation of another's name or likeness (publicity); and

      4) Unreasonable intrusion upon the seclusion of another (intrusion).

B. PUBLIC DISCLOSURE OF PRIVATE FACTS

1. **Elements.** If a reasonable person would find the disclosure of the private facts highly objectionable, then the plaintiff has a cause of action.

a. **Private facts.** Matters to be distinguished here are the following:

    1) **Matters of public record.** Matters of public record are not actionable since they are already public.

    2) **Public occurrences.** Public occurrences are not actionable since anyone present would have seen them. They also are already public.

b. **Revelation of previous misconduct--**

Haynes v. Alfred A. Knopf, Inc., 8 F.3d 1222 (7th Cir. 1993).

Facts. The Hayneses (Ps) sued the author and publisher (Ds) of a journalistic history which focused upon Ruby Lee, Luther Haynes's ex-wife. Part of the description involved Lee's relationship with Luther, who was depicted as an unfaithful alcohol abuser who neglected his children, was often unemployed, and eventually left Lee for Dorothy (Johnson) Haynes. Luther admitted to many of the alleged incidents, but argued that they had taken place 25 years earlier, and that since that time he had reformed and now "lived an exemplary life." The trial court granted Ds summary judgment, and Ps appeal.

Issue. Did Ds' book invade Ps' right of privacy?

Held. No. Judgment affirmed.

♦   The phrase "right of privacy" encompasses many distinct wrongs (*see supra*).

♦   Ds' book did not invade Ps' privacy by publicizing personal facts; it did not reveal intimate details, but only previous misconduct.

♦   There is no detail of the book that Ps claim invades their privacy that is not germane to the story, which is a story not only of legitimate but of transcendent public interest.

---

2. **State-Protected Privacy Interests--**

The Florida Star v. B.J.F., 491 U.S. 524 (1989).

Facts. In violation of its internal policy of not publishing the names of sexual offense victims, *The Florida Star* (D) published the full name of B.J.F. (P), who had reported a sexual assault to the sheriff's department. P sued both the newspaper and the sheriff's department. The latter settled for $2,500. D's motion to dismiss was denied. At trial, P testified that she had suffered emotional distress, her mother had received threatening phone calls from a man who had said he would rape P again, and P had been forced to change her phone number and residence and to seek mental counseling. D put forth evidence that it had learned P's name from a police report and that its violation of its internal rule was inadvertent. D moved for directed verdict and was denied. At the close of D's defense, P was granted a directed verdict on the issue of negligence. The jury considered causation and damages upon the judge's instruction that it could award P punitive damages if it found that D had acted with reckless indifference to the rights of others. P was awarded $75,000 in compensatory and $25,000 in punitive damages. The court of appeals affirmed. The Florida Supreme Court denied discretionary review, and D appeals.

Issue. May the state impose sanctions on the accurate publication of the name of a rape victim obtained from judicial records, which are maintained in connection with a public prosecution and which themselves are open to public inspection?

Held. No. Judgment reversed.

♦ We hold only that when a newspaper publishes truthful information that it has lawfully obtained, punishment may lawfully be imposed, if at all, only when narrowly tailored to a state interest of the highest order, and that no such interest is satisfactorily served by imposing liability under the facts of this case.

♦ The information involved here comes from a report prepared at a time when no criminal adversarial proceedings had begun.

♦ We articulated the considerations underlying our decision in the instant case in *Smith v. Daily Mail Publishing Co.*, 443 U.S. 97 (1979). First, only lawfully obtained information is protected, and the government retains ample means of safeguarding significant interests that may be impinged upon by publication. Second, punishing the press for dissemination of information that is already publicly available is not likely to advance the interests upon whose behalf the state seeks to act. It is a limited set of cases indeed where, despite the accessibility of the public to certain information, a meaningful public interest is served by restricting its further release by other entities, like the press.

---

3.   **Breach of Confidentiality--**

Humphers v. First Interstate Bank of Oregon, 289 Or. 706, 696 P.2d 527 (1985).

Facts. Humphers (P), unmarried at the time, gave birth to a child (Dawn) she immediately put up for adoption. She had been registered in the hospital under an alias by her physician, Dr. Mackey. The medical records concerning the birth were sealed. P later married and raised a family. Twenty-one years later, Dawn sought out Dr. Mackey in her attempt to make contact with her biological mother. Dr. Mackey informed Dawn in a letter that he had registered P at the hospital. To further help Dawn breach the confidentiality of the records, he also stated untruthfully that he recalled administering diethylstilbestrol to P, and that the possible consequences of this medication made it important for Dawn to find P. Dawn gained access to the medical records and she located P, who was upset. The development caused her emotional distress. P sued First Interstate Bank (D) as Dr. Mackey's personal representative. P's claims were dismissed and judgment was entered for D. The appeals court reversed the dismissal of two of P's claims, breach of a confidential relationship, and invasion of privacy. D appeals.

Issues.

(i)   Has P stated a claim for damages for breach of confidentiality in alleging that her former physician revealed her identity to a daughter whom she had given up for adoption?

(ii)   Has P stated a claim for damages for invasion of privacy in alleging that her former physician revealed her identity to a daughter whom she had given up for adoption?

Held. (i) Yes. (ii) No. Judgment affirmed in part; reversed in part and remanded.

♦   Breach of privacy and wrongful disclosure of confidential information claims have as a common denominator the right to control information, but they differ in other respects. All secrets do not concern personal or private information; commercial and governmental secrets are not personal, and governmental secrets are not private. The distinction we are concerned with is that one who holds information in confidence can be charged with a breach of confidence. A tortious invasion of privacy theoretically could be committed by anyone. Dr. Mackey's professional role in this case is relevant to a claim that he breached a duty of confidentiality, but he could be charged with an invasion of P's privacy only if anyone else who told Dawn the facts of her birth without a special privilege to do so would be liable in tort for invading P's privacy.

♦   Statutes that close adoption records to inspection without a court order establish P's interest as a privacy interest. That categorization alone is not enough to collect damages from anyone who causes injury to that interest. Dr. Mackey helped Dawn find her biological mother, but we are not prepared to find Dawn liable for invasion of privacy in so doing. Nor would anyone who knew the facts without an obligation of secrecy commit a tort simply by telling them to Dawn. Dr. Mackey did not try to discover any facts he did not know; if he had informed P that Dawn was trying to find her, we could not describe that communication as an invasion of privacy. The point of P's claim against Dr. Mackey is not that he pried but that he failed to keep a secret.

- Several courts have held that "unauthorized and unprivileged disclosure of confidential information obtained in a confidential relationship can give rise to tort damages." Courts have found several sources of the nonconsensual duty of confidentiality in the medical profession, *e.g.*, statutory exclusion of medical testimony in litigation, professional regulations. Where there are "no obligations undertaken expressly or implied in fact in entering a contractual relationship," the parameters of the duty of confidentiality are determined by a "legal source external to the tort claim itself." If a statute is alleged to have been violated, the rule must validly apply to the facts.

- Because the duty is determined by standards outside the tort claim for breach, so are the defenses of privilege or justification. Members of confidential professions may be statutorily obligated to report information, *e.g.*, child abuse. Defenses are determined in the same way as the existence and scope of the duty itself and will differ from one occupation to the other.

- The relevant state statute imposes a duty on physicians to keep medical information confidential in a medical relationship and disqualifies or otherwise disciplines physicians for breach of this duty. The appeals court thought that breach of this statutory provision could not lead to civil liability when such liability would be quite inappropriate to other provisions of the statute, but the court's reasoning misses the point. The statute establishes the duty only in a medical relationship, not in a confidential relationship.

- If only this statute were involved, we do not know how the disciplining board would judge a physician who assists at the birth of a child and 20 years later reveals to that person her parentage. But there are other statutes that specifically mandate the secrecy of adoption records. Court records in adoption cases may not be inspected or disclosed except upon court order, and a court order is required before sealed adoption records may be opened by the state registrar. Given these clear legal constraints, there is no privilege to disregard the professional duty solely to satisfy the curiosity of the person who was given up for adoption.

C. FALSE LIGHT PRIVACY

1. Constitutional Requirements--

Cantrell v. Forest City Publishing Co., 419 U.S. 245 (1974).

Facts. Mrs. Cantrell's (P's) husband, the father of four, was killed along with some 40 other people when a bridge collapsed. Forest City (D) assigned a reporter to do a feature story focusing on the husband's funeral and the impact of the death on the Cantrell family. Five months later, the reporter returned to the Cantrell home to write a follow-up story. P was not home, but her children were interviewed and photographed. The story stressed the family's poverty, the house's deterioration, and the children's poor clothing. It is conceded that the story had a number of inaccuracies and falsehoods. The case went to the jury on the "false light" theory of invasion of privacy. The district judge, on D's motion, struck the claims relating to P's three youngest children. P and her oldest son received a judgment. D appealed, and the Sixth Circuit held that D's motion for a directed verdict should have been granted as to all of the Cantrells and set aside the verdict.

Issue. Is a newspaper's reckless disregard for the truth, which sheds false light on a plaintiff, actionable?

Held. Yes. Judgment reversed and case remanded.

♦ The jury was properly instructed that D was liable only if it was shown that D published the article with knowledge of its falsity or reckless disregard of the truth. This is the constitutional "actual malice" standard used in defamation cases.

♦ The district court dismissed the demand for punitive damages on the grounds that P had not proved common law malice. There was, however, a finding of actual malice.

♦ There was sufficient evidence for the jury to find that the reporter knew of the falsity of the story. D can be held on the basis of respondeat superior since it approved and published the story.

Dissent (Douglas, J.). The collapse of the bridge placed the Cantrells in the public eye. First Amendment guarantees of freedom of press should not turn on differences between common law malice and actual malice.

D. INTRUSION

1. **Physical Solitude.** Intrusion into one's physical solitude, as by a peeping tom, is an actionable invasion of privacy, as is searching another's handbag or spying with high-powered binoculars or a motion picture camera.

2. **Unreasonable Intrusion--**

Nader v. General Motors Corp., 255 N.E.2d 765 (N.Y. 1970).

Facts. Ralph Nader (P), an author and lecturer on automotive safety and a critic of General Motors (D), brought suit alleging that D conducted a campaign of intimidation against him in order to suppress his criticisms and prevent his disclosure of information about D's products. Among other things, P alleged that D had tapped his phone, eavesdropped on his private conversations, and kept him under surveillance. D moved to dismiss P's complaint. Two courts upheld the legal sufficiency of P's cause of action. The appellate court certified the question to the New York Court of Appeals as to whether the alleged conduct would constitute a tort for invasion of privacy.

Issue. Does the seeking of confidential information through wiretapping, eavesdropping, and surveillance constitute an actionable invasion of privacy?

Held. Yes. Order appealed from affirmed.

♦ There is a cause of action for invasion of privacy based on the right to be free from intrusions in private matters.

♦ To constitute an actionable intrusion, there must be more than a mere gathering of information. The information sought must be of a private nature.

♦ Conduct that merely harasses or attempts to uncover information that P has already revealed to others is not an actionable invasion.

♦ "Overzealous" surveillance designed to obtain private information may be actionable, as well as the wiretapping and eavesdropping.

---

3. **Injunctive Relief for Public Figure--**

Galella v. Onassis, 487 F.2d 986 (1973).

Facts. Photographer Galella (P) sued Jackie Onassis (D) for false arrest and malicious prosecution after he was arrested by secret service agents protecting D's children. D denied the charges and counterclaimed for injunctive relief against P's constant efforts to photograph her and her children. The court of appeals affirmed the dismissal of P's claim. This portion of the opinion deals with the injunctive relief granted to D and the government, which had intervened as protector of the children.

Issue. Is the injunctive relief granted to D and to the government appropriate?

Held. Yes. Judgment affirmed as modified.

♦ P "insinuated himself into the very fabric of [D's] life," interrupting the children at play, invading their private schools, bribing doormen and a family servant. Evidence showed that P had occasionally intentionally touched D and her daughter and caused fear of physical contact in his attempts to get pictures.

- Legitimate countervailing social needs may warrant some intrusion into an individual's privacy, but P's actions, when weighed against the slight public importance of D's daily activities, went beyond reasonable bounds of newsgathering.

- P has stated his intention to continue covering D and continued his harassment while the temporary orders were in effect. There is no indication that a voluntary change in his techniques can be expected.

- The injunction, however, is too broad. It should be tailored to protect D from the behavior P exhibits that is different from other photographers, but should not infringe on the rights of other photographers to cover D. As modified, the relief granted fully allows P to photograph and report on D.

---

4. **Concealed Cameras--**

Desnick v. American Broadcasting Cos., 44 F.3d 1345 (7th Cir. 1995).

Facts. Desnick Eye Center and two doctors (Ps) sued ABC and Sam Donaldson (Ds) following a *Prime Time Live* television show expose of Ps. Ds claimed that Ps performed unnecessary eye surgery, overcharged, and tampered with machines so that tests would lead patients to believe that they had cataracts. Ds also reported an administrative proceeding that charged Dr. Desnick with "malpractice and deception." The district court dismissed Ps' complaint for failure to state a claim, and Ps appeal.

Issues.

(i)   Did Ds' use of test patients and concealed cameras support Ps' claims for trespass, infringement of the right of privacy, and illegal wiretapping?

(ii) Did Ds' alleged conduct support Ps' claim for promissory fraud?

Held. (i) No. (ii) No. Judgment affirmed in part and reversed in part, and case remanded.

- Entering another person's land without consent is trespass, and there is no "journalists' privilege" to trespass. However, the test patients here entered Ds' offices that were open to anyone considering ophthalmic services, and they videotaped physicians who were engaged in professional communications; no intimate details of any person's life were publicized.

- Ds' use of concealed cameras did not violate Illinois or federal wiretapping statutes, which allow a party to a conversation to record that conversation unless the purpose is to commit a crime, tort, or "other injurious acts." Public disclosure of alleged misconduct at medical clinics cannot be considered an "injurious act."

♦ Illinois does not provide a remedy for promissory fraud unless there is a "scheme to defraud." In this case, there was no showing of such a scheme.

---

5. **Concealed Microphone--**

Shulman v. Group W Productions, Inc., 955 P.2d 469 (Cal. 1998).

Facts. The Shulmans, mother and son (Ps), whose activities and position did not otherwise make them public figures, were trapped inside their car when it went off the highway. The medical rescue helicopter crew that came to Ps' assistance was accompanied by Group W's (D's) cameraman. He filmed Ps' extrication from the car, the efforts to give them medical care during the extrication, and their transport to the hospital in the helicopter. Conversations with rescue workers and with the mother were picked up by a microphone worn by the flight nurse. Months later, in a documentary television show, *On Scene: Emergency Response,* the accident/rescue events were broadcast. Ps had not consented to the filming, the recording, or the broadcast. Ps sued for intrusion and public disclosure of private facts. Ps stipulated that car accidents on public highways and publicly provided medical rescue were matters of public interest and public affairs. The trial court granted D's motion for summary judgment. The appeals court reversed, finding triable issues of fact exist as to the mother's claim for publication of private facts and legal error on the trial court's part as to both Ps' intrusion claims. The case is now before the state supreme court.

Issues.

(i) Do triable issues exist as to whether D invaded Ps' privacy by accompanying Ps in the helicopter?

(ii) Do triable issues exist as to whether D tortiously intruded by listening to the mother's confidential conversations with the rescue nurse at the rescue scene without the mother's consent?

(iii) Did D have a constitutional privilege to intrude on Ps' seclusion and private communications?

Held. (i) Yes. (ii) Yes. (iii) No. Judgment affirmed in part; reversed in part and remanded.

♦ In an action for intrusion, a plaintiff must prove: (i) intrusion into a private place, matter, or conversation, (ii) in a manner highly offensive to a reasonable person. A great portion of the public travels often, and automobile accidents are of interest to them, as are rescues and medical treatment of accident victims. The subject matter of the broadcast, an automobile accident, the rescue, and the mother's appearance were of legitimate public concern. Ps have not shown they had an objectively reasonable expectation of seclusion or solitude on a public way. The mere presence of a camera operator at the accident scene and his filming of the events occurring there are not bases for a cause of action for intrusion.

♦ However, a triable issue exists as to whether the cameraman's presence in the helicopter, which served as an ambulance, intruded on Ps' reasonable expectation of privacy. Reporters at an accident scene are expected, but it is not customary for members of the public or media to ride in an ambulance.

♦ The camera operator may not have intruded into the zone of privacy by being present where he could hear conversations between Ps and medical personnel, but by placing a microphone on the nurse and listening to what she and others said, he may have listened to conversations reasonably expected to be private.

♦ The leading California decision, *Miller v. National Broadcasting Co.*, 187 Cal. App. 3d 1463 (1986), explained that offensiveness of an intrusion requires consideration of all the circumstances of the intrusion, including the intruder's motives and objectives. There is a strong societal interest in effective and complete reporting of events, but the constitutional protection afforded the press does not justify an intrusion that would otherwise be offensive. Here, a reasonable person could find D's recording of the mother's comments to her rescuers highly offensive. Ps were severely injured, vulnerable, and disoriented. D should have foreseen Ps would not know their words were being recorded and would not have the opportunity to object or consent.

♦ In the area of constitutional protection, the common law reflects a general rule of nonprotection: the press in its newsgathering activities enjoys no immunity or exemption from generally applicable laws. California's intrusion tort and statute apply to all private investigative activity, whatever its purpose and whoever the investigator. The media may even enjoy some favorable treatment based on a reporter's motive to uncover socially important information. There is no basis for finding the California laws place an "impermissible burden" on the press in general or in this case. Newsgathering does not depend on hidden microphones; reporting on automobile accidents also does not.

♦ The rule D seeks, that when intrusion claims are brought in the context of newsgathering conduct, that conduct be deemed protected so long as (i) the information being gathered is about a matter of legitimate concern to the public and (ii) the underlying conduct is lawful (*i.e.*, was undertaken without fraud, trespass, etc.), is too broad a privilege and unsupported by both tort law and constitutional precedent. Several cases have found reporters tortiously intruded on the plaintiffs' privacy because their conduct was highly offensive to a reasonable person, not because they had committed any independent crime or tort, *e.g.*, reporter tells small children that their neighbors have been killed and films their reaction.

♦ The state may not tell the news media what to publish and broadcast, and the media may not unlawfully spy on the public under the cover of newsgathering.

Concurrence. I agree with the premise of the holding, but I do not agree that a trier of fact could find D's conduct highly offensive. Others could hear the conversations between the mother and the nurse, D did not interfere with the rescue, and the helicopter ride was routine.

---

6. **Intercepted Cell Phone Conversation--**

Bartnicki v. Vopper, 532 U.S. 514 (2001).

Facts. During contentious union negotiations between a Pennsylvania teachers' union and the school board, Bartnicki (P), the union's chief negotiator, used a cell phone to talk with Kane (P), the union's president. Ps discussed the status of the negotiations, which were contentious and were covered in the media. An unknown person intercepted and recorded Ps' conversation. During the call, Kane said, "If they're not gonna move for three percent, we're gonna have to go to their, their homes . . . To blow off their front porches, we'll have to do some work on some of those guys." Vopper (D), a radio commentator, had previously criticized the union. When the union and school board reached a settlement, Vopper played a tape of the intercepted conversation on his radio show. The media then further publicized it. Vopper had received the tape from Yocum (D), the leader of a taxpayers' organization that opposed the union's demands, who had discovered the tape in his mailbox. Yocum had played it for members of the school board before delivering it to Vopper. Ps sued for damages. Both parties sought summary judgment. The district court denied both parties' motions. On interlocutory appeal, the Third Circuit remanded the case with instructions to enter summary judgment for Ds. The Supreme Court granted certiorari.

Issue. Does the First Amendment protect the disclosure of a communication concerning matters of public concern if the communication had been illegally intercepted by someone other than the person disclosing it?

Held. Yes. Judgment affirmed.

♦ Title 18 U.S.C. section 2511(1)(c) provides that it is unlawful to intentionally disclose to another person the contents of a wire, oral, or electronic communication, knowing or having reason to know that the information was obtained through the interception of a wire, oral, or electronic communication. Pennsylvania has a similar statute.

- We accept Ps' submission that Ds intentionally disclosed the contents of the illegally recorded conversation and that they knew or had reason to know that the recording was illegal. Under section 2511 and the Pennsylvania statute, Ps would be entitled to recover damages from Ds.

- We also accept Ds' submissions that: (i) they played no role in the interception but found out about it after it occurred and never learned who had done it; (ii) their access to the tape was lawful even though the information on the tape was obtained unlawfully by another person; and (iii) the subject matter of the conversation was a matter of public concern.

- The statutes at issue are content-neutral laws of general applicability. They do not distinguish based on the content of the intercepted conversations. The communications in this case were singled out because they were illegally intercepted—because of the source, rather than the subject matter. The prohibition against disclosures is a regulation of pure speech.

- The government has a legitimate interest in protecting privacy, which it protects by prohibiting an interceptor from using information acquired illegally. If the sanctions are inadequate to deter illegal actions, perhaps they should be made more severe, but the government cannot suppress speech by a law-abiding possessor of information in order to deter the conduct of a non-law-abiding third party.

- The government claims that it is necessary to protect the privacy of confidential communications to encourage the uninhibited exchange of ideas and information; the fear of public disclosure of private conversations might have a chilling effect on private speech. Nevertheless, in balancing the competing interests, privacy concerns must yield to the interest in publishing matters of public importance.

Concurrence (Breyer, O'Connor, JJ.). The majority's holding is correct based on the special circumstances of this case. Ps had little or no legitimate interest in maintaining the privacy of the conversation; Ps were limited public figures; Ds acted lawfully prior to their disclosures; and the material published involved a matter of unusual public concern. The holding should not be read to extend beyond these circumstances.

Dissent (Rehnquist, C.J., Scalia, Thomas, JJ.). This decision diminishes, instead of enhances, the purposes of the First Amendment by chilling the speech of millions who rely on electronic technology to communicate each day.

E. RIGHT OF PUBLICITY

1. Appropriation of One's Performance--

Zacchini v. Scripps-Howard Broadcasting Co., 433 U.S. 562 (1977).

Facts. Zacchini (P) had a "human cannonball" act where he was shot from a cannon into a net. The entire act lasted 15 seconds. Scripps-Howard Broadcasting Company (D) filmed the act, without consent, and showed it on a news program. P sued, claiming that his whole act had been appropriated. D was granted summary judgment, and P appeals.

Issue. Does the news media have a right to show P's whole act?

Held. No. Judgment reversed.

♦ The right to one's own work is like copyright or patent law. The performance is a talent that should be respected.

♦ The false light and public disclosure cases are distinguishable. Those cases protect reputation. There was no attempt in those cases to publish an entire act for which someone normally paid.

♦ This appropriation was a threat to the economic value of the performance.

Dissent (Powell, Brennan, Marshall, JJ.). The First Amendment should protect the news media absent a showing of an attempt to exploit the value of an act.

---

2. Transforming Creative Elements--

Winter v. DC Comics, 69 P.3d 473 (Cal. 2003).

Facts. DC Comics (D) published a comic book series with a volume entitled "Autumns of Our Discontent." This volume featured Johnny and Edgar, the Autumn brothers, depicted as villainous half-worm, half-human creatures who were born from the rape of their mother by a supernatural worm. At the end of the next volume, the anti-hero kills the brothers in a gun battle. Johnny and Edgar Winter (Ps), well-known musicians, sued D, alleging, among other things, appropriation of their names and likenesses under Civil Code section 3344. Ps claim that D chose the names Johnny and Edgar Autumn to let readers know that Ps were being portrayed and that D gave the Autumn brothers physical features similar to Ps', such as long white hair and albino features. Ps also allege that D falsely portrayed them as vile, stupid, cowardly subhumans who committed wanton acts of violence and bestiality for pleasure. The trial court granted D summary judgment. The appellate court originally affirmed. The supreme court granted Ps' petition for review and later remanded the case. On remand, the appellate court affirmed summary judgment for all causes of action except the one for misappropriation of likeness, because the court found that triable issues of fact existed. It reversed the judgment and remanded for further proceedings on that cause of action. The supreme court granted D's petition for review.

Issue. Did the comic books contain significant creative elements that transformed them into something more than mere celebrity likenesses so that they were entitled to protection under the First Amendment?

Held. Yes. Reversed and remanded.

- ◆ Civil Code section 3344 provides: "(a) Any person who knowingly uses another's name, voice, signature, photograph, or likeness, in any manner, on or in products, merchandise, or goods, or for purposes of advertising or selling, or soliciting purchases of, products, merchandise, goods or services, without such person's prior consent . . . shall be liable for any damages sustained by the person or persons injured as a result thereof."

- ◆ There is tension between this right of publicity and the First Amendment. However, the right of publicity is essentially an economic right, not a right of censorship, and is not a right to control the celebrity's image by censoring disagreeable portrayals.

- ◆ In *Comedy III Productions, Inc. v. Gary Saderup, Inc.,* 21 P.3d 797 (Cal. 2001) (*Comedy III*), we determined that when a celebrity's right of publicity clashes with constitutional free speech rights, there must be a balancing between the First Amendment and the right of publicity, based on whether the work adds significant creative elements so that it is transformed into something more than a mere celebrity likeness. Whether a work merely appropriates a celebrity's economic value, and thus is not entitled to First Amendment protection, or whether it has been transformed into a creative product that the First Amendment protects depends on whether the work has become primarily the defendant's own expression rather than the plaintiff's likeness. In *Comedy III*, we found that lithographs and T-shirts displaying the likeness of The Three Stooges were not sufficiently transformative to receive First Amendment protection.

- ◆ The transformative elements or creative contributions that invoke First Amendment protection can take many forms, including factual reporting, fictionalized portrayal, lampooning, or subtle social criticism, as long as the depiction is more than a trivial variation. The determination of whether a work is transformative is not based on the quality of the artistic contribution. The inquiry is more quantitative than qualitative because the question is whether the literal or the creative elements predominate in the work.

- ◆ When an artist is faced with a right of publicity challenge to his work, he may raise an affirmative defense that the work is protected by the First Amendment because it contains significant transformative elements or that its value does not derive primarily from the celebrity's fame. However, if an artist uses his skill and talent to create a conventional portrait of a celebrity that commercially exploits the celebrity's fame, the artist's right of free expression is outweighed by the right of publicity.

♦ In this case, Ps were only part of the raw materials used to synthesize the comic books, and the books did not depict Ps literally. The drawings were distorted for purposes of lampoon, parody, or caricature. As such, they did not threaten Ps' right of publicity. Fans wanting pictures of Ps would not find the drawings to be good substitutes for conventional depictions.

♦ Unlike the drawings of The Three Stooges, the comic books contain significant creative elements that transform them into something more than mere celebrity likenesses. Therefore, they are entitled to First Amendment protection.

———————

XV. INTENTIONAL ECONOMIC HARM

A. MISREPRESENTATION

1. **Introduction.** Misrepresentation is a specialized area of the law in which the plaintiff is seeking damages for some economic loss suffered because of reliance on a false statement. Although some recovery for a negligently made false statement is allowed, the traditional common law action for fraud or deceit required a knowingly made false statement.

2. **Basic Elements for Fraudulent Misrepresentation.** The basic elements for fraud are:

    a. A false representation of a material fact;

    b. Scienter or knowledge that the statement is false;

    c. Intent to induce reliance;

    d. Justifiable reliance on the statement; and

    e. Damages.

3. **Basic Elements for Negligent Misrepresentation.** A negligent misrepresentation occurs when there is:

    a. A false representation of a material fact;

    b. Failure on the part of the defendant to use reasonable care to determine the truth of the statement;

    c. Duty to the plaintiff who relied;

    d. Justifiable reliance; and

    e. Damages.

4. **Deceit Actions Based upon Innocent Misrepresentations.**

    a. **Majority rule of no liability.** Under the majority rule, if the defendant innocently misrepresents a material fact by mistake, he will not be liable. The maker of the statement must have actual knowledge of its falsity, or negligent ignorance as to its truth or falsity.

    b. **Minority rule of liability.** However, a growing minority position in cases involving the sale of land or chattels is that the good faith of the maker is immaterial. All that need be shown is that the statements were false and intended to induce reliance and that damages resulted from the plaintiff's justifiable reliance thereon.

5. **Nondisclosure--**

Ollerman v. O'Rourke Co., 288 N.W.2d 95 (Wis. 1980).

Facts. Ollerman (P), a noncommercial purchaser, alleged in his complaint that he would not have purchased from O'Rourke Company (D) or would have purchased at a lower rate a residential building lot which held an underground well. D allegedly failed to disclose the existence of the well. The trial court dismissed P's claim. The court of appeals overruled the dismissal, and D appeals.

Issue. Does the complaint state a cause of action for intentional misrepresentation?

Held. Yes. Judgment affirmed.

◆ Failure to disclose a fact does not constitute intentional misrepresentation unless the party has a duty to disclose. If there is such a duty, a failure to disclose is treated as the equivalent of a representation that the fact does not exist.

◆ In this case, D did have a duty to disclose any facts of which D had knowledge and that were material to the transaction and not readily discernible to a purchaser such as P.

◆ A vendor has knowledge of a fact if he had actual knowledge of the fact or acted in reckless disregard as to the fact's existence.

◆ A fact is "material" if a reasonable purchaser would attach importance to its existence or nonexistence in determining whether to enter into the transaction, or if the vendor knows or has reason to know that the particular buyer is likely to regard the matter as important, although a reasonable purchaser would not so regard it.

Comment. The court deferred a ruling on the validity of P's negligence claim until the case had been tried.

B. INTERFERENCE WITH CONTRACT

1. **Common Law Origin.** Originally, this action was intended to protect master-servant relationships. A master could seek damages if a servant was induced to leave his position.

2. **Modern Elements.** The modern development of this action recognizes several elements:

   a. There must be an existing contractual relationship;

   b. The defendant must have been aware of that relationship; and

   c. The defendant must have acted to cause a breach of that relationship.

3. **Defenses--**

Imperial Ice Co. v. Rossier, 112 P.2d 631 (Cal. 1941).

Facts. Imperial Ice (P) had a contract to sell ice with a covenant by S.L. Coker not to compete. Rossier (D) induced Coker to breach that covenant, buy ice from D, and resell it. P sued D for this act, and the trial court sustained D's demurrer. P appeals.

Issue. May P maintain an action for the inducement to breach the contract when D's sole purpose was his own personal gain?

Held. Yes. Judgment reversed.

♦ There are defenses or justifications that will prevent recovery when a defendant induces a breach of contract. Where the public good outweighs the contract interest, inducing a breach is justifiable.

♦ An induced breach may also be justified when a defendant seeks to protect a contract already in force on his behalf. In addition, lawful competitive means are permissible even though other contracts may not be reversed.

♦ Where, however, a defendant induces a party to breach a contract in order to gain a future competitive advantage, an action will lie.

♦ Here, D induced Coker to breach a contract with P in order to favor D. This is actionable.

Comment. While recognizing the action for inducement to breach a contract, this case discusses available defenses. Merely seeking future economic advantages, however, is not a defense.

C. INTERFERENCE WITH PROSPECTIVE ECONOMIC ADVANTAGE

1. **Basic Elements.** The action for interference with the prospective advantage differs from inducement to breach a contract in one distinct manner. This

action does not require a presently enforceable contract. It is sufficient if some prospective or future relationship is disturbed. The elements of this action, therefore, are as follows:

a.   A prospective or future advantageous relationship;

b.   The intentional interference with that relationship; and

c.   Damage caused by that interference.

2.   Burden of Proof--

Della Penna v. Toyota Motor Sales, U.S.A., Inc., 902 P.2d 740 (Cal. 1995).

Facts. Among the steps that Toyota Motor Sales, U.S.A. (D) took to prevent Lexus automobiles from exportation to Japan was the compiling of a list of "offenders" and the warning of its dealers that D would sanction dealers who did business with any offenders. Della Penna (P) was a wholesaler who bought Lexus automobiles from retailers at retail prices and exported them to Japan. As a result of D's efforts, P lost its supply. P sued D. The trial court granted D's motion for nonsuit on P's antitrust claim and found for D on the interference claim. P appeals.

Issue. Does a plaintiff seeking recovery for alleged interference with prospective economic relations have the burden of pleading and proving that a defendant's interference was wrongful by some measure beyond the fact of the interference itself?

Held. Yes. Judgment reversed and case remanded.

♦   After examining divergent rulings from the appeals court, a doctrinal evolution among other state courts, the elements of the tort of "interference with prospective contractual relations," and the allocation of the burden of proof between the parties to such an action, we conclude that the tort requires proof of a "wrongful act," and that the plaintiff bears the burden of proof.

♦   These requirements sensibly redress the balance between providing a remedy for predatory economic behavior and keeping legitimate business competition "outside the bounds of litigation."

Concurrence. The common law is nearly incoherent on the tort of intentional interference. Reformulation is necessary, but I would not adopt the "standard" of "wrongfulness." Such a standard is ambiguous. Were I to adopt such a standard, however, I would not allow it to remain undefined.

D. CONTRACT AND TORT IN THE ECONOMIC SPHERE

1. Economic Loss Doctrine--

All-Tech Telecom, Inc. v. Amway Corporation, 174 F.3d 862 (7th Cir. 1999).

Facts. All-Tech (P) claims that Amway (D) lured it into a losing business venture involving telephones intended for hotel and restaurant customers. The customer would use a credit card or telephone calling card to pay for a long-distance call, and the line charges would be divided among D, the hotel or restaurant, and the long-distance phone companies. P was created for the very purpose of being a distributor of the phones and the associated telephone service. P bought a lot of phones and for reasons beyond P's control (equipment problems, regulatory impediments, the obsolescence of the phones) P withdrew the product from the market. P claims D misrepresented that it had thoroughly researched the product, that the service would be the "best" in the nation, that any business telephone line could be used with the phone, that the service had been approved in all 50 states and did not require the approval of any telephone company, that each phone could be expected to generate an annual revenue for the distributor of $750, and that the carrier that D had retained to handle the calls and billings for the phones was the largest company of its kind in the nation. The district court granted summary judgment for D on P's claims of intentional and negligent misrepresentation and promissory estoppel. P appeals.

Issue. Did the district court err in granting summary judgment to D on P's claims of intentional and negligent misrepresentation and promissory estoppel?

Held. No. Judgment affirmed.

♦ The "economic loss" doctrine of the common law originally limited who could bring a tort suit for the consequences of a personal injury or damage to property to the injured person himself, or the owner of the damaged property himself, and not parties with commercial links to the owner. The underlying theory is that remedy is available in contract to suppliers.

♦ This point has implications for commercial fraud as well as for business losses that are secondary to physical harms to person or property. There is no need to provide tort remedies for misrepresentation where there are well-developed contractual remedies, such as the remedies that the Uniform Commercial Code provides for breach of warranty of the quality, fitness, or specifications of goods. Contract law has been shaped to allow the jury to resolve factual disputes and the parties to contracts to rely on the written word and not be exposed to the unpredictable reactions of lay factfinders to witnesses who testify that the contract means something different from what it says. The parol evidence and "four corners" rules and the Statute of Frauds limit the scope of jury trial contract disputes. Tort law does not have these screens. In recognition of this omission, the "economic loss" doctrine forbids commercial contracting parties (as distinct from consumers, and other individuals not engaged in business) to escalate their contract dispute into a charge of tortious misrepresentation if they could easily have protected themselves from the misrepresentation of which they now complain.

♦ Product warranty cases best illustrate the function of the economic loss doctrine in confining contract parties to their contractual remedies. If the seller makes an oral representation that is important to the buyer, the buyer has only to insist that the seller embody that representation in a written warranty. The warranty will protect the buyer, who will have an adequate remedy under the Uniform Commercial Code if the seller reneges. To allow him to use tort law in effect to enforce an oral warranty would unsettle contracts by exposing sellers to the risk of being held liable by a jury on the basis of self-interested oral testimony and perhaps made to pay punitive as well as compensatory damages.

♦ The representations challenged in this case are in the nature of warranties, and because the warranted "product" was a mix of a product and a service, that should not affect the application of the doctrine. D also has a solid alternative ground for affirmance: P presented no evidence of actionable misrepresentation. Some of the alleged misrepresentations were corrected before P bought its first phone (the phone could be installed on any business line and regulatory approval had been obtained in all 50 states). If the victim of a misrepresentation about a product learns the truth before he relies, but decides to buy the product anyway, he cannot complain about the misrepresentation.

♦ One of the representations was made by D's independent contractor distributor at a trade meeting. Independent contractors do not bind their employer by force of the doctrine of respondeat superior. He was speaking about his own experience and there is no evidence that he was speaking with D's actual or apparent authority or that D ratified his remarks.

♦ Some representations were puffing or sales patter (*e.g.*, that the service was "the best").

♦ The promise that P emphasizes as the basis for its promissory estoppel claim, that D had thoroughly researched the phone program before offering it to distributors, is not forward-looking. It warrants a past or existing condition rather than promising some future action and is thus more a warranty than a promise. But a warranty is a type of promise—in this case a promise by D to pay for the consequences should the research that went into the development of the phone service not have been thorough after all. Since a warranty can induce reasonable reliance, it can be the basis for a promissory estoppel claim in limited cases. A promisee cannot be permitted to use the doctrine to do an end run around the rule that puffing is not actionable as misrepresentation, or around the parol evidence rule.

◆ The economic loss doctrine protects contract doctrines and prevents the piling on of duplicative remedies. Promissory estoppel is meant for cases in which a promise, not being supported by consideration, would be unenforceable under conventional principles of contract law. When there is an express contract governing the relationship out of which the promise emerged, and no issue of consideration, there is no gap in the remedial system for promissory estoppel to fill.

◆ Here, the parties had a contract and the alleged warranty of thorough research was either one of the warranties of the contract or it was not (by virtue of disclaimer, the puffing exemption, or the parol evidence rule). If it was not (and it was not), we cannot think of any reason for using the doctrine of promissory estoppel to resuscitate it. Promissory estoppel is not a doctrine designed to give a party a second bite at the apple in the event it fails to prove a breach of contract.

———————————

TABLE OF CASES
(Page numbers of briefed cases in bold)

NOTES

NOTES

NOTES

NOTES

NOTES

NOTES

NOTES